State Propaganda in China's Entertainment Industry

Most current research on the evolution of China's propaganda discourse only touches upon recent variations of official propaganda rhetoric grounded in popular media. Here, the research is extended by tapping into the most recently released popular cultural media narratives such as online documentaries, films, TV drama serials and education programs, all of which are enlisted and co-opted by the state for propaganda goals.

This book maps out the cutting-edge expansions of official propaganda that are embedded in the entertainment industry of contemporary China. Its case studies bring to light the progression of the mainstream propaganda discourse in terms of its merging, cooperation and compromise with the commercial features of both the traditional and the newly emerging entertainment media. In particular, it examines a group of mass entertainment products which include two bestselling mainstream blockbusters, two online commercial web documentaries, the China Central Television Moon Festival Gala series, revolutionary nostalgia TV drama serials, and a prime time science and education program. In so doing, it forefronts the up-to-date developments and novelties of state propaganda: its motives, reasoning and approaches within the media sphere of today's China.

Illustrating how the CCP (Chinese Communist Party) propaganda apparatus and tactics evolve and become embedded in popular media products, this book will be of interest to students and scholars of Chinese Studies, Media Studies and Popular Cultural Studies.

Shenshen Cai is a lecturer in Chinese Studies at the University of Melbourne, Australia. She has recently published articles in journals such as *Social Semiotics* (2015), *Asian Studies Review* (2016), and *Asian Theatre Journal* (2016).

Routledge Contemporary China Series

For a full list of titles in this series, please visit www.routledge.com

145 **The Identity of Zhiqing**
   The lost generation
   Weiyi Wu and Fan Hong

146 **Teacher Management in China**
   The transformation of educational systems
   Eva Huang, John Benson and Ying Zhu

147 **Social Entrepreneurship in the Greater China Region**
   Policy and cases
   Yanto Chandra

148 **China's Approach to Central Asia**
   The Shanghai Co-operation Organisation
   Weiqing Song

149 **China's Peasant Agriculture and Rural Society**
   Changing paradigms of farming
   Jan Douwe van der Ploeg and Jingzhong Ye

150 **China's Changing Economy**
   Trends, impacts and the future
   Edited by Curtis Andressen

151 **China's Energy Security**
   A multidimensional perspective
   Edited by Giulia Romano and Jean-François Di Meglio

152 **Chinese Muslims and the Global Ummah**
   Islamic revival and ethnic identity among the Hui of Qinghai Province
   Alexander Blair Stewart

153 **State Propaganda in China's Entertainment Industry**
   Shenshen Cai

State Propaganda in China's Entertainment Industry

Shenshen Cai

LONDON AND NEW YORK

First published 2016
by Routledge
2 Park Square, Milton Park, Abingdon, Oxon OX14 4RN

and by Routledge
711 Third Avenue, New York, NY 10017

Routledge is an imprint of the Taylor & Francis Group, an informa business

© 2016 Shenshen Cai

The right of Shenshen Cai to be identified as author of this work has been asserted by her in accordance with sections 77 and 78 of the Copyright, Designs and Patents Act 1988.

All rights reserved. No part of this book may be reprinted or reproduced or utilised in any form or by any electronic, mechanical, or other means, now known or hereafter invented, including photocopying and recording, or in any information storage or retrieval system, without permission in writing from the publishers.

Trademark notice: Product or corporate names may be trademarks or registered trademarks, and are used only for identification and explanation without intent to infringe.

British Library Cataloguing in Publication Data
A catalogue record for this book is available from the British Library

Library of Congress Cataloging-in-Publication Data
Names: Cai, Shenshen, author.
Title: State propaganda in China's entertainment industry / Shenshen Cai.
Description: Milton Park, Abingdon, Oxon ; New York : Routledge, 2016. | Series: Routledge contemporary China series ; 153 | Includes bibliographical references and index.
Identifiers: LCCN 2016001395 | ISBN 9781138639614 (hardback) | ISBN 9781315637082 (ebook)
Subjects: LCSH: Mass media and propaganda—China. | Mass media—Political aspects—China. | Performing arts—Political aspects—China. | Politics and culture—China. | Propaganda, Chinese—History—21st century. | Nationalism—China—History—21st century.
Classification: LCC P96.P722 C635 2016 | DDC 303.3/750951—dc23
LC record available at http://lccn.loc.gov/2016001395

ISBN: 978-1-138-63961-4 (hbk)
ISBN: 978-1-315-63708-2 (ebk)

Typeset in Times New Roman
by Apex CoVantage, LLC

Contents

	Acknowledgements	vi
	Introduction	1
1	The Chinese Moon Festival Gala 2009–2014: political marketing using imagery and sensory laden messages	15
2	*Founding of a Republic* and *Beginning of the Great Revival*: propaganda-infused blockbusters in present-day China	38
3	The Cultural Revolution: how TV Drama Serials create collective amnesia	59
4	*The Search for Modern China* and *The Pillar Standing in Midstream*: two examples of the nationalist genre of Chinese commercial media	83
5	A rising star professor: Yu Dan and her interpretation of the *Analects*	106
6	A cultural reading of three contemporary Chinese revolutionary spy-themed TV drama serials: *Undercover*, *Plotting* and *All Quiet in Peking*	127
	Conclusion	147
	Index	151

Acknowledgements

I would like to express my sincere gratitude to Dr William Lakos (Bill) and Dr Emily Dunn for their kind help and advice during the writing process of this book. Bill was my sharp-eyed critic and insightful interlocutor, who provided enormous help in terms of polishing my arguments, editing my grammar, and most importantly being finicky with my mistakes and errors, and he contributed much to the completion of this work. He has been my mentor since our time together at the University of Tasmania, where I started my PhD research. Bill generously dedicated his time and help as a true friend and colleague.

I would also like to thank Emily for her careful editing of some of the chapters, which I know is time-consuming and tedious. Also, I would like to thank the Asian Studies editors at Routledge – Ms Stephanie Rogers and Ms Rebecca Lawrence – for their kind support during the reviewing and production process of the book. Finally, and most importantly, I want to thank my family for accompanying me during the writing process of the manuscript.

The author thanks the following publishers for granting permission to reprint material from the following articles. They include: Shenshen Cai, "The Cultural Representation and Politics of the Chinese Moon Festival Gala: Nostalgia, Romance and Nationalism" (*East Asia: An International Quarterly* 31, 3 [2014], 249–267), some sections of which are included in chapter 1; Shenshen Cai, "An Unconventional Mainstream Film: *The Founding of a Republic*" (*Asian Cinema* 25, 2 [Winter 2014], 183–203), a few segments of which are incorporated, with revisions, in chapter 2; Shenshen Cai, "Contemporary Chinese TV Serials: Configuring Collective Memory of Socialist Nostalgia through the Cultural Revolution" (*Visual Anthropology* 29, 1 [2016], 22–35), an revised and updated version of which forms the basis for chapter 3; Shenshen Cai, "Analyzing the Nationalist Genre of Chinese Commercial Media: Case Study of Sohu Web Documentary – the Search for Modern China" (*China Media Research* 11, 1 [2015], 36–45), some sections of which are included, with adjustments, in chapter 4; Shenshen Cai, "'White Collar' Academia and 'Exemplar' Cultural Product: Yu Dan and Her Confucius from the Heart: Ancient Wisdom for Today's World" (*Sungkyun Journal of East Asian Studies* 15, 1 [2015], 89–108), which, with some revisions, forms the basis for chapter 5.

Introduction

Since the beginning of the People's Republic of China (PRC), propaganda has been an integral part of the Chinese Communist Party's (CCP) strategy of political control and ideological manipulation. The government promotes its policies through the news media and also through other means such as study groups and workshops organized by government institutions and work units; however, the state propaganda machine is also very adroit at utilizing mass entertainment to publicize official doctrine and spread Party ideology. The CCP's inventive and adept appropriation of popular artistic forms, such as the New Yangge Movement (*xin yangge yundong*) that was launched in the Shan-gan-ning area in the 1930s and 1940s before the CCP took over rule of mainland China, "demonstrated how the north Chinese peasant dance-drama yangge underwent dramatic political transformations in the hands of the communist propagandists in their attempt to realize the Maoist goal of 'facing the masses'" (You 2012: 260). Since the beginning of communist rule of China, the CCP propaganda continues this tradition of appropriating a wide range of mass cultural and entertainment practices to mobilize and educate the masses of Chinese people. Consequently, a plethora of mass entertainment and popular cultural activities and pursuits have been employed as a practical tool by the official propaganda bodies. These cultural forms include collective dancing, revolutionary films, celebratory events, Peking Opera, folk literature, and performing arts forms such as storytelling (*pingshu*), crosstalk (*xiangsheng*), rhythmic comic talk (*kuaibanr*), and musical storytelling art of Suzhou (*tanci*), and all were used at various times to disseminate socialist education and promote socialist policy (Mackerras 1981; Kaikkonen 1990; Holm 1991; Link 2007; Gerdes 2008; Webster-Cheng 2008; You 2012).

In particular, the practice of the CCP's propaganda of merging ideology with the utility of folk literature and performing arts genres became a distinctive feature of the Party publicity in the post-liberation period. Based on their entertainment value and immense public appeal, indigenous Chinese performing art such as crosstalk, storytelling and musical storytelling art of Suzhou are typical ruses that were recruited by the propaganda institutions to convey Party ideology and policy. The founding of the PRC in 1949 marked the beginning of a new social system, and, in this new proletariat society, street performers, who were once exploited and discriminated against, were seen for the first time as artists or artisans (Xue 1985: 120). In keeping with the new social rules and socio-political reality, and to help with the propagation of the CCP's policies, street performers took an active part in political studies and worked hard to improve their political awareness.

In 1950, under these new circumstances, and with Chairman Mao Zedong as the prime mover, "[t]he Small Group for the Improvement of *Xiangsheng*" (*Beijing xiangsheng gaijin xiaozu*; hereafter "the Group"), which was headed by one of China's most famous *xiangsheng* performers, Hou Baolin, was organized. Other *xiangsheng* writers and scholars, such as Lao She and Luo Changpei, acted as advisers to the Group (Wang, Wang and Teng 1995). The Group modified many old *xiangsheng* pieces and removed any pornographic or risqué jokes, references to inappropriate class attitudes, and other ideological flaws that were originally part of the works (Link 1984: 97; Xue 1985: 124; Xiang 2008: 155), so that the content reflected the opinions of the ruling authorities. Most of the reformed works lampooned society's remnants of feudalism, eulogised the new regime, and promoted optimism among the people (Ma 1980: 26). *Xiangsheng* was no longer intended to only make people laugh; it was intended to have "educational value" (Kaikkonen 1990: 76). Some examples of this didactic use of *xiangsheng* are shown below. In order to promote China's participation in the Korean War, the Group wrote and performed *Such America* (*Ruzi meiguo*) and *Paper Tiger* (*Zhi laohu*). To promote the new Marriage Law, they performed *Liu Qiao Raises Pigs* (*Liu Qiao yangzhu*) and *Marriage and Superstition* (*Hunyin yu mixin*). As propaganda for the new Transport Security Movement, they wrote *Travel at Night* (*Yexing ji*).

Apart from crosstalk, the Party adopted other mass entertainment fork-art forms such as storytelling and musical storytelling to be used as propaganda. Starting from 1962, the official propagation tools renovated the traditional folk performing arts genre storytelling into a New Storytelling Movement (*xin gushi yundong*) as part of a program to preach the Chinese people. In this movement, customary oral storytelling performance was appropriated by the CCP to work as a medium for spreading socialist messages and principles, which reconfigure the tradition of it into a novel political vehicle to legitimatize the power of the Party (You 2012: 260). These new stories were widely circulated as revolutionary tales (*geming gushi*), which has obvious ideological implications. During this movement, popular storytelling events that were used for propaganda purposes, such as class struggle, had become trendy in the fields, teahouses, and work and entertainment places in Shanghai, where over two thousand amateur storytellers were employed. While the masses were attracted by these events for entertainment, these storytelling routines became a practice of socialist tutelage (You 2012: 263). Besides storytelling events, the political control of the arts and individual agency by the Party is also found in the enlistment of the musical storytelling art of *Suzhou tanci*, most notably from the outset of the founding of the PRC to the eve of the breakout of the Cultural Revolution (Webster-Cheng 2008; cited in You 2012: 261).

Similar to folk literature and preforming arts, elite national essence Peking Opera performances, a classical performing arts genre, was appropriated and transformed by the CCP (partly under the organization and instructions of Jiang Qing, Mao's third wife and a member of the Gang of Four) into a popular mass recreational tool to be used to sell their political doctrines and ideologies to the people. During the Cultural Revolution time, the Eight Model Operas, which called for and celebrated continuous class struggle, became almost the only entertainment source available to the public.

Another mass entertainment and popular cultural form that was commissioned by the Party propaganda machine were revolutionary films. They were produced during the initial decades of socialist China, and these revolution-themed movies extolled the virtues and spirit of the Chinese communist revolutionaries, their courageous endeavours and sacrifices for the people and the country, and their heroic deeds signifying the collective and patriotic ethos. These propaganda films foreground Mao's Yan'an injunctions, which was to praise and glorify the achievements of the Chinese revolutions and its stars, and the new society (Lee 1991: 15).[1]

This revolutionary movie pattern evolved into the so-called mainstream / main melody film genre (*zhuliu / zhuxuanlu dianying*)[2] in the post-socialist, post-revolutionary new era. These mainstream melodies are, according to many scholars, a recurrent political ploy by the CCP (Rao and Pei 1997; Wang 2003), as it continues to grasp for "cultural leadership" by the Party and a nuanced "partnership" between the state propaganda and mass entertainment. Mainstream films have consistently served as authorized propaganda as they help mould and remould the Party's ideological control.

At the 1987 National Conference for Cinematic Production, the official slogan, "propagate the main melody and uphold diversity," was articulated, which was quickly taken up by propaganda and cultural institutions and by literary organization and television creators. In the cultural-media domain of contemporary China, a main melody is found in literary, filmic, TV, or other comparable texts, which are synthesises of theme and CCP ideology (Zhang 1994; cited in Zhu, Keane and Bai 2008: 5). The main melody narrative exemplifies the cultural and artistic expressions of the orthodox ideology that is upheld and sponsored by the Party. Mainstream narrative refers largely to official culture and the culture of the Party, and its mission is to promote the rule of the Party and to spread revolutionary traditions and propagate the spiritual construction of socialism (Meng 2003: 147; Xu 2010: 47). Most importantly, mainstream propaganda work has to fulfil some core responsibilities, including verifying the legality and effectiveness of CCP's rule and its intimate bond with the well-being of the Chinese people.

Building on Williams's (1980: 38) argument, the Chinese mainstream, official and orthodox ideology may be interpreted as the "overriding and active discourse" comprising "a central system of practices, meanings and values" in socialist and post-socialist China. The strength, durability, and scope of this mainstream discourse have become the social consciousness. In the current Xi Jinping epoch, CCP propaganda values highly the worth and potency of the mainstream paradigm that concentrates on "positive propaganda" (*zhengmianxuanchuan*).[3] As Xi has pointed out, the CCP is facing an enormous struggle at this historical juncture, and the Party is bravely confronting many extraordinary problems; thus the propaganda work should stay in line with the right political position, and that is to advocate the Party governance, to uphold the authority of the central government, and to spread the Party policy and line (Xi Jinping: xionghuaidaju bawodashizhaoyandashi nulibaxuanchuangongzuozuodegenghao 2013).

Dr Ye, the president of the Sino-American Association of Science, Technology and Cultural Exchange, remarked that since Xi Jinping took over power in 2013, the previously comparatively relaxed ideological environment has been tightened. Xi does not allow speeches and opinions that divert from those of the government leaders to be published. Liu Nianchun, another critic on Chinese affairs, observed that Xi Jinping mainly tackled two issues after he gained power – one is the army, and the other is public opinion – and that Xi's political ideas were formed during the Mao era (Meiguo pinglunjie renshi dianping Xi Jinping de xinwenlinian 2015). Since Xi Jinping's rule began, the "struggle for public opinion" has been re-employed by the CCP in order to achieve positive propaganda outcomes for Party policies and ideology (Xi Jinping xuanchuan sixianglingyu "yulundouzheng" xintifa yinguanzhu 2013). This more sombre and politically coded catchphrase has replaced "public opinion guidance" to designate the CCP's will to reinforce its command by propaganda. In so doing, Xi foregrounds the weight of ideological monitoring and propaganda and stresses that the Party must grip firmly the leadership, the management, and the "right of discourse" of ideological propaganda, as once the Party loses control over these fields, it will unavoidably make irretrievable historical mistakes (Xi Jinping tan xuanchuangongzuo: bu rixinze bi ritui 2014). Xi further instructs that the integration of media resources – including broadcasting, TV, newspaper and the internet – play a key role in promote "positive propaganda" amongst the ordinary Chinese people (Sanshengqu xuanchuanbuzhang bitan: xuanchuan sixiang gongzuo xu chuanbo zhengnengliang 2013). Xi's directive reconfirms the Party's propaganda machine's continuing engagement with and appropriation of mass media genres and the entertainment vehicles to manipulate and direct public opinion and to propagate its policies along ideological lines.

In the recent decades, a much more energetic and competitive era in many grounds of China's socio-cultural creation emerged, and this era has nurtured a more multifarious and prosperous mass entertainment cultural landscape. However, the influence and appeal of mainstream cultural products is gradually waning. This loss of impact of the official propaganda in modern-day China's cultural-media sphere is a combination of a number of causal agents. First, the fourth of June Tiananmen Square demonstration marked a watershed in the contemporary history of China which hugely damaged the image and reputation of the CCP. In addition, the widening economic and social gap between China's nouveau riche and the poor, officialdom corruption, numerous social malaises, and injustice greatly reduces the authority and legitimacy of the CCP as the ruling party. Although propaganda then became an imperative for the Party-state, so as to repair and rebuild its impaired image during the post-1989 period, other factors impinged on the Party's propaganda agenda.

The waning of revolutionary passion and the loss of revolutionary tradition among the Chinese people, in particular among the young generation people, contributed to the lack of attraction of mainstream texts as a certain part of this cultural discourse eulogies the CCP's revolutionary past and its heroes. If we take the mainstream film genre as an example, revolutionary films produced in the 1950s, 1960s and 1970s achieved great popularity among the filmgoers as they were manufactured at a time when political excitement and wrath was prolific across China. However, mainstream films made in the following decades did not earn much responsiveness from the film audience. As a result, these films do not have many voluntary spectators, but instead they have obligatory audiences organized by schools, work units and companies who are required to view them. Also, they are seen as being monotonous and solemn, and their strict form, their educational intent, and their superior and sanguine themes – mainstream cultural creation fostered by the Party-state – have become abstract symbols with little temptation to the contemporary Chinese people (Meng 2003: 147; Wu and Xu 2005: 154). The reception of mainstream cultural creations is also severely affected by the implementation of the free market economic system, which evokes ferocious competitiveness in the cultural market in modern-day China. Noticeably, in the socio-cultural context of today's China, both elite and official cultures are recoiling, and popular culture has assumed the domination (Yin 1998, cited in Lu 2005: 120). In order to retain a living space in the cultural landscape, producers and distributors had to readjust their attention to sales and profit margins. The lack of selling points and entertainment value are the disadvantages of many mainstream cultural products.

In order to reverse the dwindling situation of the mainstream cultural products and retrieve the dominant position of official ideological discourse in the cultural-media arena of modern-day China, and to win the "struggle for public opinion," desperate efforts are required in terms of lifting the effectiveness of state propaganda through improving its quality and standard and making it more appealing to the general public. The concern about the declining effectiveness of mainstream cultural products and their propaganda utility have long been a focus of the CCP government's agenda of ideological works, which has been re-stressed lately by the Xi Jinping administration.

In the post-Tiananmen era, creative efforts have been made to repackage the mainstream rhetoric into TV drama narratives, and this has achieved some success. In post-reform China the consumption of TV programs and other popular cultural practices has progressively become the route through which people are contacted and engaged (cited in Rofel 1994: 702). Many very successful TV serials have been used as conduits to disseminate official rhetoric and mainstream ideology, which is a sort of "cultural governance," as TV dramas continue to be one of the most popular TV formats in China (Zhu 2008a; Schneider 2012). The political leadership in China attributes a very high grade of impact to TV in general and to TV dramas in particular (Schneider 2012: 180). Although the market now has much to say in recognizing which programs are profitable and popular, "both the institutionalization and ideological contours of state power" have the final say in determining what can be aired on the screen (Rofel 1994: 703).

Yearnings (*Kewang* 1990), a record-breaking domestic drama serial, is about two ordinary Chinese households during the period from the Cultural Revolution and up to the post-reform era, and its popularity caused the CCP propagandists to realize that a workable and effective official cultural product should first be accepted and liked by the people before it is used as a tool for propaganda. While viewers enjoyed *Yearnings* as a domain unattached from those topics usually associated with the state, post-Mao political ideas that have been steadily waning in the entertainment domain were threaded throughout the TV drama's account (Rofel 1994: 715). In other words, the TV show, "as both a narrative and an event, is inseparable from the apparatus of Chinese television as a site for objectification of 'state desires' in post-Mao China," and it "reminds us that the production of meaning is a process that never stands outside of power, so that spectators' needs are often contained within dominant political and cultural agendas" (Rofel 1994: 702–703). Embedded in different facets of its narrative, *Yearnings* embodies, in its character design and building, the Party's efforts to further construct socialist morality in response to the people's demands and desires (Rofel 1994: 704). Following its broadcast, the then Politburo member in charge of culture and ideology, Li Ruihuan, applauded the serial for "providing a new model of social relations which represented 'socialist ethics and morals'" (Feng 1991; cited in Zhu, Keane and Bai 2008: 6). Moreover, in its echoing of mainstream ideology, *Yearnings* purposely turns intellectuals into offensive figures, which is in line with the official discourse that brutally suppressed intellectuals' open and courageous challenge to state power during the Tiananmen demonstration.

A more recent state's appropriation of TV drama has been the so-called revisionist Qing dramas such as *Yongzheng Dynasty* (*Yongzheng wangchao* 1999) and *Kangxi Dynasty* (*Kangxi wangchao* 2001). They have gained huge admiration among TV viewers, but it also reveals the Chinese entertainment industry's subservient rapport to the state (Zhu 2008b: 28). Focusing on palace infightings and power struggles, the revisionist Qing dramas were extremely popular; however, the narrative of revisionist Qing dramas has taken clues from different political strands including Neo-authoritarianism, Neo-conservatives and the New Left schools. While partly incompatible on the economic and political model for China's modernization, these main intellectual camps agree on the necessity for a tougher central government that would safeguard China's interests internationally and eliminate social and economic troubles locally (Zhu 2008b: 28). Converging in support for strong central government, these intellectual ideologies echo the Confucian thought of nurturing restrained individuals and accountable leaders who obey rules and rituals for the sake of the larger society (Zhu 2008b: 27). Serving as personifications of the strong central government, the Emperors Yongzheng and Kangxi were accordingly portrayed as "representatives of an age of determination and confidence, of cultural and political unity, and above all of economic equality and incorruptibility." This rehabilitation of Yongzheng bears a close similarity to the remythologization of Mao during the post-Tiananmen era, which is also suggestive of former premier Zhu Rongji, who was "an upright reformer tough on corruption and passionate about the well-being of ordinary people" (Zhu 2008b: 31). By planting these mainstream political values into the make-up of characters and plot design, the revisionist Qing dramas react to the political and cultural ethos of the time and demonstrate their ideological positioning clearly, which remains close to popular views endorsed by the state (Zhu 2008b: 28).

The mainstream paradigm also cleverly appropriates the TV drama narrative in anti-corruption dramas. Given the tight political control over prime-time TV, the "positive propaganda" rhetoric continuingly dominates the storyline and plots of anti-corruption shows. In combating public opinion that suspects the ruling party of gross corruption, this TV subgenre intelligently and skilfully grafts the image of an honest Party and government official to a longstanding, but still formidable and pervasive, ideology of "clean official" (*qingguan*). By creating a minor group of "clean officials" who are trustworthy and fair-minded, who care for the needy, and who pit themselves against mighty criminals to preserve the interests of common people, society is ameliorated and justice is reinstated in the show's narratives (Bai 2008: 49). In so doing, the anti-corruption drama creates an imagined "moral community" where "moral consensus" is shared by the viewers. Being heroes of this hypothetical "moral community," "clean officials" "mediate and reduce the gap between the propaganda and the popular," and "they blend the Party's need for good publicity with a powerful popular belief in and desire for the redemptive power and heavenly justice embodied by clean officials" (Bai 2008: 57). Further, from an ideological perspective, the "clean official" cultural icon, acting as representative of the Party-state, helps "anchor the Party in the role of moral leadership and create a sense of moral unity between the Party and the people," which is "central to the remoulding of the Party's image in the mass media" (Bai 2008: 49) and provides "the moral basis for the Party leadership of the community" (Bai 2008: 57).

Apart from those above-mentioned single research articles that examine popular TV drama texts which have been directly or indirectly enlisted by the state propaganda apparatus to spread Party lines and policies, Florian Schneider's *Visual Political Communication in Popular Chinese TV Series* (2012) provides a systematic and detailed discussion and update on the Chinese state's cultural governance through TV drama serials. Schneider foregrounds the visual collaboration of TV dramas with the dominant ideological discourse with a focus on building images of proficient and decent officials and public servants, and justifying the political legitimacy and accountability of the state. However, the analysis focuses only on the visual political communication in popular Chinese TV dramas and does not cover the broader infiltration of the visual mainstream propaganda rhetoric into the comprehensive and dynamic cultural entertainment industry of modern-day China.

Besides Schneider, other scholars have also made efforts to offer fresh and insightful research and analysis in keeping up with the evolution and developments of contemporary China's propaganda discourse and its policies and devices. For example, Xiaoling Zhang's *The Transformation of Political Communication in*

8 Introduction

China: From Propaganda to Hegemony (2011) maps out the changes and updates of the Party-state's controlling and monitoring systems and institutions in the media world. Anne-Marie Brady's *Marketing Dictatorship: Propaganda and Thought Work in Contemporary China* (2008) addresses the role of the Chinese propaganda system, its methods of control and its modernization. Daniel C. Lynch's *After the Propaganda State: Media, Politics, and "Thought Work" in Reformed China* (1999) analyses the commercialization, globalization and pluralization of thought work in contemporary China and the state's struggle to reassert control over the media sphere. Daniela Stockmann's *Media Commercialization and Authoritarian Rule in China* (2013) offers analyses and insights on the phenomenon "propaganda for sale – marketized media as instruments of regime stability and change," with a focus on news reporting. Anne-Marie Brady's edited volume *China's Thought Management* (2012) provides up-to-date information and discussion on the state's new approach to propaganda via national events, cultural traditions and social malaises – such as adopting the 2008 Olympic Games and Confucian concepts, and through the People's Liberation Army and even prostitutes – to renovate and revamp its propaganda devices. Edney Kingsley's *The Globalization of Chinese Propaganda: International Power and Domestic Political Cohesion* (2014) examines the Chinese propaganda system in the era of globalization and the power of propaganda in China's domestic political system, with a concentration on exploring the connections between the CCP's desire for domestic political control and its vision for the development of China's international power.

Most of this academic research reflects the state propaganda discourse of contemporary China; however, these attempts at scholarship are mostly seen as readings that only mirror the policies, institutional organizations and systems of the CCP propaganda machinery. Moreover, they do not provide a detailed account of the recent variations of official propaganda rhetoric embedded in the popular media texts, and they did not pay adequate attention to the intersections and interactions between state propaganda and commercial interests reflected in the prevailing popular cultural products of today's China. Although many aspects of the renovation and progress of the mainstream propaganda paradigm have been identified and touched on by the above-mentioned manuscripts, they nonetheless do not offer sufficient case studies to concretely and practically show how the makeovers are being implemented or their intended effects.

Further, these research manuscripts do not specify and tap into the most recently released popular cultural media narratives and sensations, particularly those that are active and admired in the energetic visual media arena such as online documentary, film, TV drama serials and education and science programs, which are enlisted and co-opted by the state for propaganda goals. This work addresses the holes left by the above endeavours made by other scholars. Through examining a group of representative popular cultural media texts and spectacles, the manuscript will map out the cutting-edge and inventive expansions and evolutions within the field of official propaganda that are embedded in the entertainment industry of contemporary China, and it will illustrate how the CCP propaganda apparatus and tactics refashion and revamp themselves.

In so doing, the proposed book foregrounds the latest advances and novelties of state propaganda: its motives, reasoning and approaches within the entertaining media sphere of today's China. It textually examines a group of carefully chosen mass entertainment products, which include two bestselling mainstream blockbusters, two online commercial web documentaries, the China Central Television Moon Festival Gala series, socialist revolutionary nostalgia TV drama serials, and a prime-time science and education program, in order to bring up-to-date the current knowledge about how the official propaganda machine has evolved and how it operates. Through content analysis and decoding of the production process of these media texts, the book will explore the cutting-edge subtlety of the state propaganda regarding its merging with commercial features, its fresh encroachments and originalities, which on one hand humanize and soften the serious, solemn, grand themes and topics usual and classical to official propaganda rhetoric; on the other hand it allows commercial media practitioners to reap the rewards of the mainstream ideology through repackaging and remodelling the official propaganda elements to suit the demands of the marketplace.

Following this brief introduction, the rest of the book interprets the latest movements of official propaganda as embedded in the popular cultural media narratives of contemporary China. Chapter 1, "Nationalism, nostalgia and romance: the politics of the Chinese Moon Festival Gala," examines the China Central Television Moon Festival (Mid-Autumn Festival) Gala series. Nationalism has been a consistent feature of modern Chinese politics and society, though its form has changed over recent times. The CCP has started to appropriate China's cultural nationalism as a tool for propaganda. Through imagery and sensitively laden political marketing that favours Party policy and rule, this form of nationalism indicates a more nuanced and ingenious mode of propaganda; and the CCTV Moon Festival Gala is a prime example. The Gala is a moon-inspired traditional Chinese cultural event that merges nostalgia and romance with nationalist sentiment.

Chapter 2 investigates two blockbuster movies from modern-day China: *Founding of a Republic* (*Jianguodaye* 2009) and *Beginning of the Great Revival* (*Jiandangweiye* 2011). They were released to coincide with the sixtieth anniversary of the founding of the People's Republic of China and the ninetieth anniversary of the CCP respectively. In contrast to previous mainstream films, from both the socialist and the post-socialist periods, *Founding* and *Beginning* are more commercial, but nevertheless they have still been useful to the CCP's more nuanced approach to propaganda. This chapter shows the novel ways enlisted by the CCP in its efforts to achieve ideological control of the Chinese people. By cleverly focusing on casting high-profile stars and also many comedians, and by employing a more objective and empathetic humanist approach to historical figures, the commercial success of *Founding* and *Beginning* are exemplary cases of how commercially successful films and CCP propaganda can coexist and benefit each other in contemporary Chinese entertainment industry. This kind of political remoulding of commercial mainstream film has produced "blockbusters with Chinese characteristics." As the arts are an embodiment of ideology, so *Founding* and *Beginning* denote "a great leap forward" in official discourse and propaganda.

Chapter 3 analyses the popular socialist revolutionary nostalgia genre on television, a unique type of TV drama serial in modern-day China. Using the Cultural Revolution as a representative historical event, this chapter examines how the collective memory and popular history revolving around it are reconfigured and reinterpreted via televisual media narratives. The collective memory of the Cultural Revolution is constructed and not preserved, and it is moulded by a collective framework of memory: this being the predominant thoughts and the governing ideological rhetoric of society – the state, official and mainstream ideology promoted by the CCP. A textual analysis of a group of typical socialist revolutionary nostalgia TV drama texts featuring *The Place Where Dreams Start* (*Meng kaishi de difang* 1998), *Bloom of Youth* (*Yu qingchun youguan de rizi* 2006) and *Crimson Romance* (*Xuese langman* 2003) will expose the process of manufacturing collective memory concerning the Cultural Revolution for what it is – a cultural amnesia which caters to the current propaganda and ideological goals of the Chinese government. This drastic reversion and reshaping of the Cultural Revolution moderates the critical and reflective power given to it by Scar Literature, and it is a distraction to a detached judgement of the Cultural Revolution.

Chapter 4 is about two online commercial web documentaries released on Sohu Web: *The Search for Modern China: Looking Back at Historical Moments* (*Zhuixun bainianzhongguo: huiwanglishishunjian* 2009) and *The Pillar Standing in Midstream: The Great Backstage Battlefield of the War of Resistance against Japan* (*Dizhuzhongliu: weida de dihoukangzhan* 2014). These two Sohu Web documentaries reveal a strong connection between Chinese state propaganda and China's non-state commercial media practitioners. They expose a concerted campaign of patriotism and nationalism marketed towards the Chinese people, in particular the online population. China's domestic private internet industry cannot overtly challenge Party authority, and the CCP is determined to manipulate a pliable media in order to uphold and propagate its policies and ideology.

Chapter 5 is an examination of Yu Dan and her book *Yu Dan lunyu xinde*, (English version title: *Confucius from the Heart: Ancient Wisdom for Today's World*). It questions why the book is so successful, and it explores the links with the popularity of people's interest in the Chinese classics and national studies. There is intense debate about the book's contents and Yu's elaboration of the *Analects*, and also the subtle collaboration of this understanding with official discourse and ideology. The chapter also addresses the impact that the Yu Dan phenomenon plays in changing the social status and functions of China's intellectuals.

Chapter 6 uncovers the nexus between the TV serials and official ideology and features another popular subgenre on Chinese television, the revolutionary suspense TV drama. It examines three popular revolutionary suspense TV drama serials – *Plotting* (*Ansuan* 2006), *Undercover* (*Qianfu* 2008), and *All Quiet in Peking* (*Beiping wuzhanshi* 2014), and much like other Red classics and revolutionary-themed films and TV dramas, the revolutionary suspense TV drama is also trending towards depoliticization and humanization. The chapter will show that these spy-themed dramas use suspense and mystery to achieve propaganda outcomes by hijacking the viewers into a position of "dominant" reading. This nuanced merging of "mainstream melody" with popular spy-themed dramas reveals a new pattern of official and commercial co-opted propaganda. This chapter will also probe the relationship between spy-themed dramas, topical social issues, official ideology, and the "aesthetic public sphere" where ordinary citizens are able to discuss and criticise civil and political issues.

The concluding chapter highlights the main research findings of the book and foregrounds the continuing efforts by the CCP to firmly grasp the "cultural leadership" through an intense "struggle for public opinion" and through a "positive propaganda" agenda via the use of mass entertainment vehicles.

Glossary

Ansuan 暗算
Beijing xiangsheng gaijin xiaozu 北京相声改进小组
Beiping wuzhanshi 北平无战事
Dizhuzhongliu – weida de dihoukangzhan 砥柱中流 – 伟大的敌后抗战
Hunyin yu mixin 婚姻与迷信
Jiang Qing 江青
Jiandangweiye 建党伟业
Jianguodaye 建国大业
Kangxi wangchao 康熙王朝
Kewang 渴望
kuaibanr 快板儿
Liu Qiao yangzhu 刘巧养猪
Meng kaishi de defang 梦开始的地方
pingshu 评书
Qianfu 潜伏
qingguan 清官
Ruzi meiguo 如此美国
Shan-gan-ning 陕甘宁
tanci 弹词
Xi Jinping 习近平
xiangsheng 相声
xin yangge yundong 新秧歌运动
Xuese langman 血色浪漫
Yexing ji 夜行记
Yongzheng wangchao 雍正王朝
Yu Dan 于丹
Yu Dan lunyuxinde《于丹论语心得》
Zhi Laohu 纸老虎
zhuliu / zhuxuanlu 主流 / 主旋律
Yu qingchun youguan de rizi 与青春有关的日子

zhengmianxuanchuan 正面宣传
Zhu Rongji 朱镕基
Zhuixun bainianzhongguo – huiwanglishishunjian 追寻百年中国 – 回望历史瞬间

Notes

1 Mao's Talks at the Yan'an Forum on Literature and Art (1942) is most notable for its promotion of literature and art to serve political ends of the Party, which emphasizes that all art should reflect the life of the working class and should serve politics, in particular the advancement of socialism.
2 The "mainstream / main melody" (*zhuliu / zhuxuanlu*) paradigm used here was first introduced into the cultural lexicon of contemporary China in the 1980s. It refers to official ideology that continues the revolutionary traditions of the Mao eras and promotes the rule of the CCP.
3 The promotion of "positive propaganda" indicates the CCP's determination to promulgate the advantages of the CCP rule, together with the legitimacy, authority, and prestige enjoyed by the Party among the Chinese people.

References

Bai, Ruoyun. (2008) "'Clean Officials,' Emotional Moral Community and Anti-corruption Television Dramas," in Y. Zhu, M. Keane and R. Bai (eds) *TV Drama in China*. Hong Kong: Hong Kong University Press: 47–60.
Brady, Anne-Marie. (2008) *Marketing Dictatorship: Propaganda and Thought Work in Contemporary China*. Lanham, MD: Rowman & Littlefield.
Brady, Anne-Marie. (ed.) (2012) *China's Thought Management*. Abingdon, Oxon; New York: Routledge.
Cao, Guoxing. (2013) "Xi Jinping xuanchuan sixianglingyu 'yulundouzheng' xintifa yinguanzhu," (Xi Jinping's Wording "the struggle for public opinion" Attracts Attention), RFI, published on 6 Sept 2013, accessed on 12 Jul 2015, available at: http://cn.rfi.fr/中国/20130906-习近平宣传思想领域"舆论斗争"新提法引关注
Edney, Kingsley. (2014) *The Globalization of Chinese Propaganda: International Power and Domestic Political Cohesion*. New York: Palgrave Macmillan.
Feng, Yingbing. (1991) "Li Ruihuan deng lingdao tongzhi yu Kewang juzu tan fanrong wenyi zhi lu." (Li Ruihuan and Other Leaders Stalk with the Production Team of Kewang About the Road for the Flourishing of Literature and Art) *Renmin Ribao* (People's Daily), Overseas Edition, 9 January, p. 1.
Gerdes, Ellen. (2008) "Contemporary Yangge: The Moving History of a Chinese Folk Dance Form." *Asian Theatre Journal* 25(1): 138–147.
Holm, David. (1991) *Art and Ideology in Revolutionary China*. Oxford: Clarendon Press.
Kaikkonen, Marja. (1990) *Laughable Propaganda: Modern Xiangsheng as Didactic Entertainment*. Doctoral Dissertation, Stockholm Unversity Institute of Oriental Languages, Stockholm, Sweden.
Kangxi wangchao (*Kangxi Dynasty*). (2001) TV drama serial, directed by Chen Jialin and Liu Dayin, first broadcast via CCTV's (China Central Television) Channel one.
Lee, Leo Ou-fan. (1991) "The Tradition of Modern Chinese Cinema: Some Preliminary Explorations and Hypotheses," in C. Berry (ed.) *Perspectives on Chinese Cinema*. London: BFI: 6–20.

Link, Perry. (1984) "The Genie and the Lamp: Revolutionary *Xiangsheng*," in B. S. McDougall (ed.) *Popular Chinese Literature and Performing Arts in the People's Republic of China 1949–1979.* Berkeley: University of California Press: 83–111.
Link, Perry. (2007) "The Crocodile Bird: *Xiangsheng* in the Early 1950s," in J. Brown and P. G. Pickowicz (eds) *Dilemmas of Victory: The Early Years of the People's Republic of China*. Cambridge, MA: Harvard University Press: 207–231.
Lu, Sheldon H. (2005) "Chinese Film Culture at the End of the Twentieth Century: The Case of *Not One Less* by Zhang Yimou," in S. H. Lu and E. Y. Yeh (eds) *Chinese-Language Film: Historiography, Poetics, Politics*. Honolulu: University of Hawaii Press: 120–140.
Lynch, Daniel C. (1999) *After the Propaganda State: Media, Politics, and "Thought Work" in Reformed China*. Stanford, CA: Stanford University Press.
Ma, Ji. (1980) *Xiangsheng yishu mantan* (Informal Discussion on Xiangsheng). Gangdong: Guangdong People's Press.
Mackerras, Colin. (1981) *The Performing Arts in Contemporary China*. London, Boston: Routledge & Kegan Paul.
"Meiguo pinglunjie renshi dianping Xi Jinping de xinwenlinian 2015." (American Critics Momment on Xi Jinping's Concept of News Reporting) RFA, published on 8 Jan 2015, accessed on 16 Sept 2015, available at: http://www.rfa.org/mandarin/yataibaodao/meiti/sd-01082015104127.html
Meng, Fanhua. (2003) *Chuan mei yu wenhua lingdaoquan: dangdai Zhongguo de wenhua shengchan yu wenhua ren tong* (Media and Cultural Leadership: The Cultural Production and Recognition of Contemporary China). Jinan: Shangdong Education Press.
Rao, Shuguang and Pei, Yali. (1997) *Xinshiqi dianying wenhua sichao* (Reflection on Film Culture in the New Era). Beijing: China Radio and Television Press.
Rofel, Lisa B. (1994) "'Yearnings': Televisual Love and Melodramatic Politics in Contemporary China." *American Ethnologist* 21(4): 700–722.
"Sanshengqu xuanchuanbuzhang bitan: xuanchuan sixiang gongzuo xu chuanbo zhengnengliang." (Essays of Ministers of the Department of Propaganda of Three Provinces: Propaganda Work Should Spread "positive energy") China News and Media Web, published on 17 Oct 2013, accessed on 18 Sept 2015, available at: http://news.xinhuanet.com/zgjx/2013–10/17/c_132805599.htm.
Schneider, Florian. (2012) *Visual Political Communication in Popular Chinese TV Series*. Leiden, Boston: Brill.
Stockmann, Daniela. (2013) *Media Commercialization and Authoritarian Rule in China*. New York: Cambridge University Press.
Wang, Jue, Wang, Jingshou and Teng, Tianxiang. (1995) *Zhongguo xiangshengshi* (History of Xiangsheng in China). Beijing: Yanshan Publishing House.
Wang, Xiaoyu. (ed.) (2003) *Zhongguo dianying shigang*. Shanghai: Shanghai Antique Books Press.
Webster-Cheng, Stephanie. (2008) Composing, Revising and Performing Suzhou Ballads: A Study of Political Control and Artistic Freedom in *Tanci*, 1949–1964. PhD Dissertation, University of Pittsburg.
Williams, Raymond. (1980) *Problems in Materialism and Culture: Selected Essays*. London: Verso.
Wu, Xiaoli and Xu, Shenmin. (2005) *Jiushi niandai zhongguo dianying lun* (Reflection on 1990s Chinese Films). Beijing: Culture and Art Publishing House.
"Xi Jinping tan xuanchuan gongzuo: burixinzhe biritui." (Xi Jinping Comments on the Propaganda Work: Move Forward or You Will Fall Behind) China Military Web, published

on 11 Aug 2014, accessed on 6 Sept 2015, available at: http://www.81.cn/jmywyl/2014-08/11/content_6087761_2.htm.
"Xi Jinping: xionghuaidaju bawodashi zhaoyandashi nuli ba xuanchuan sixianggongzuo zuodegenghao." (Xi Jinping: Having the Overall Situation in Mind, Seizing the Big Issues, and Making an Effort to Improve Propaganda Work) People's Daily Online, published on 21 Aug 2013, accessed on 6 Sept 2015, available at: http://cpc.people.com.cn/n/2013/0821/c64094-22636876.html.
Xiang, Shi. (2008) "Lun Xiangsheng chuantong de jicheng yu fazhan." (Commentary on the Inheritance and Development of the Traditions of *Xiangsheng* Performance) *Hunan diyi shifan xuebao* 8(3): 155–157.
Xu, Jianfeng. (2010) "Zhuxuanlu dianying de yishu yu jishu ronghe." (The Merging of Techniques and Arts in Mainstream Films) *Wenyi pinglun: Xueshu Ban* 11: 47–48.
Xue, Baokun. (1985) *Zhongguo de chuantong xiangsheng* (*Traditional* Xiangsheng *Performance of China*). Beijng: People's Press.
Yin, Hong. (1998) *Jing xiang Yuedu: jiushi niandai yingshi wenhua suixiang* (Reading in the Mirror: Reflection on 1990s Film and Entertainment Culture). Shenzhen: Hainan chubanshe.
Yongzheng wangchao (*Yongzheng Dynasty*). (1999) TV drama serial, directed by Hu Mei, first broadcast via CCTV's (China Central Television) Channel one.
You, Ziying. (2012) "Tradition and Ideology: Creating and Performing New Gushi in China, 1962–1966." *Asian Ethnology* 71(2): 259–280.
Zhang, Jiabing. (1994) "Strike Up the Music of the Times: On the Main Melody and Television Drama." *Chinese Television* 9: 2–5.
Zhang, Xiaoling. (2011) *The Transformation of Political Communication in China: From Propaganda to Hegemony*. Singapore; Hackensack, NJ: World Scientific Pub. Co.
Zhu, Ying. (2008a) *TV in Post-Reform China: Serial Dramas, Confucian Leadership and the Global TV Market*. London; New York: Routledge.
Zhu, Ying. (2008b) "*Yongzhong Dynasty* and Totalitarian Nostalgia," in Y. Zhu, M. Keane and R. Bai (eds) *TV Drama in China*. Hong Kong: Hong Kong University Press: 21–32.
Zhu, Ying, Keane, Michael and Bai, Ruoyun. (2008) "Introduction," in Y. Zhu, M. Keane and R. Bai (eds) *TV Drama in China*. Hong Kong: Hong Kong University Press: 1–18.

1 The Chinese Moon Festival Gala 2009–2014

Political marketing using imagery and sensory laden messages

Introduction

Nationalism has been a prominent feature of modern Chinese politics and society, although its form has altered over the past decade or so as the CCP has appropriated China's cultural nationalism through its broad use of propaganda. This move symbolizes the thoughtful manipulation that state nationalism is wielding on cultural signs and perceptions in China. Through imagery and sensitively laden political marketing that favours Party policy and rule, this form of nationalism indicates a more nuanced and ingenious mode and use of propaganda than what we have previously encountered. On 19 August 2013, the Chinese president Xi Jinping made an important speech at a national conference on propaganda where he emphasized that innovation in ideas, devices and methods are the most significant points in the development and progress of the CCP's propaganda work (Xi Jinping: xionghuaidaju bawodashi zhaoyandashi nuli ba xuanchuan sixianggongzuo zuodegenghao 2013). Using the China Central Television (CCTV) Moon Festival / Mid-Autumn Festival Gala (*zhongqiuwanhui*) as a case study, this chapter scrutinises Party-state appropriations of cultural nationalism. The gala is a rich pool of moon-inspired traditional Chinese cultural attractions, and the shrewd steering of these culturally bound images and iconography shows a new propaganda tactic that mixes nostalgia, romance and abstract philosophical ideas into a patriotic and nationalist symbol. These customary cultural signifiers, illusions and fantasies attend to the Party's political objective of bolstering its legitimacy by shaping a culturally bound national identity.

Nationalism as a lifeblood of the Party-state

In the political and social climate of modern China, nationalism and nationalist discourse have gradually taken the upper hand among other ideas or social movements, such as communism, revolution and modernization (Townsend 1988: 205). In particular, in the process of the Chinese Communist Party's (CCP) revolutionary march towards power on the mainland region, nationalism played a more important role than Marxism in terms of contributing to the popular anti-imperialist revolution and creation of legitimacy for the communist regime (Gries

2004: 73; Zhao 2004: 209). When China was under siege by Western countries at the end of the imperial era, nationalism, gained the greatest appeal among the Chinese compatriots, especially with young college students. They were very patriotic and enthusiastic about the possibility for change in China, and around this time there was temporary cooperation between the CCP and its political adversary – the Nationalist Party. Nationalist sentiment among the Chinese people, evoked by the invasion from the West and Japan, helped the CCP to avoid what may have been a catastrophic fate as it was encircled and being suppressed by the Nationalist Party.

Up until it took over power of the mainland region, the CCP maintained its focus on nationalism and changed it into a patriotic-only discourse that overwhelmed other national and collective campaigns and ideologies. This state-steered nationalism discourse, along with its political focus, is still active in the political, social and cultural narratives and activities of present-day China. Moreover, acting as the official rendition of patriotism, nationalism is used by the CCP government to mobilize and manoeuvre the Chinese people in order to maintain the stability of its rule (Zheng 1999; Chang 2001; Guo 2004; Zhao 2004; Zhao 2005; Brady 2008). The Chinese government officially acknowledges nationalist sentiment as *aiguo*, which translates as "'loving the state,' however, Chinese nation and the Communist state are forever 'indistinguishable'" (Zhao 2005: 78). In contemporary China, state nationalism is simply a contracted patriotism that demands adherence and loyalty to the Communist Party–state, which is assumed to represent the will of all the Chinese people and is similar to the Three Represents[1] that signify the superiority and omnipotence of the CCP.

Unfortunately, since the adoption of the Opening Up reforms and the loss of appeal of Marxism and Maoism among the Chinese people, a depoliticization process has occurred within the socio-cultural domain. Consequently, people's attention has gradually become more focused on the economy and their own affluence and materialism. Simultaneously, a mounting political and social crisis, directly or indirectly caused by the economic makeover, broke out during the 1989 Tiananmen Square protests, and the armed suppression of the peaceful demonstration led to a deterioration of reputation and legitimacy of the CCP government with the Chinese people.

In order to repair and rebuild its damaged image and authority during the post-1989 period, propaganda, in its diverse guises, became the very lifeblood (*shengmingxian*) of the Party-state, as the vital measure for ensuring the CCP's ongoing validity and hold on power (Propaganda Cadre Training Reference Materials: 131; cited in Brady 2008: 1). In particular, since Xi Jinping took over power in 2013, "the struggle for public opinion" (*yulundouzheng*) has been re-called by the CCP to highlight the importance of propaganda and positive publicity of Party policies and ideology (Xi Jinping xuanchuan sixianglingyu "yulundouzheng" xintifa yinguanzhu 2013). This more serious and politically coded phrase has replaced "public opinion guidance" and points to the CCP's determination to strengthen its power through propaganda. Different from Mao-era propaganda, the current mass education enlisted by the CCP has been revitalized and is capable of managing the content of information that is disseminated to the public (Shambaugh 2007: 27). A feature of propaganda in the post-1989 period is that the CCP has started to further strengthen patriotic admonition and nationalist appeal (Zhao 2004: 218–247; Chang 2001: 6). Nationalism has become a "political apparatus" (Guo 2004: 24) and "a new ideology" (Zheng 1999: 2) and thus underscored all attempts to reclaim the rightfulness of, and to confirm the governing of, the CCP. The use of nationalism is a versatile cure to numerous internal and external dilemmas and challenges encountered by the CCP government. For instance, to redirect concern from domestic troubles, and to feign power in the diplomatic world (Zhao 2005: 76), it has been useful in refurbishing the "state ideology of socialism" and aiding China's progression into "a socialist nationalist phase" (Xu 2001: 126).

This novel stage of the state nationalistic discourse – as fostered by the CCP government, along with its advance into the new millennium – is correlated with components of cultural nationalism and features a culturally bound national entity. Guo (2004: 15) argues that Chinese nationalism normally refers to official or state nationalism, or unofficial nationalism (which largely reflected in areas of cultural and popular nationalism), or a combination of both. As a pioneer in analysing China's cultural nationalism discourse, Guo (2004: 2) maps out the distinguishing characteristics of the cultural nationalists group in contemporary China. According to Guo's findings, for cultural nationalists, being Chinese predominantly engages sharing in conventional cultural practices and recognition of "Chinese" principles and moral standards; it does not ineluctably require love of the Party or devotion to its "four cardinal principles." Therefore, culture, rather than allegiance to the Party-state, has become the most fundamental yardstick for outlining the national community.

Different from cultural nationalism, state nationalism defines the nation to be first of all a political-territorial entity, where Party rule and a dominant centralized state are of utmost significance in upholding national independence, concord and identity. Even if state nationalists sponsor traditional culture in state-nation construction, culture is only a means that serves a political goal instead of being a goal in itself (Guo 2004: 17). But under the rule of Deng Xiaoping, Jiang Zemin, Hu Jintao and Xi Jinping, the CCP's nationalist claims have been increasingly challenged by the unofficial nationalist discourse. The unofficial and bottom-up popular nationalist discourse repeatedly speaks of the "motherland" (*zuguo*) and the "Chinese race," (*zhonghua minzu*), without reference to the Party. Even the People's Liberation Army (PLA) affiliated writers have commenced to accentuate the estrangement of the Chinese notions of state (*guojia*) and motherland, and argue that "there are 'two Chinas': the Chinese people's 'motherland,' and the rulers' 'state'" (Gries 2004: 133).

The post-Tiananmen era witnessed the escalation of an indisputably popular nationalism in China that should not be conflated with state or official nationalism (Gries 2004: 20). With the expansion of online content and the increased use of the internet in China, this popular nationalism is growing stronger (Reilly 2010: 62). The popular nationalism discourse is motivated by a victimization sentiment held by contemporary Chinese people, and it is the attacks and degradations by the imperialist powers from the West and Japan which have been inflicted upon China over the past one hundred years that are considered the main cause of this mental trauma, as evidenced in the *China Can Say No* (*Zhongguo keyi shuobu*) series by popular nationalist author Song Qiang. This xenophobia was exacerbated by the American bombing of the Chinese embassy in Belgrade in 1999, which elicited sweeping street protests against the U.S. government and instigated cyber-nationalists to hack into the U.S. embassy's website in Beijing. Comparable demonstrations also followed the downing of an American spy plane off the coast of Southern China in 2001 and the boycott of the 2008 Beijing Olympics torch relay in Europe and America, marking the summit of the popular nationalist movements. Popular nationalist sentiment first surfaced in the mid-1990s from the bottom-up and was later appropriated by the CCP to serve its nationalist propaganda and to promote its "apolitical politics." This is also the case of cultural nationalism, which has been enlisted to serve the state's own ideology.

Akin to its rapport with popular nationalism, there also exists a convoluted correspondence between state nationalism and cultural nationalism. The association between cultural nationalism and state nationalism is vacillating, inter-reliant and open to argument. Zhao (2004: 227–228) observes a revitalization of customary Chinese cultural insignia and argues that such examples as the Great Wall and Confucianism are used as propaganda tools of the CCP. Tsu (2005: 3) further suggests that cultural nationalism constantly and instrumentally assists political propaganda and that "a state-imposed ideology" is underlined by ethnic kinship. When nationalism is turned into "a product of culture," the latter is commonly "relegated to a mobilized rather than mobilizing status."

Former CCP chairman Hu Jintao said in an address to the Congress that "[i]n the current period, culture is becoming an ever more important source of national cohesion and creativity and an ever more important component of comprehensive national power competition" (Hu 2007; cited in Edney 2012a: 139). Edney (2012b: 910) further argues that the cultural composition agenda implied by Hu's speech on culture's role is not only boosting extension and inspiration but also spawning unity and augmenting the Party-state's aptitude to direct the manufacture of cultural symbols. President Xi Jinping correlates the traditional Chinese culture with the soft power of contemporary China. Furthermore, socialism with Chinese characteristics, which according to him stems from conventional Chinese cultural heritage, caters to the needs of China's development and reflects the wishes of the Chinese people (Xi Jinping: xionghuaidaju bawodashi zhaoyandashi nuli ba xuanchuan sixianggongzuo zuodegenghao 2013).

The state endeavours to wield power on components of cultural nationalism such as cultural entities, cultural images and Chinese customs by conjoining with political inducement and propaganda is an elusive but sensitively enthralling approach. When perceived in such detail, it becomes clear that state propaganda is more nuanced and inventive than is frequently assumed. This Party-state appropriation of cultural nationalism not only bolsters the development and potency of cultural nationalism but also projects harmony and lifts the Party-state's faculty to direct the erection of cultural icons. In the following sections of this chapter, I will conduct an in-depth textual analysis of the CCTV Moon Festival Galas that spans the period from 2009 to 2014. It will trace the way in which the CCTV Moon Festival Galas have been fashioned to comply with the Party-state appropriation of cultural nationalism. The CCTV Moon Festival Galas embody a lush reservoir of moon-inspired traditional Chinese culture which is displayed via tasteful and delicate nostalgia and poignant romance. These cultural elements are adroitly woven into a patriotic and nationalist petition where cultural politics are reflected in the moon and the Moon Festival.

Moon/Mid-Autumn Festival Gala – a novel signature program of CCTV

In the ever-escalating competition within contemporary China's media sphere and entertainment industry, CCTV's domination and near-monopoly is being challenged by the provincial stations and satellite channels, although it still maintains much of its ideological and moral influence. In order to compete with the growing rivalry with the other less-powerful stations, CCTV's programs must change in order to be appealing to the audiences. Beginning in 2004, the creative and production team of *Our Chinese Heart* (*zhonghuaqing*) from the CCTV Overseas Centre initiated a new style of Moon Festival (the Mid-Autumn Festival) Gala, which aimed to transform the "Autumn Gala" into a massive fête that would be as significant and powerful as the "Spring Gala" (the Spring Festival Gala, *chunwan*). Different from the Spring Festival Galas that are shot in the CCTV television studios, the Autumn Galas are produced on-location and are therefore labelled as "holographic landscape shows." From their beginning in 2004, the Autumn Galas have been staged at different cities across China, all chosen for their rich cultural and historical heritage. The stages used in the performances of the galas were set at well-known historical landmarks in the cities.

For example, the 2005 Autumn Gala used the Yellow Crane Tower in Jiangcheng City (*jiangcheng*) of Hubei Province as its background landscape. The Yellow Crane Tower (*huanghelou*) is depicted in many famous ancient Chinese poems and prose and is therefore rich in historical and cultural symbolism and significance. In 2007 the gala was performed at the Imperial Summer Villa of Chengde in Hebei Province. The Qing Dynasty emperors and their families frequently visited the Imperial Summer Villa of Chengde (*bishushanzhuang*) during the summer due to Beijing's hot days. The stage was built in front of the Pavilion of Mist and Rain (*yanyuting*), a building that is often depicted in historical writings and adopted in contemporary television dynasty dramas. In 2009, the gala was held outdoors at the foot of the Bright Moon Mountain in Yichun County, Jiangxi Province. According to an ancient Chinese legend, it was from Bright Moon Mountain (*mingyueshan*) that Chang'e (an ancient beauty of China) flew to the moon. This ancient fairy tale and its ageless beauty add an enigmatic and oriental essence to the overall atmosphere of the gala.

Erected around these chosen landmarks were pavilions, terraces, rockeries, ponds and small bridges to create a fantasy-like atmosphere, which is distinctively traditional Chinese and also phantasmagorical. The decorations employed at the gala symbolize traditional Chinese landscape paintings, which themselves are attached to the image of a serene and harmonious society of ancient times. It is a "peach blossom garden existence" (*taohuayuan*) in which people can forget the pressure and plights of their everyday lives, enjoy delectable wine and chat freely with friends. In ancient China, people who chose to live in a "peach blossom garden" usually did not interfere with politics. The great poet and official of the East Jin Dynasty, Tao Yuanming, is one example. After Tao retired to a secluded life, he merely engrossed himself in a bucolic lifestyle and had no interest in politics anymore. Therefore, through the "peach blossom garden" scenery of the gala, the CCP conveys a symbolic message to the Chinese people which gently hints that they should not concern themselves with how the country is run, nor should they interfere too much with politics. Instead, the Chinese people would do better to enjoy a tranquil and affluent life in a "harmonious society" and to focus on realizing their "Chinese dream" (*zhongguomeng*), a phrase coined by the Xi Jinping administration to indicate the great resurrection of the Chinese nation. This romantic imagery of an ideal Chinese society is woven through the CCTV Moon Festival Galas and loosely shrouds the ideological intent behind it.

At night, when the galas are performed, the stage and the whole scene, assisted by the special lighting and sound effects created by the newest holographic 3D audio-visual technology, turn into a fairyland. The exquisite towers, rockeries and bridges with sparkling water running underneath are all scattered under the serene night sky. The water refracts the light, thus illuminating the pavilions, corridors, bridges and boats floating above it, while enchanting songs and music permeate the glow of the water and the shadows of the boats. After watching the galas, the chairman of the Houston International Film Festival found it incredible that the stages were built among real scenes and the performances were shot on location, and he praised the CCTV Autumn Galas as being extremely impressive and imaginative. The chairman had to admit that the Chinese holographic landscape shows were much more enjoyable than those American programs of the same kind.

These rich visual and aural representations of traditional Chinese cultural features and surroundings epitomise the quintessence of the great Chinese civilisation, which has vast appeal for both Chinese locally and those in the diaspora. Here, the shared inheritance gives rise to emotional identification from the audience, which confirms the cultural link between its members. This cultural bond contributes to the construction of a national identity, which is described by Gries (2004: 9) as "that aspect of individuals' self-image that is tied to their nation, together with the value and emotional significance that attach to the membership in the national community."

The producers creatively combine the natural and cultural landscape to create a "real" fairy-tale scene, which helped to win the CCTV Autumn Gala series numerous international awards. Among these awards, the most outstanding ones were gained at the thirty-ninth session (best TV entertainment program), fortieth session (special jury award for best director) and forty-third session (Remi Award and best director) of the Houston International Film Festival. The Houston

International Film Festival enjoys enormous reputation among TV and film producers and directors (Steven Spielberg and Ang Lee have won their first best director award at Houston International Film Festival). The director of the CCTV Autumn Galas, Guo Jihong, has become the second Chinese director to win this award after Ang Lee. The Remi Award is the top award for film, TV and new media programs at the film festival. Among more than five thousand participating works at the forty-third session of the festival, only four were awarded this prize, and the 2009 CCTV Autumn Gala was the only TV program which was awarded this prize. Further, Guo Jihong has become the only TV program director who has received this prize in the past forty-three years. The jury agreed that the 2009 CCTV Autumn Gala manufactured unbelievable on-location effects through spectacular scenes and outstanding artistic creativity.

The director of the CCTV Overseas Centre believes that the Autumn Gala has already become another signature program of CCTV and that it is well known for its poetic and elegant themes and styles, and, alongside its romantic scenes and stage design, it has become very popular with TV audiences. Guo Jihong has directed the CCTV Autumn Gala series for a continual six years, and she believes that the most important goal of the galas is to promote the image of contemporary China to the rest of the world. The CCTV Autumn Gala is a stereotypical example of the central objective of CCP propaganda. As Xi Jinping has said, propaganda should spread the most fundamental cultural ideals of the Chinese nation through popular means that engage broad participation; and it should make these cultural elements rich in long-lasting charm that crosses spatial and temporal limits and also be compatible with contemporary culture and society (Xi Jinping tan xuanchuan gongzuo: burixinzhe biritui 2014).

The Moon Festival Gala as a platform of "softened" state propaganda

In the Chinese milieu of politics and culture, celebratory events are frequently hijacked by the official ideology of the government (Yu 2009). Arranging celebratory fêtes and tribute events is understood as the best means by the official propaganda instrument to circulate ideas and ideals of patriotism and to expedite the patriotic fervour among the Chinese commoners (Zhao 2004: 223). Zhao (1998: 46; cited in Lu 2009: 112) explains that festival galas have become a platform to gain consensus via propaganda and official ideology. Starting from the CCTV Spring Festival Gala, which is the "most extravagant form of 'indoctritainment,' that is, indoctrination and entertainment in a single package" (Sun 2003; cited in Zhao 2008: 83), the Chinese people have formed a habit of viewing the festival galas while family members come together to celebrate traditional Chinese holidays, and it has become a regular folk custom (Lu 2009: 111). Therefore, most festival galas, such as the Spring Festival Gala and the Moon Festival Gala, are typically planned and presented by CCTV, and almost all the local satellite TV stations in China broadcast the national CCTV relay. Although many local satellite TV stations have in recent times organized their own Spring Festival and Moon Festival Galas, the CCTV versions remain the most popular. Although CCTV has ventured down a path of commercialization over the past three decades, its primary mission is to carry out the political directives of the Party and to serve as the Party's mouthpiece, and this has remained unchanged (Hong, Lu and Zou 2009: 41; Zhu 2012: 22). Gao and Pugsley (2008) provide a typical example of this argument in their article "Utilizing Satire in Post-Deng Chinese Politics: Zhao Benshan *Xiaopin* vs. the Falun Gong," where they examine the anti-Falun Gong campaign launched by the official propaganda institutions that is embedded in the Zhao Benshan *Xiaopins* (the Zhao Benshan–style short comedy skits). In the 2006 Spring Festival Gala, a large number of short comedy skits about the three problems concerning farmers, agriculture and the rural areas were underlined, through which the creators of the skits attempted to "use mainstream ideology to bridge the rural-urban gap" (Lu 2009: 121). These short comedy skits are the most popular entertainment genre of performing arts in contemporary China, and they are consistently performed during the CCTV Spring Festival Gala. However, "[c]reating sketches for the *Spring Festival Gala* each year is more difficult than walking a tightrope. They are subject to not only repeated censorship and revision by the state authorities, but social pressure to be 'politically correct'" (Lu 2009: 121).

Aside from the Spring Festival Gala, the Moon Festival Gala is more appropriate for incorporating cultural (in particular, traditional cultural) features, and it has thus been preferred by the CCP as a medium for spreading its state-steered mainstream ideology and nationalist discourse. If we take the 2009 Moon Festival Gala as an example, we see this show was given special consideration because it coincides with the sixtieth anniversary of the founding of the PRC. Moreover, the achievement of the 2008 Beijing Olympic Games has provided the central government with the extra bonus of an elevated and confident profile, within and outside China. Thus, the 2009 Moon Festival Gala was seen as the perfect graphic stage to boost the identity, unity and revival of the Chinese nation (CCTV.com). Television is an effective way of transmitting ideas, both directly and through symbols, and, with its romantic and poetic scenes and themes, the CCTV Autumn Galas conveyed the mainstream melody and zeitgeist of contemporary China.

This Party-state appropriation of cultural nationalism (as a genre or discourse) uses abstract cultural emblems, ideas and customs, and it saturates them with imagery and poignant political inducement that favours Party policy and rule. This propaganda strategy is tailored to the cultural palate of the embryonic middle class in contemporary Chinese society. In the Moon Festival Gala, the moon and moon-related subjects and scenes are converted into a symbolic reservoir of nostalgic emotion, romance, traditions and nationalism. Therefore, through the medium of television, the Moon Festival Gala achieves a specific social function in Chinese society. It helps to bolster traditional ideology targeted at the family and intended to unite families into the "imagined community" of the nation (Lu 2009: 112), the family writ large, which is governed by the state and the Party.

The Moon Festival Galas have been extremely popular with Chinese audiences across the globe. Following the broadcasting of the 2009 Moon Festival Gala, a posting on the Sina Web (*xinlangwang*) Culture and History BBS (bulletin board service which had a focus on the discussion of the gala) attracted a total of 2,213 follow-up postings, and the majority of postings were opinions of netizens who were very satisfied and enjoyed watching the gala. The Sina.com website is host to the biggest and most dynamic Chinese-language internet community in the world and home to over one hundred thousand postings every day (Reilly 2010: 49). Some of the most representative responses towards the gala were:

> "This year's gala is really gorgeous, perhaps it is due to the celebration of the National Day"; "It is really wonderful and unforgettable"; "It is as good as the Spring Gala"; "It is unbelievable that it was produced by CCTV"; "On such a good day, united with all the family members, and watching such a terrific gala, I really feel the happiness"; "I finally realized that life could be this pretty, and I want to celebrate the Moon Festival everyday"; "Because of CCTV, I did not feel lonely on this Moon Festival"; "This year's Moon Festival Gala is really meaningful"; "Many thanks for your hard work, CCTV"; "CCTV is progressing with the time."
>
> (The Cultural and History BBS on Sina Web 2009)

Each year, the CCTV Moon Festival Gala has been broadcasted live via three of its channels, CCTV-1, CCTV-4 and CCTV-9. CCTV reaches a huge audience and can be "beamed into virtually every corner of China" (Brady 2008: 140). In 1993, the CCP propaganda authorities set as their goal the renovation of CCTV into a media platform with a global influence (Brady 2008: 141), which resulted in the establishment of satellite TV channels CCTV-4 and CCTV-9. These two satellite TV channels were targeted at foreign and overseas Chinese viewers, particularly those in Taiwan, Hong Kong and Macau. It was also aimed at foreigners in China and in English-speaking countries. Both CCTV-4 and CCTV-9 serve as the mouthpiece for the Chinese government's standpoints on international matters and on the Party's perspectives on China's own affairs (Brady 2008: 167), and the state propaganda body, via its CCTV arm, is able to reach all parts of the world.

The ethnic attraction of the moon: ancient and present

In traditional Chinese culture, moon, moonlight and the circular image of the moon have long been classical and important motifs. The moon is understood to foster pleasure and accord, and it was often used by ancient Chinese poets and literati to express their prayers and hopes as the moon itself is a highly condensed symbol of conventional Chinese beliefs and philosophy. In the CCTV Moon Festival Galas, the CCP's propaganda apparatus cleverly manipulated the moon's primeval allegory, as the moon's traditional implications of fullness, cheerfulness and harmony fit precisely with the official political sermon of "building a harmonious society"[2] and "realizing the Chinese dream."

At the CCTV Moon Festival Galas, Hu Jintao's call for building a harmonious society and Xi Jinping's call for realizing the "Chinese dream" have been converted into imaginative and sentimental illustrations of the moon and associated cultural components. This inventive trial of instigating mainstream rhetoric exhibits a variation in the CCP's tactics for steering its ideological message. Anderson (1983) has remarked that shared language contributes to building the "imagined community," and, I argue, shared cultural images and concepts also help to create an "imagined harmonious society" and the "wonderful Chinese dream." Anderson (1983: 20–21) points out that Chinese characters have efficaciously shaped a community out of signs and ideograms. Like these pictograms, the Moon Festival Gala uses patterns and images to generate shared ideas and to render the imagined harmonious society and Chinese dream proposed by the CCP.

It is a well-known aspect of propaganda that it seeks the "control of opinion by significant symbols, or to speak more accurately by stories, rumours, reports, pictures, and other forms of social communication" (Lasswell 1927: 221; cited in Brady 2008: 9). Propaganda has within it the supervision of minds and the use of cultural symbols to pilot public opinion. The CCP has over recent time espoused Western notions on public relations in order to better run its propaganda and to generate homogeneous views on topics. In an extraordinary process of cultural exchange, China's propaganda system has harnessed the power of political public relations, mass communications and other modern methods of mass persuasion frequently used in Western democratic societies (Brady 2008: 3; cited in Veg 2012: 41). This new means of public persuasion is indicative of the Party's tactic of public communications and demonstrates that it has "moved from a Leninist model that functioned as a 'tool of mass propaganda and agitation' to a more 'public relations' style that is more suited to 'ruling by popular consent'" (Zhu 2012: 15), or, as Brady calls it, "popular authoritarianism" (Brady 2008: 68, 72). Propaganda strategies now incorporates pop music as a vehicle for political tutelage, in an attempt to make China's propaganda more appealing, enjoyable and motivating (Brady 2008: 74), and the similar use of galas and festivals fits neatly into this latest rationale of propaganda.

One example of this new mode of propaganda is found in the impressionist song about the moon "Moon Enchanting Bird" (*Yuemenglong niaomenglong*), which was performed at the 2009 Autumn Gala. The melody and lyrics of the song were adapted to suggest classic images of moon, moonlight and the moonlit night, and they convey the feelings and ambience of gentleness, peace and harmony.

The moon is fascinating, bird sweet	月朦胧 鸟朦胧
The night sky twinkles with fireflies	萤光照夜空
The forests and mountains are indistinct	山朦胧 树朦胧
The autumn worms are restless	秋虫在呢哝
The flowers at night seem flimsy	花朦胧 夜朦胧
The night breeze knocks at the window	晚风叩帘笼
The lanterns are hazy and the people lovesick	灯朦胧 人朦胧
Dreaming something sweet	但愿同入梦[3]

In the lyrics, the moon itself only appears once; however, the scenes around it are intensely portrayed. The sky, forests, mountains and flowers form a static background for the moonlit night, and birds, fireflies, autumn worms, a night breeze and people introduce vibrant scenes. Together, these traditional culturally entrenched images and scenes generate a poetic and romantic atmosphere and paint a miniature harmonious society.

Another musical item in the 2009 Moon Festival Gala was "Moonlit Night on Spring River" (*Chunjiang huayueye*). Played on the classical zither, it is full of pleasant melody, and the rhyming was adopted to emulate the tranquil and harmonious atmosphere.

Leaning on the railing to view the river tower	江楼上独凭栏
Hearing the sounds of bells and drums	听钟鼓声传
Lingering in the setting sun	袅袅娜娜散入那落霞斑斓
Spring river flows languidly	一江春水缓缓流
Looking around at the quiet and solitude	四野悄无人
Enveloped in a light fog	唯有淡淡袭来薄雾青烟

Upon hearing the ancient and graceful tune, and when relishing the delicate and elegant artistic conception of the verse, the audience becomes intoxicated by, and immersed in, the tender and delicate ambiance weaved by traditional cultural symbols and concepts. In other words, the audience is greatly enchanted by the romance and charm of Chinese traditional culture. Thus, a sense of cultural belonging and pride is spawned and strengthened, which prompts the shared nationalist sentiment in the Chinese people, which is highly regarded by the Party-state in its attempts to promote cohesion (Edney 2012a: 49).

Two themes in the up-to-date state nationalist discourse: nostalgia and love

Two distinguishing themes observed in recent Chinese cultural products are nostalgia and romance, and both are cleverly utilized by CCP propaganda to promote its official ideology. There is a tradition in the history of the CCP's propaganda where it enlists love and romance to spread its political ideas. The main propaganda method employed by the leftist literary movement during the May Fourth era and the periods immediately following it was the revolution model with an added component of love (Wang 2004). In that movement, revolution informed and liberated love, and love personified and romanticized revolution. The "love" module in this case was a cultural adaptation to changing political and social patterns in those eras, and it is an example which highlights the validity and merits of the revolution led by the CCP which claims itself the saviour of the suffering Chinese masses.

Similarly, the CCTV Moon Festival Gala is an archetypal nostalgic cultural product with an added love constituent, which is regularly implemented to deliver the gentle and poignant directives of the novel mainstream propaganda discourse. In this case, nostalgia implies a return to, and a yearning for, traditions, and the traditions mediate cultural identification and nationalist sentiment, which is the ultimate goal of the Party-state appropriations of cultural nationalism. Here, love exudes a romantic trace that mollifies, emotionalizes and romanticizes the political factors and caters to the cultural demands of the emergent middle-class. Alternatively, themes of love, romance and nostalgia are a measure through which the Party-state buttresses its role as the spokesperson for the will of the entire Chinese nation. For instance, in the pop song performed at the 2010 Autumn Gala "Jiang Cheng Zi" (*Jiangchengzi*), love and culture are juxtaposed, and love becomes culture – a shared culture of the Chinese people:

Relentless time	岁月忘
Scent of the rogue at night long gone	弹指哪夜胭香
Mirror of melancholy	铜镜叹
Farewell to the beauty by the dressing table	依稀轩窗梳妆
Sad autumn flowers	花怨秋
Is the bright moonlight to blame?	你会否怨明月光
Dreams never-ending	幽梦长
Only shattered by the tears that awake you	醒来拭泪几行
Brows knitted in sorrow	攒眉憾
Ravaged face with grey at the temples	纸上尘面鬓霜
Moon obscured by clouds	云掩月
What pain are you hiding in your letter?	你悬笔欲掩何伤
A castle in the air where to meet you	再逢若遥想
Two souls now separated forever	执手怎永相望
Remembering her faint smile	回眸谁浅笑
Yet her likeness has become so vague	音容渺惘
Ten years apart	你挥墨十年
One living yet the other dead	生死两茫茫
However the love is remembered	你怎会不思量
You cannot stop thinking of her	纵然流芳
In your life	而今生
You've seen through all the vicissitudes	崖边望穷千叠浪
Unchanged commitment	多少人
Followed by so many lovers before	恍然似你情难忘
Wishing you two souls	只愿两心
To be free from the constantly changing world	了却世事无常
To love the way you used to love	仍爱于
Even after ten years apart	十年生死两茫茫

"Jiang Cheng Zi" was originally a classical Chinese poem written by the North Song Dynasty poet Su Shi to commemorate his deceased wife. The lyric adaptation in the pop song sticks to the theme and scenery of the poem; however, it changes the traditional writing convention to a vernacular expression which is easy to understand by contemporary Chinese people. In the poet's imagined re-encounter with his wife in his dreams ten years after her death, he sees her sitting at the dressing table putting on her make-up. The tenderness and love of the situation is demonstrated by imagined scenes from timeworn Chinese culture. For example, bronze mirror, dressing table, traditional Chinese calligraphy awaken a nostalgic sentiment and stimulate the audience's craving for traditional culture and customs shared by all Chinese, forming an invisible bond among them. The cultural emblems depicted in the lyrics call for a joint hindsight of the identity and image of a China full of pleasure, serenity and love. The tenderness between the two lovers adds to the romantic sentiment of the whole gala and evinces the shared nostalgic warmth towards the bygone memory of a joyful and quiet, old China. Here, the nostalgic sentiments conjure a sense of cultural togetherness, while love personifies and romanticizes this nationalist discourse. Thus, nostalgia and love de-ideologise the tone of the statist cultural nationalism, building harmony and bliss the paramount ethos of contemporary China, overtaking the ideological grandiloquence of the CCP government.

"A Thousand Rivers" (*Qianjiangshui*), performed at the 2010 Autumn Gala provides another example:

A thousand rivers, the wine sways in the cup	千江水摇晃手中杯
To whom will you drink?	你敬谁？
Beneath the arch bridge the full moon is bright	拱桥下一轮皎洁
Be my companion	对邀明月
The distant sound of the flute	远方的洞箫
Lingering in my yearning heart	牵引思念往心里绕
As I fish by the river	我在水面上
I think of your smile	垂钓你的微笑
A thousand rivers sorrow furrows your brow	千江水轻蹙柳叶眉
Who are you thinking of?	你想谁？
Head bowed I embroider the shoes	低头绣着鞋
I wait for you as if awaiting the full moon	万里婵娟你在等满月
The pipa's melody still lingers	琵琶声 声声敲 绕梁绕
As I chant the Qingping ode	随我吟唱清平调
Reeds swaying in the moonlight	芦苇弯腰月色摇
Hand-in-hand we cross the bridge	执子之手共渡桥

The lyric of "A Thousand Rivers" was written by Vincent Fang (Fang Wenshan), a Taiwanese pop-song writer. As a lyricist, Vincent Fang has himself become a cultural phenomenon. He is an enthusiastic admirer of traditional Chinese culture and is best known for writing lyrics for some of Jay Chou's (Zhou Jielun) most popular songs, such as "Green Flower Porcelain" (*Qinghuaci*) and "Chrysanthemum Flower Bed" (*Juhuatai*).[4] The songs that were co-produced by Vincent Fang and Jay Chou have made a significant contribution to the "Chinese style" of music (*Zhongguofeng yinyue*).[5] This "Chinese style" of music combines lyrics that contain the quintessential elements of traditional poetry and ancient culture such as traditional Chinese painting and calligraphy with contemporary singing techniques and music composition (sometimes with components played on traditional Chinese musical instruments). This mixture of elements generates a nostalgic sentiment that is subtle and elegant.

Vincent Fang's lyrics are best known for their focus on anecdotes of love from ancient China. The love aspect of Fang's lyrics employs a variety of traditional images and icons to create scenery that is rich in nostalgic flavour and refined taste: such as a small bridge, flowing water, pipa (stringed Chinese lute), moon, chrysanthemum, attic and sanders. In "A Thousand Rivers," a traditional Chinese arch bridge, a flute, an image of a woman embroidering shoes, a pipa's melody, and the Qingping ode (*qingpingdiao*) are employed to create the old-style scenery of ancient China. In the tranquil moonlit night, a lady is waiting for her lover or husband to return home. Here, the sound of the flute and the pipa's melody linger in the longing hearts of the lovers, creating a very subtle and refined feeling that only people with a love for traditional Chinese culture would sense. Therefore, the love and romance mediate cultural bonding and furthermore the nationalist appeal, which serves the ideological goal of the Party-state.

Another well-known traditional Chinese poem about the moon, which has also been adapted into a pop song and has been repeatedly performed at the CCTV Autumn Galas, is "May You Live Long" (*Danyuan renchangjiu*), written by the Northern Song Dynasty poet Su Shi:

Bright moon, when will you be full?	明月几时有
Holding my wine cup I ask the blue sky	把酒问青天
Up there in the Moon's palaces	不知天上宫阙
Not knowing what year it is tonight	今昔是何年
If only I would ride the wind	我欲乘风归去
To the jade mansions of the moon	又恐琼楼玉宇
Though it may be so high up	高处不盛寒
Dancing alone with my shadow	起舞弄清影
I am better off in the earthly world	何似在人间
Retiring to the red chamber	转朱阁
Moonlight beneath the carved window	低绮户
Teasing through the sleepless night	照无眠
The moon should not know sadness	不应有恨
Why is it always full when we part?	何事长向别时圆
In joy or sorrow, in reunion or parting	人有悲欢离合
The moon waxes and wanes, bright or dims	月有阴晴圆缺
The way things have been since of old	此事古难全
May those living far apart live long	但愿人长久
And share the bright moon with their beloved ones	千里共婵娟

Su Shi's ancient poem describing the moon has become the most often used piece within this theme. The legendary Hong Kongese female singer Faye Wong (Wang Fei) transformed the poem into a popular hit song with her gentle and surreal voice. In her rendition, the sophisticated and quixotic storylines penned by Su Shi are transposed into delicate pop love music. Each year, a popular singer from the mainland, Hong Kong or Taiwan performs Faye Wong's song at the CCTV Moon Festival Galas. Another feature of Su Shi's poem is its abstract way of dealing with emotions. The phrases "playing with wind" and "dancing with the shadow" suggest the casual and elegant peculiarities of classical Chinese philosophy. The concluding part of the poem, "In joy or sorrow . . . with their beloved ones," renders the munificence of Chinese culture and thinking, as well as its ethos and pursuit of harmony, which is acutely implanted in the storylines and the artistic conception of the poem. This harmonious pursuit not only echoes the official discourse of "building of a harmonious society"; it also conforms to the peaceful rise of a great, modern Chinese nation in the international political arena that is embedded in the "Chinese dream" and that extols the virtues of the CCP government.

The "cultural-cum-state" nationalist discourse

The directors and producers of the CCTV Moon Festival Galas endeavoured to attach the features of cultural nationalism into the discourse of state nationalism by including the promotion of nostalgia; the innovative pageant and elucidation of cultural signs, perceptions and legacies; renovation of traditional cultural and philosophical classics; and the poetic and quixotic representations of love and intimate sentiments. Through this freshly moulded Party-state appropriated cultural nationalism discourse, moderate and poignant political persuasion is enacted. The governing motif of the gala remains state nationalism, a type of nationalism which is state-centred, Party-centred and concerned most with the "stability for the Party-state" (Guo 2004: 24). The pop song "Country" (*Guojia*), performed at the 2009 Autumn Gala by the Hong Kongese Kungfu actor Jackie Chan (Cheng Long) (accompanied by mainland singer Liu Yuanyuan), demonstrates this argument well:

China, the "guo" of the Chinese nation	一玉口中国
Where every family is called a "jia"	一瓦顶成家
They say China is a big country	都说国很大
But China is also a family	其实一个家
Where the people love their "guo"	一心装满国
And work diligently for their "jia"	一手撑起家
Each family is a tiny country	家是最小国
Numerous families make up China	国是千万家
China is a "guo" in the world	在世界的国
The family is a "jia" in the universe	在天地的家
And only when China is strong	有了强的国
Can its families lead a better life	才有富的家
The "guo" as a family is in the heart	国的家住在心里
The "jia" as a country living in harmony	家的国以和矗立

"Guo" is a place blessed with glory	国是荣誉的屹立
The family is a place blessed with happiness	家是幸福的洋溢
Every inch of the country's land	国的每一寸土地
Every footstep by the country's families	家的每一个足迹
Country and families are tightly linked	国与家连在一起
Together creating miracles on earth	创造地球的奇迹
My "guo" is my country	国是我的国
My "jia" is my family	家是我的家
I love my country	我爱我的国
I love my family	我爱我的家
I love my "guojia" (nation-state)	我爱我国家

As the most famous Chinese martial arts actor in the international film industry, Jackie Chan has established his image as a daring, trustworthy and patriotic "big brother." It is an image which is supported by the many martial arts themed movies in which he starred. Chan is widely known by the Chinese film audience, and thus a readily suitable and well-qualified symbol to act as an agent for the entire Chinese nation. Over the past decade, Jackie Chan has performed at many important national celebrations where he always sings patriotic songs at the end of the celebratory events. Besides acting as the spokesperson of the entire Chinese nation, Chan also shows his inclination to be the voice of the CCP government. China's number-one blogger Han Han (2009) sees Chan's motives in another way as shown by his blog entry titled, "We Should Learn from Jackie Chan on How to Read the Emperor's Mind." He writes, "Jackie Chan said 'Is it a good thing for us Chinese to have freedom? . . . We are currently in a big chaos, we have too much freedom, so that Hong Kong is a mess, and Taiwan is also a mess.'"

It is obvious from Han Han's analysis that Chan's words fall squarely into the expectations of the official ideology endorsed by the CCP government, which has strict censorship regulations in areas such as the media and publication spheres in order to dispossess the Chinese people of their autonomy. Han Han's purpose in writing the blog post about Chan is to reveal Chan's role as a collaborator with CCP ideology that is seeking to suppress the Chinese people's right to enjoy social and political freedom. There is a recent phenomenon within the broader Chinese entertainment industry, where performers from Hong Kong and Taiwan who seek to develop their career in mainland China, first need to ensure that what they say, and how and whom they identify with, is in line with the official ideology. Some of those official ideologies may include support for the one China policy and support for the rule and legitimacy of the CCP. For example, in the case of the Hong Kong singer and actor Andy Lau (Liu Dehua), Lau's admission to mainland China required him to convert into a pan-Chinese icon that was politically desirable in China (Fung 2003). Since the mid-1990s, Lau has been portrayed as an "icon of Chineseness" whose celebrity suggests Hong Kong's political allegiance to the PRC" (Stenberg 2013).

Jackie Chan's song "Country" skilfully deploys the connection between country and family by playing on words and obscuring the boundary of the two notions. It is a seamless mixture stemming from twisting the relation between one's country and one's family, and it catapults the nationalist and patriotic appeal of the gala to a high point. Kong (2008: 87) comments that "from Confucian teachings to socialist propaganda, the interchangeable and interdependent relationship between *guo* and *jia* (the family/nation or family/state) have been repeatedly exploited by those in power." Consequently, "Country" transformed the elegant and aesthetic atmosphere created by the moon-themed songs and performances preceding it, into a choir performing a eulogy to the nation and the Party-state.

According to Guo (2004: 30), China's propaganda apparatus is very adroit at playing word games:

> Of central importance to official patriotism, therefore, is the promotion of "country" or *guo* as a package, which takes advantage of the ambiguity of the term, which can be translated into "country", "the land", "nation", "state" or "nation-state". When combined with *jia* (as in *guojia*), *guo* is usually taken in every day parlance as the equivalent of "the government", which in turn means the CCP. Packed in *guo*, therefore, is not only the country, land, nation and state but also the government and the CCP. Patriotism, or love of country, thus becomes love for all these things.

The lyrics of "Country" explore the relationship between *guo* and *jia*. In juxtaposing *guo* with *jia*, *guo* is deliberately fixed on the position of the "big," the "authoritative," the "superior" and the "more important." As Guo argues, *guo* when merged with *jia* is generally implied as "the government," which in the Chinese circumstance is the CCP. The English subtitles of the song skilfully avoid the use of words such as "nation," "state" or "nation-state"; instead, it uses the specific word "country." Again, all the attention and emphasis is laid on the *guo*, which is actually the CCP government. Therefore, to love and be loyal to the CCP is the only practical choice of all families – that is, all the Chinese people. The song has made it very clear that if a strong, "big" *guo* does not exist, there will be no strong, "small" families, and, if the *guo* gains honour, families will enjoy happiness.

The pop song which concluded the 2009 CCTV Moon Festival Gala, "Riding the Wind" (*Chengfeng erlai*), also pushed nationalist sentiment to its pinnacle:

Tide and rainbow in parallel	海潮平彩虹起
Like a dragon rising from the sea	蛟龙出水万丈涟漪
Stirring heroic sentiment	波涛涌豪情满
The sea is vast and the future infinite	沧海辽阔前程无限
The red sun sets on the distant landscape	山河远红日近
Dragon flying in the clouds	飞龙在天云开云合
For thousands of years	几千载丰年里
The rain of good fortune has fallen	洒向人间都是吉祥雨
Riding the wind the dragon soars	龙乘风而来笑傲天际
In varied hues it roams above	神游长空七彩华衣
Lifted by heroic sentiment	龙一飞冲天豪情万里
Bringing good fortune to the world	已让人间沐浴吉祥气

The abstract ideas and poetic sentimentality conveyed by "Riding the Wind" fit neatly into the motif and style of the Moon Festival Gala, and together they create a fusion of the illusion generated by the moon and moon-themed signifiers and representations. With its auspicious lyrics, the song envisages a new time of harmony and fortune in China, a time that synchronizes with the theme of a harmonious society endorsed by the CCP and China's peaceful rise in the international arena. In addition, the "glorious" theme rendered by the song replicates China's goal of becoming a superpower in the international domain and the zeitgeist of present-day China, which is to revive national buoyancy and influence. By foreseeing the rebirth of a great Chinese nation and the realization of a Chinese dream, the gala smoothly transmutes the sense of concord and luck connoted by the moon into a harmonious and splendid Chinese nation detectable in the near future. "In recent years the party-state has been particularly successful in linking the goals of economic modernisation and national rejuvenation with the need for political and social stability in China" (Edney 2012a: 89). In doing so, the discourse of state nationalism finally overtakes the cultural nationalist sentiment that the CCTV Moon Festival Galas competently and tactically created.

Another mainstream song, "Beautiful Chinese Dreams" (*Meili zhongguomeng*), was performed on the 2014 Autumn Gala, which reflects a recently coined political and social propaganda phrase of the Xi Jinping administration that highlights a "Chinese dream." The "Chinese dream" is nowadays frequently mentioned to indicate the continuity of a prosperous and harmonious Chinese nation within which everybody enjoy an equal and happy life.

From the top of Mount Taishan	登泰山之巅
Embracing the sunrise and clouds	拥抱日出云海
I see a youthful China	看青春中国
Alive with the splendors of life	跳动生命精彩
My heart is soaring	我的心在飞翔
Through the hues of the sun	与霞光同在
To paint a fine picture of the world	向天地绘美景
In a colourful dreams	缤纷梦自来
Beautiful Chinese dreams, flowers of prosperity	美丽的中国梦繁荣花盛开
Beautiful Chinese dreams, the future beckons	美丽的中国梦深情向未来
Following the Yellow River to the sea	追黄河入海
The sound of the waves splits the sky	涛声响彻天外
Seeing the beautiful homes	望美丽家园
Growing happier each day	加快幸福节拍
My dreams are unfolding	我的梦正打开
Like a scented song	芳香入歌来
Telling the world of my thoughts	向世界诉情怀
My heart surges high	心潮在澎湃
Where there are dreams there's hope	有梦就有期待
Where there are dreams there's a future	有梦就有未来
There's a future	有未来

The lyrics of "Beautiful Chinese Dreams" are somewhat abstract in their interpretation of "Chinese dreams" from the official perspective; however, another pop song, "My Requirement Is Not That High" (*Wode yaoqiu busuangao*), performed at the 2015 CCTV Spring Festival Gala is less abstract when it maps out the "Chinese dreams" from an ordinary Chinese viewpoint. The song was sung by a popular Chinese actor who was dressed in a worker's uniform:

An eighty square meters apartment	八十平米的小窝
And a gentle wife	还有个温柔的好老婆
My children could go to university	孩子能顺利上大学
And find a good job after graduation	毕业就有好工作
There are no traffic jams on my way to work everyday	每天上下班很畅通
...	
I can see blue sky	看蔚蓝的天空
I can make money and I have time to go to Paris and New York and Mt Alps	我能挣钱 我还有时间去巴黎 纽约 阿尔卑斯山
...	
I have money to spend when I am old and sick	养老生病不差钱
As the government will look after everything	有政府来买单
And this is my 'Chinese dream'	这就是我的中国梦
It is very little and simple	它很小也很普通
...	
Food is safe to eat	食品安全吃得放心
The mortgage will be paid off within ten years	贷款十年就能还清
...	
The society is an equal place to live in	社会相对很公平
No matter whether one is a star or a worker	不管是明星还是工农兵
This is my 'Chinese dream'	这就是我的中国梦
It is very little and simple	它很小也很普通
...	

The symbolic and lofty nature of "Beautiful Chinese Dreams" and the practical and realistic flavour of "My Requirement Is Not That High" are apparent when the two songs are examined together. It is also easy to perceive that "My Requirement Is Not That High" exposes some controversial social problems such as food safety, environmental pollution, social welfare and equality which concern most of the ordinary Chinese people. Therefore, the abstract dealing with the "Chinese dream" in the Autumn Gala clarifies its romantic and amorous traits which present a manufactured and superficial appearance of peace and prosperity therefore intentionally camouflaging the serious and unacceptable social reality of current China.

Conclusion

As an effective and ongoing stage for the spreading of official discourse and Party ideology, festival galas are routinely appropriated by the political leadership. The

Moon Festival Gala, which flourishes with traditional Chinese cultural signs and ideas, is cleverly and creatively employed by China's official propaganda machines as a political means and as a forum for nurturing the Party-state appropriation of cultural nationalism. In the mishmash of traditional cultural imagery, nostalgic sentimentality, quixotic love and abstract philosophical ideas related to or derived from the image of the moon, a tender and poignant political coaxing and appeal to nationalism supersede rigid ideological transmission. This progression of the CCP propaganda echoes Chinese president Xi Jinping's call for renovating the propaganda apparatus so that it remains relevant in contemporary times and indicates the determination of the Party to occupy the dominant position of public opinion and to spread the official ideology through this more public and popular means. Meanwhile, this novel propaganda style assists the CCP's long-term objectives of uniting its people, lifting national morale, constructing a harmonious society and realizing the Chinese dream while at the same time it helps to stabilize the Party's rule and reconfirm its validity, which is a priority of CCP propaganda.

As shown by the analysis of this chapter, CCP's propaganda that manipulates the cultural references and politics of the moon and the Moon Festival Gala to serve its ideological goals has proven effective and fruitful by the acclaim it has garnered from the Chinese audiences and also by the recognition and praise it has gained from foreign professional critics and judges. The success of this novel Chinese propaganda strategy that manipulates China's entertainment vehicles projects a future for China's propaganda that is filled with infinite possibility and potential. Besides passively tightening its control over the internet and social media, the CCP propaganda machine renews and reorganizes itself in terms of creating new strategies, tactics and schemes, in order to guide the mainstream policy and ideology through into the daily life and mind-set of ordinary Chinese people. Just as "sun" was appropriated to establish Mao's cult in the heydays of socialist China, so "moon" is now appropriated to project a harmonious image of present-day Chinese society under the rule of the CCP government. To borrow Anne-Marie Brady's (2008: 202) words, we may conclude that the Party propagandists have succeeded in "marketing a dictatorship."

Glossary

bishushanzhuang 避暑山庄
Chang'e 嫦娥
Cheng Long 成龙
Chengfengerlai 乘风而来
Chunjianghuayueye 春江花月夜
chunwan 春晚
Danyuanrenchangjiu 但愿人长久
Deng Xiaoping 邓小平
FangWenshan 方文山
Guo Jihong 郭霁红
Han Han 韩寒
Hu Jintao 胡锦涛

huanghelou 黄鹤楼
Jiang Zemin 江泽民
jiangcheng 江城
Jiangchengzi 江城子
Juhuatai 菊花台
Liu Dehua 刘德华
Liu Yuanyuan 刘媛媛
Meili zhongguomeng 美丽中国梦
mingyueshan 明月山
Qianjiangshui 千江水
Qinghuaci 青花瓷
qingpingdiao 清平调
shengmingxian 生命线
Su Shi 苏轼
Tao Yuanming 陶渊明
taohuayuan 桃花源
Wang Fei 王菲
Wo de yaoqiu bingbugao 我的要求并不高
Xi Jinping 习近平
xiaopin 小品
xinlangwang 新浪网
Yuemenglong niaomenglong 月朦胧鸟朦胧
yulundouzheng 舆论斗争
Zhongguo keyi shuobu 《中国可以说不》
Zhongguofeng yinyue 中国风音乐
zhongguomeng 中国梦
zhonghua minzu 中华民族
zhonghuaqing 中华情
zhongqiuwanhui 中秋晚会
Zhao Benshan 赵本山
Zhou Jielun 周杰伦
zuguo 祖国

Notes

1 Jiang Zemin's Three Represents literally mean the CCP represents advanced social productive forces, the progressive course of China's advanced culture and the fundamental interests of the majority.
2 "Harmonious society" (*hexieshehui*), is a phrase devised by President Hu Jintao and widely fostered in the state-controlled media since 2005 as a perfect realm of economic success and social cohesion under Party-state rule.
3 The 2009 CCTV Moon Festival Gala is available online at http://v.ku6.com/show/IDqqQk1NG-VCIt8y.html (accessed 2 Nov 2012). All the English subtitles of the song lyrics cited in this paper are the CCTV version.
4 Jay Chou was born in Taiwan and is one of the most popular music composers and singers in the sinophone music world. Some of the co-produced songs of Fang and Chou are representative of Chinese style music, a genre which has become a cultural sensation in both Taiwan and mainland China.

5 Chinese-style music has long been an established music subgenre in popular music of the Chinese-language speaking world; however, it was the combination of Jay Chou's music composition and Vincent Fang's lyric writing that pushed the trend to an unprecedented peak of popularity.

References

Anderson, Benedict. (1983) *Imagined Communities: Reflections on the Origin and Spread of Nationalism*. London: Verso.

Brady, Anne-Marie. (2008) *Marketing Dictatorship: Propaganda and Thought Work in Contemporary China*. Lanham, MD: Rowman & Littlefield.

Cao, Guoxing. (2013) "Xi Jinping xuanchuan sixianglingyu 'yulundouzheng' xintifa yinguanzhu." (Xi Jinping's Wording "the struggle for public opinion" Attracts Attention), rfi, published on 6 Sept 2013, accessed on 12 Jul 2015, available at: http://cn.rfi.fr/中国/20130906-习近平宣传思想领域"舆论斗争"新提法引关注.

Chang, Maria Hsia. (2001) *Return of the Dragon: China's Wounded Nationalism*. Boulder, CO: Westview Press.

The Cultural and History BBS on Sina Web (2009). "Seisei tiwei zongsuan shizai zhongjiu wanhui shang langman le yiba" (CCTV finally creates "romantic" Moon Festival Gala), posted on The Cultural and History BBS on Sina Web in Oct 2009; available at: http://club.history.sina.com.cn/thread-1980546-51-1.html?sudaref=www.google.com.hk&retcode=0, viewed on 10 June 2014.

Edney, Kingsley. (2012a) Managing the Globalisation of Ideas: Propaganda, Power, and Cohesion in Chinese Domestic and International Politics. School of Social and Political Sciences: The University of Melbourne, PhD Thesis.

Edney, Kingsley. (2012b) "Soft Power and the Chinese Propaganda System." *Journal of Contemporary China* 21(78): 899–914.

Fung, Anthony. (2003) "Marketing Popular Culture in China: Andy Lau as a Pan-Chinese Icon," in Chin-Chuan Lee (ed.) *Chinese Media, Global Contexts*. London: Routledge, Curzon: 257–269.

Gao, Jia and Pugsley, Peter. (2008) "Utilizing Satire in Post-Deng Chinese Politics: Zhao Benshang *Xiaopin* vs. the Falun Gong." *China Information* XXII(3): 451–476.

Gries, Peter. (2004) *China's New Nationalism: Pride, Politics, and Diplomacy*. Berkeley: University of California Press.

Guo, Yingjie. (2004) *Cultural Nationalism in Contemporary China: The Search for National Identity under Reform*. New York: Routledge Curzon.

Han, Han. (2009) Han Han's blog at Sina Web. "We Should Learn from Jackie Chan on How to Read the Emperor's Thought", posted on 21 Apr, available at: http://blog.sina.com.cn/twocold, viewed on 9 June 2014.

Hong, Junhao, Lu, Yanmei and Zou, William. (2009) "CCTV in the Reform Years: A New Model for China's Television?" in Ying Zhu and Chris Berry (eds) *TV China*. Bloomington: Indiana University Press: 40–55.

Hu, Jintao. (2007) "Gao ju Zhongguo tese shehui zhuyi weida qizhi, wei duoqu quanmian jianshe xiaokang shehui xin shengli er fendou – zai Zhongguo gongchandang de shiqi ci quanguo daibiao dahuyi shang de baogao." (Raise High the Great Banner of Socialism with Chinese Characteristics, Struggle to Capture the New Victory of Building an Overall Prosperous Society – Report to the Chinese Communist Party 17th National Party Congress).

Kong, Shuyu. (2008) "Family Matters: Reconstructing the Family on the Chinese Television Screen," in Ying Zhu, Michael Keane and Ruoyun Bai (eds) *TV Drama in China*. Hong Kong: Hong Kong University Press: 75–88.

Lasswell, Harold. (1927) *Propaganda Technique in the World War*. London: Kegan Paul, Trench, Trubner.
Lu, Xinyu. (2009) "Ritual, Television, and State Ideology: Rereading CCTV's 2006 *Spring Festival Gala*," in Ying Zhu and Chris Berry (eds) *TV China*. Bloomington: Indiana University Press: 111–125.
The Official Website of the 2009 CCTV Moon Festival Gala, available at: http://ent.cctv.com/special/zhongqiu/01/, viewed on 9 June 2014.
Reilly, James. (2010) "China's Online Nationalism Toward Japan," in Simon Shen and Shaun Breslin (eds) *Online Chinese Nationalism and China's Bilateral Relations*. Lanham, MD: Rowman & Littlefield Publishers: 45–73.
Shambaugh, David. (2007) "China's Propaganda System: Institutions, Processes and Efficacy." *The China Journal* 57: 25–58.
Stenberg, Josh. (2013) "Are You Still Chinese? Negotiations of Cultural Identity in the Yang Lijuan Affair." *Reception: Texts, Readers, Audiences, History* 5: 41–60.
Sun, Wanning. (2003) *Leaving China: Media, Migration, and Transnational Imagination*. Lanhan, MD: Rowman & Littlefield.
Townsend, James. (1988) "Nationalism Chinese Style." *The Antioch Review* 46(2): 204–220.
Tsu, Jing. (2005) *Failure, Nationalism, and Literature: The Making of Modern Chinese Identity 1895–1937*. Stanford, CA: Stanford University Press.
Veg, Sebastian. (2012) "Propaganda and Pastiche: Visions of Mao in Founding of a Republic, Beginning of the Great Revival, and Let the Bullets Fly." *China Perspectives* 2: 41–53.
Wang, David Dewei. (2004) *The Monster that is History: History, Violence, and Fiction Writing in Twentieth-Century China*. Berkeley: University of California Press.
"Xi Jinping tan xuanchuan gongzuo: burixinzhe biritui." (Xi Jinping Comments on the Propaganda Work: Move Forward or You Will Fall Behind) China Military Web, published on 11 Aug 2014, accessed on 6 Sept 2015, available at: http://www.81.cn/jmywyl/2014–08/11/content_6087761_2.htm.
"Xi Jinping: xionghuaidaju bawodashi zhaoyandashi nuli ba xuanchuan sixianggongzuo zuodegenghao." (Xi Jinping: Having the Overall Situation in Mind, Seizing the Big Issues, and Making an Effort to Improve Propaganda Work) People's Daily Online, published on 21 Aug 2013, accessed on 6 Sept 2015, available at: http://cpc.people.com.cn/n/2013/0821/c64094–22636876.html.
Xu, Ben. (2001) "Chinese Populist Nationalism: Its Intellectual Politics and Moral Dilemma." *Representations* 76(1): 120–140.
Yu, Haiqing. (2009) *Media and Cultural Transformation in China*. Abingdon, Oxon; New York, NY: Routledge.
Zhao, Bin. (1998) "Popular Family Television and Party Ideology: The Spring Festival Eve Happy Gathering." *Media, Culture, and Society* 20(1): 43–58.
Zhao, Suisheng. (2004) *A Nation-State by Construction: Dynamics of Modern Chinese Nationalism*. Stanford, CA: Stanford University Press.
Zhao, Suisheng. (2005) "Nationalism's Double Edge." *The Wilson Quarterly* 29(4): 76–82.
Zhao, Yuezhi. (2008) *Communication in China: Political Economy, Power, and Conflict*. Lanham, MD: Rowman & Littlefield Publishers.
Zheng, Yongnian. (1999) *Discovering Chinese Nationalism in China: Modernization, Identity, and International Relations*. Cambridge; Melbourne: Cambridge University Press.
Zhu, Ying. (2012) *Two Billion Eyes: The Story of China Central Television*. New York: The New Press.

2 *Founding of a Republic* and *Beginning of the Great Revival*
Propaganda-infused blockbusters in present-day China

Introduction

Released to coincide with the sixtieth anniversary of the founding of the People's Republic of China and the ninetieth anniversary of the Chinese Communist Party (the CCP) respectively, *Founding of a Republic* (*Jianguodaye* 2009; hereafter *Founding*) and *Beginning of the Great Revival* (*Jiandangweiye* 2011; hereafter *Beginning*) were both huge box-office successes and cultural hits in mainland China in 2009 and 2011. In contrast to previous mainstream films, from both the socialist and the post-socialist periods, which were both times of immense transformation in Chinese society, *Founding* and *Beginning* have a more commercial flavour, as demonstrated by their more nuanced approaches to the CCP's policies and ideology. This chapter examines *Founding* and *Beginning* and reveals the novel ruses enlisted by the CCP and its shifting route of official propaganda, as the Party reaches for ideological control of the Chinese people. This chapter will illustrate that the panoramic history depicted in both films incorporates official propaganda that is very delicately fused with commercial devices. By concentrating on the use of film stars in combination with a more balanced and objective approach to historical figures, I argue that the commercial and critical success of *Founding* and *Beginning* are prototypes for future mainstream films in terms of breaking through the blockade of commercial blockbusters and reforming CCP's propaganda policy.

In the cultural domain of contemporary China, mainstream or main melody (*zhuliu / zhuxuanlu*)[1] narrative, whether it is in literature or in film, or other similar mediums, embodies the cultural expressions of the orthodox ideology endorsed by the ruling regime – the CCP. In the post-socialist Chinese cultural environment, mainstream culture refers largely to official (sanctioned, condoned and promoted) culture, Maoist culture, the culture of the Party. Mainstream culture's mission is to promote the rule of the Party and to spread revolutionary traditions and propagate the spiritual construction of socialism (Meng 2003: 147; Xu 2010: 47). Over the past decades, mainstream narrative has become official narrative and a conduit through which the Chinese people are ideologically controlled and politically manipulated. Borrowing Williams's (1980: 38) argument, this mainstream, official and orthodox ideology may be understood as the "dominant and effective discourse" made up of "a central system of practices, meanings and values" in socialist and post-socialist China. The authority and power of this mainstream discourse and its embedded ideology, along with its relentless implementation and ubiquitous reach, has become the social consciousness. Over the history of socialist China, in particular during the Mao era, the social members have compromised and submitted to the orthodox dogma. Whoever challenges the restrictions of the governing discourse becomes a social pariah and is discarded by society and the ruling regime. In the current Xi Jinping era, the propaganda policies of the CCP government, public and apparent, emphasize and enhance the significance and strength of "positive propaganda" (*zhengmianxuanchuan*) which foregrounds the function of mainstream thinking and opinion and highlights the main "melody" themes of the time. As Xi has remarked, the CCP is conducting a great struggle at an important historical point, and the Party is confronting unprecedented challenges and difficulties; thus, propaganda should maintain the correct political stand, and that is to support the Party leadership; to maintain the authority of the central government; and to spread the Party policy and ideology. The critical point of improving the efficiency of the propaganda is to lift its quality and standard and to increase its attractiveness and appeal to the general public (Xi Jinping: xionghuaidaju bawodashi zhaoyandashi nuli ba xuanchuan sixianggongzuo zuodegenghao 2013).

Generally, there are two basic categories or streams of Chinese mainstream and official cultural expression. The first is that which is embodied by revolutionary idealism; and the second is the recounting of the life stories of heroes, models and advanced individuals (*xianjingeren*), and the promotion of their values (Meng 2003: 147). Over time, the themes and topics of the mainstream and official cultural discourse have increased on the peripheries; however, the discourse's most representative examples still fall into either or both of these two categories. By the end of the 1980s, there emerged the so-called mainstream film genre (Zhang 2010: 97–98), which was one of the consequences of official Party policy of carrying on mainstream beliefs and strengthening the legitimacy of the ruling party due to the negative social problems caused by the Opening Up reforms. In this post-socialist Chinese socio-cultural backdrop, "mainstream film" became a newly coined political phrase denoting one of the more nuanced arts and mass culture praxis that the CCP had enlisted to carry out its ideological and official propaganda (Wu and Xu 2005: 146).

Another more general understanding sees the mainstream film genre as a continual political ploy by the CCP where it uses the genus for propaganda of its ideology (Rao and Pei 1997: 142; Wang 2003: 232). The origin of mainstream films can be traced back to the revolutionary films produced in the 1950s, 1960s and 1970s. Examples of these films include *Eternity in Flames* (*Liehuo zhong yongsheng* 1965), *Battle of Triangle Hill* (*Shangganling* 1956), *The Eternal Wave* (*Yongbu xiaoshi de dianbo* 1958), *Song of Youth* (*Qingchun zhi ge* 1959), *Dong Cunrui* (1955), *Little Soldier Zhang Ga* (*Xiaobing zhangga* 1962) and *Lei Feng* (Dong 1964). Films such as *Battle of Triangle Hill*, a depiction of the gallant deeds of the People's Liberation Army soldiers in the Korean War, and *The*

Eternal Wave, a depiction of the life and achievements of the CCP secret agents in Shanghai before liberation, extol the revolutionary optimism of the times. Other films, such as *Lei Feng* and *Dong Cunrui*, narrate the sagas and life trajectories of the communist soldiers and promote their values.

These above-mentioned revolutionary films are the early versions of mainstream films, as they foster revolutionary principle and passion and enlarge archetypal heroes and heroines with a salient degree of glossiness and glamour (Clark 1987: 94). This conspicuous aspect is congruent with the traditions of propaganda driven films initiated during Mao's Yan'an injunctions, which celebrate and eulogize the brilliance of the Chinese revolutions and its heroes, and the new society (Lee 1991: 15).[2] Further, as these films are driven by propaganda motives and goals (Zhu and Rosen 2010: 1), they consequently turned the cinema and artists into simple functionaries in the revolutionary machinery (Zhang 2003: 12).

Following the Opening Up reform period from the late 1970s, a much more vibrant and liberal era in many fields of China's socio-cultural life emerged. This included filmmaking, where the tradition of producing propaganda-oriented films, a tradition that was carried on during the early period of socialist China, became re-invigorated and reinvented itself, thus enabling it to carry on the task of disseminating the established official discourse of the CCP. Examples of post-1980s mainstream films are *Steel Meets Fire* (*Liehuo jingang* 1991), *The Founding Ceremony of a Nation* (*Kaiguo dadian* 1989), *Decisive Engagement* (*Dajuezhan* 1991), *The Days without Lei Feng* (*Likai leifeng de rizi* 1997) and *Kong Fansen* (1995). As a conduit, mainstream films have continuously served as the official propaganda apparatus that modelled and remodelled its ideological control, both during and after Mao's reign, which is consistent with Shambaugh's (2007: 26–27) argument that film is recruited as authorized propaganda and has become a form of "thought control" which remains an important part of Chinese political and cultural life.

In post-socialist China, mainstream films concur with and revitalize the time-honoured conventions of revolutionary film through revisiting the struggling and progressive history of the CCP, creating role models and reconstructing an underpinning ethic at a time when people had lost faith in grand ideologies (Lu 2005: 121). Revolutionary films of the 1950s, 1960s and 1970s enjoyed great popularity as they were produced at a time when political fever was rampant across China and when the artistry of film and its unique socio-historic features fed the propaganda machine. However, mainstream films made in recent decades do not garner much attention from the film audience (and especially from the younger generation), as the celebrated revolutionary history of the CCP, together with the legitimacy and authority of the Party itself, have been gradually fading, particularly since the 1989 Tiananmen Square demonstrations, and after the collapse of belief in Marxism and Maoism among the Chinese people. Due to their dull and sombre topics, their rigid form, their didactic intent, and their haughty and optimistic themes, mainstream films sponsored by the state have become abstract symbols with little appeal to the contemporary film audience (Meng 2003: 147; Wu and Xu 2005: 154). As a result, newly produced mainstream films do not have many voluntary spectators, but, instead, they have obligatory audiences organized by schools, work units and companies who are required to view them.

Another important factor that contributed to the decline in the privileged status of mainstream films is the adoption of the free market economic system. There is, in present-day China, a cultural phenomenon, where authoritarian politics parallel a consumer economy that manufactures a cultural sphere in which ideological supervision and market rules overlap in the production arena (Cui 2003: 72). Consequently, the official discourse is required to make a compromise with market pressure in order to turn out profitable cultural products; and both elite culture and official thought are in retreat, and popular culture has assumed the hegemony (Yin 1998; cited in Lu 2005: 120). This hegemony has been reflected in China's film industry since the end of the 1970s, where it "legitimizes, and indeed valorizes, entertainment films with commercial value" (Zhu 2003: 1). Subsequently, in order to maintain a living space in the cultural landscape, producers and distributors had to shift their attention to audiences, sales and profit margins. To survive and succeed in a cultural domain that is manipulated by both "an ideologically controlled mass culture" and "a market-driven popular culture," artists and investors have struggled to find the middle ground where official discourse and audiences' interest can both be satisfied and have economic triumph ensured. *Founding* and *Beginning* are two examples of the attempts to accommodate both ideology and consumerism through commercializing the red classics and redefining nationalism.

To be viable in the increasingly commercialized and competitive Chinese film market while at the same time achieving mainstream film functionality as propaganda, *Founding* and *Beginning* had to be ingenious and audacious. This chapter will examine these two "unconventional" and "controversial" mainstream films, by exploring their creational inspirations, which is a mixture of comedy and commodity of historical facts and figures, and intertextuality between historical personnel and movie stars. It will do this by foregrounding their non-traditional and contentious effects and their status in the Chinese cultural landscape. This chapter will also consider the films' value as a mainstream-cum-commercial production experiment embodying the renewal and innovation of the official propaganda devices and discourse. The amalgam of official creed and commercial enterprise provides a fresh model of the political leadership's exploitation of consumerism as it harnesses the power of the marketplace to serve its own ideological purposes. The switch of propaganda modes from conceptual diffusion to mass consumption creates an unpredicted association between socialist and consumerist systems of mass communication (Dal Lago 1999; cited in Cui 2003: 73).

Founding of a Republic and *Beginning of the Great Revival*

Founding (2009) and its sequel, *Beginning* (2011), were respectively released in the year of the sixtieth anniversary of the People's Republic and the ninetieth anniversary of the CCP. The timing of the production and release of *Founding* was a cultural signifier of the emergence of China in the global arena (Xu 2009: 49).

Further, the scheduling of the creation and screening of *Beginning* served as a political signifier of the CCP's firm grip on power. Both of the movies have a propaganda utility and a responsibility to boost unity among Chinese citizens. A cluster of ostensibly haphazard and coincidental elements and features of the films reveal the well-timed and attentive updates of the propaganda devices by the CCP government as it endeavours to catch up with the prevailing trend of commercialization in the cultural-media sphere.

As representative mainstream blockbusters, the production teams of the two films were "hyper-luxurious" (*chaohaohua*) – to borrow a fashionable phrase from the contemporary Chinese cultural lexicon – meaning that the teams were comprised of a group of A-list Chinese film directors and actors. This instance of the broad engagement of film stars and directors may be compared to a line-up of prominent performers (*quanliangshangba*) in the Peking Opera shows, which gather together the best actors of each role into one opera, thereby maximizing its appeal to fans. The Peking Opera stars are the key determining aspect in an opera's popularity. In *Founding* and *Beginning*, the plethora of stars thus mirrors the line-up of notable performers in a Peking Opera production, which further corroborates and underlines the upshot of a particular performance.

The producer and co-director of the two movies, Han Sanping, was the chair of the China Film Group Corporation (CFGC, *Zhongguo dianying jituangongsi*) Board (Han stepped down as its chair in early 2014), a government body that is the driving force behind the scenes of the Chinese film industry. The CFGC is the most comprehensive and extensive film enterprise in China, facilitating the entire process of film production, distribution and exhibition. It has many fully funded subsidiaries, proprietary and joint stock companies, and a movie channel. In an address on the CFGC official website by Han, the significance and political and social function of the state-owned CFGC was clarified:

> We will provide timely reports on the Chinese film industry, the propaganda policy of the Party and the government, build a strong platform for domestic films and serve the prosperous development of national films.[3]

The official claims by Han makes it clear that his two co-directed films co-produced and released by CFGC, which both commemorate the pivotal accomplishment in the history of the CCP and socialist China, serve a propaganda goal for the state government. In one of his speeches in 2014, the current Chinese president Xi Jinping proposed to establish several new-type, powerful and competitive mainstream media corporations, which have considerable propagation force, credibility and influence with the public. Noticeably here, CFGC certainly belongs to and acts as a forerunner of these modern advanced mouthpiece media organizations fostered by the CCP administration (Shibada yilai Xi Jinping zongshuji guanyu "sixiangxuanchuan gongzuo" huatide lunshuzhaibian 2015).

The other co-director of the two films, Huang Jianxin, is another "big cheese" (an important and powerful person) in China's film circle, and one who is renowned for his symbolic cinematic language that is full of black humour. Huang is highly dexterous in depicting the intrigues within Chinese officialdom; however, he never openly or directly challenges or criticises the Chinese official circle and bureaucracy. The fierce political infighting and corrupt environment within the Chinese officialdom are coded in the complex personality and the intricacy of the human characters in Huang's films. Similarly, in *Founding* and *Beginning*, Huang shows his sharp wit and his gift of being able to present the serious as funny when he transforms the solemn and vicious political and military wrangling into light-hearted hilarious anecdotes. When Han Sanping was assigned the challenging task of producing *Founding*, he at first had misgivings about whether he was capable of such a huge undertaking,[4] so he decided to invite his good friend, Huang Jianxin, to act as the co-director. In order to turn out a groundbreaking, compelling and stylish product, the two directors heeded the advice of the internationally famed director Chen Kaige, which was to cast a large number of established film stars in the movie.

During the initial phases of production, *Founding* did not instantly interest many film stars, particularly those with a high profile, until media attention about the movie increased and their interests were gradually awoken. Also it was reported that the participation of well-known movie stars in the film was mainly down to Han's influence and status in the Chinese film and entertainment circle (Yu 2009b: 39). However, after more than thirty film stars agreed to join the film, others too began to be interested. For example, the famous Hong Kong director-actor Stephen Chow (Zhou Xingchi) called the directors to express personally his keenness to play a role in *Founding*.[5] Despite the paucity of interest shown by stars during its inception, by the end of the shooting, the film was awash with movie stars, which in turn led to an unmatched event in the history of the Chinese film: 172 noteworthy actors performed in *Founding*, and the average on-screen performance time of each less than one minute (Zeng 2010: 61). Most of the celebrities performed in less than three scenes, with the most significant roles having only five or six scenes (Yu 2009a: 27).

The stars' involvement in the films created a win-win situation, which not only gave screen time to the celebrities but also neutralized the overt notion of any Party propaganda. When the stars took on the persona of important historical figures in the films, and thus contributed to the celebration of their nation, the propaganda role of the mainstream film was hidden from the audience as the stars' performances tinted the commercial elements and the effects they produced. At the same time, when a mainstream blockbuster becomes a huge "celebratory event," it also turns itself into a valuable occasion for the public images of the stars to be raised among the masses. The stars who appeared in the two films received no remuneration for their performances, as they all agreed to act for free in the name of duty and loyalty to their nation (Li 2010: 61).

At the time of its making, a popular greeting among film stars was: "Did you act in *Founding*?" And when spectators became aware of the number of stars in the *Founding*, the commercial value of the film increased. This courageous experiment and its adventurous bid to be a profitable and entertaining mainstream film was validated by its success. *Founding* took a staggering CN¥ 400 million at the box office, setting a new record for a mainstream movie.[6] In 2011, imitating the production and marketing methods, the sequel to *Founding*, *Beginning*, achieved similar attainment. Over 150 stars participated in the film, and the box office received CN¥ 412 million. Internationally famed stars from across the mainland, Hong Kong and Taiwan regions – including Jackie Chan (Cheng Long), Jet Li (Li Lianjie), Andy Lau (Liu Dehua), Chow Yun-fat (Zhou Runfa), and the best domestic actors and idols such as Liu Yunlong, Angela Baby (Yang Ying), Zhao Benshan, Fan Bingbing, Chen Daoming, the Hollywood director John Woo (Wu Yusen), and the Russian pop song singer Vitas – all contributed to the acting of the film. As the movie poster says, there are over twenty best actresses and actors in the cast, and it was an all-star historical epic starring over 150 top actors.

The success of *Founding* and *Beginning* marks the conversion from contemporary mainstream film with propaganda features into a film without overt political proselytizing and moralizing. The sensation created by the two films illustrates Brady's (2006) and Esarey's (2005; cited in Shambaugh 2007: 27) argument that the Party has been very skilled at utilizing commercialization to boost and reinforce the propaganda apparatus. The Party propaganda machine has effectively been able to integrate, appropriate and domesticate the seditious popular culture elements (Lu 1996: 160; Lu 1997: 75). In *Founding* and *Beginning*, the Party propaganda machinery responded in a timely and adroit manner to the general drift of commercialization in the contemporary Chinese film ground.

"Rehabilitation of reputation" of historical figures

The storyline of *Founding* concerns the four-year period in China's history from the Chongqing Negotiations to the founding of the People's Republic. The narrative of *Beginning* spans from the breakout of the 1911 Xinhai Revolution to the convening of the First National Congress of the CCP. It relates the chaos at the beginning of the Republican period, the May Fourth Movement and the establishment of the CCP. Trying to portray all the events of those hectic times would be an unrealistic task for a single movie, so the directors had to be resolute in their paring down of the history while still maintaining a standard of authenticity. Apart from emphasizing the grand occurrences and scenes, such as wars and negotiations, the directors chose to focus on depicting important historical figures and their anecdotes to mirror the political and social vicissitudes of history. Despite the divergence in policy and faith between political parties and forces, the two directors attempt to overcome the established discrimination and be fair and objective in their accounts of each historical character. One of the most distinguishing features of the films lies in their rehabilitating recount of "antagonist" figures in the history of modern China. For example, Chiang Kai-shek's defeat on the mainland is no longer exaggerated as the great victory of the CCP over its political rival, the Nationalist Party – and this begins the course of a more unprejudiced and realist approach to the portrayals of historical persons and the recuperation and normalisation of their reputations.

In particular, the dispassionate and independent rendering of Chiang Kai-shek and his elder son Chiang Ching-kuo can be considered as an inventive reading of history (Guo and Zhao 2009: 62; Han 2009: 11). Habitually, Chiang Kai-shek is painted in socialist historical and cultural texts as a defector, the number-one counter-revolutionary and biggest rival of the CCP, which is not a true and fair account of the man, given that Chiang also achieved much and had many personal merits. In *Founding*, Chiang is shown as a weary and beaten old man who warrants commiseration. From the appearance of his solitary figure in the shadows, his moans and his frank conversations with his son, Chiang is seen as a politician who is concerned about the fate and future of his nation, who is more common than extraordinary, more miserable than hideous, and more a gentle father than a cruel despot. In portraying this way, *Founding* asks audiences to become mindful that the political beliefs of a person do not necessarily equate with the person's moral qualities. A political opponent is not essentially bereft of morals, and, vice versa, a politically advanced character may not be ethically unfailing (Fang 2009: 27). Here, the audience may relate the renovation of Chiang's character to the reconsideration of the life and achievements of Mao during the socialist revolutions and construction of China, given that his story is still debated and many historical facts and moral actions regarding him are still contested.

Besides the more detached reading of Chiang Kai-shek, the representation of his elder son, Chiang Ching-kuo, is a highlight of *Founding*. Instead of painting a portrait of a shallow dandy and anti-Communist figurehead, Chiang Ching-kuo is depicted as a young, spirited and highly motivated politician with venerable veracity. From his settled and earnest look, and his genuine concerns about the destiny of the nation, to his stringent and non-discriminating crackdown on corrupt officials, and his frustration about the infighting within the Nationalist Party, Chiang Ching-kuo is constructed as a positive figure who is tolerant, diligent, fair-minded and ardent. This attitude adjustment in the mainstream ideology towards Chiang Kai-shek and Chiang Ching-kuo implies an overall trend of defining China from a "people's China" directed by class differences and struggles to a "citizen's China" that is open and progressing towards democracy (Xu 2009: 51–52). The CCP has begun to assume an unbiased outlook towards history and historical figures, and this manner of describing the historical figures is an adventurous ploy; however, it also demonstrates an obligation towards historical truth which denotes not only a maturity of art but also the wisdom of a national-state (Han 2009: 10).

Beginning is similar to *Founding*, in that it depicts many historical figures who were once presented as negative but are now seen in a much more positive manner. Take, for example, Yuan Shikai, a most controversial character in modern China. Yuan is regarded by some as the arch usurper of state power, an autocrat, and a traitor, for reinstating monarchy and proclaiming himself the emperor of the Chinese Empire (which lasted for only eighty-three days between December 1915 to March 1916), after the overthrow of the Qing Dynasty by the Xinhai Revolution led by Sun Yet-sen. In the history books of mainland China, Yuan is always seen as a disreputable person due to his outrageous bid for imperial restoration. However, from the early 2000s, scholars have noticed that there has been an effort to restore Yuan's honourable place in history in the popular TV drama serial *Marching towards the Republic* (*Zouxiang gonghe* 2003), where Yuan's self-proclamation as emperor is perceived as mainly the result of external forces, such as his underlings and his own son who was keen to be the crown prince (Zhu 2008: 52). Further, in this TV show, Yuan is portrayed as an open-minded leader, and an economic and educational reformer for his efforts to create a modern army, to create the Ministry of Education, and to introduce Western technology and economic infrastructure to China (Zhu 2008: 53). In *Beginning*, Yuan Shikai is depicted as a courageous and passionate nationalist who is not afraid to confront the Japanese invaders. Starring Chow Yun-fat, an established Hong Kong–based actor, the Yuan Shikai figure also received a positive revamp in the film.

Another historical figure in the history of modern China that receives an upbeat overhaul is Hu Shi. Hu Shi is widely regarded as one of the most important figures of the May Fourth Movement and the New Culture Movement, which promoted the replacement of traditional Chinese writing with vernacular language, and the end of Confucianism by replacing its learning and values with Western science and democracy. Due to the personal antagonism between Hu Shi and Mao Zedong (Hu has said that, when Mao first arrived in Peking, based on Mao's scholastic level, he was not qualified enough to be admitted by the Peking University) and Hu's political stand which were closer to the Nationalist Party, Hu fled to Taiwan from the mainland after the Nationalist Party was defeated by the CCP in 1949. Hu Shi held many important educational posts under the Nationalist Party rule, both in the mainland and in Taiwan. Hu believed that there was no freedom under the rule of the CCP, and he was thus criticised in a nationwide movement, initiated by Mao in the 1950s, which intended to destroy his fame. During his lifetime, Hu Shi supported democracy and planned to form a party to promote his political ideas after he arrived in Taiwan; however, this plan was suspended due to objections by Chiang Kai-shek. In much of the socialist historical and propaganda works, Hu Shi is painted as a right-wing intellectual who is often juxtaposed with Lu Xun in order to foreground the correct left-wing political consciousness of the latter.

If the previous images and judgements of Hu Shi are often seen through coloured spectacles, in *Beginning*, they are given an objective and vivid refurbishment. In the scene where Hu Shi opposes Chen Duxiu and Li Dazhao's (two of the early Marxist thinkers and theorists of China) proposal to copy the revolution model of the Soviet Union to revive the Chinese nation, Hu is not depicted as a conservative thinker and scholar who would impede the spread of communist thought in China. On the contrary, he is shown as a clear-minded rational thinker who articulates his concerns about the radical reformation and violent revolution. Played by the American-based Chinese actor Daniel Wu (Wu Yanzu), the Hu Shi character in *Beginning* is full of elegance, intelligence and charm. This restoration of image and fame of Hu Shi illustrates how the CCP government revises its approach to comment and judge on historical figures and how it rethinks its previous path and political upholding.

Reconstructing historical figures: a conformist approach

There are two diverging and contrasting approaches enlisted in *Founding* and *Beginning* to reconfigure crucial historical figures. One is the conformist approach, and the other is the heretical approach, and together they have proven to be inspiring, inventive and engaging. The orthodox or conformist method underlines the positive characteristics of the heroic or influential individuals in the history of modern China and remakes them into likable figures with charisma and appeal to the contemporary filmgoers. The audience's understanding and knowledge of historical personages and events will usually be coloured, to some degree, by the viewers' previous identification with the actor playing the role. In *Founding* and *Beginning*, the correlation between actor and historical entity is more pronounced due to the plethora of very well-known stars employed throughout the shows. As I have argued in the previous sections, instead of underscoring the many significant episodes of the history of modern China covered by the film narratives, the directors preferred to concentrate on portraying vital historical figures and their tales to echo the political and social fluctuations of their times. In so doing, *Founding* and *Beginning* endeavour to resuscitate the historical persons by relying heavily on the image and character presented by the film stars.

As both of the films display more than 150 key historical figures and as the average performance time for each star is often less than one or two minutes, there is little time for each character to be known through the scripts; therefore, the customary on- and off-screen persona of the stars lends more clues for the audience to understand the character and disposition of the historical figures than what is available through the background narrative and the script. In other words, the audience's identification with the star not only provides an understanding of the historical person portrayed by the star but also heightens the interest of the films; and given the amount and status of the stars in the films, the interest is enormous. The collaboration between the on-screen image and off-screen persona of the Hong Kong film star Chow Yun-fat displayed in films and commercial endorsements starring him fuelled the formatting process of self-perception of the Hong Kong audience and, moreover, the interpenetration between the star's personae and consumer culture (Lin 2011: 279).

Film and TV stars have the potential to shape the public's viewing habits and moreover to create a bond with the audience in a consumer cultural context. An interactive nexus between stars and the viewing public can be detected in both *Founding* and *Beginning*, where the star's image and personae mediate and manipulate the viewers' cognition and understanding of historical figures, and, vice versa, the audience's viewing expectations leave an impact on how influential persons in history are remodelled via the medium of celebrities. This inter-reliant and cooperative liaison increases viewers' inquisitiveness and inclination to view the film, and it helps mould their watching routines and anticipation towards a commercial mainstream movie, while it opens more space for stars to gratify both the ideological discourse and the consumerist rationale. According to Wang (2009: 58), the employment of such cultural materials – taking celebrities as an example in the mainstream film production – lessens the signs of political proselytization and achieves a kind of "political unconsciousness." This elucidates the suppleness of the Party propaganda apparatus in adapting to altered statuses by using the appeal, magnetism and reputation of film stars. Consequently, the excessive presence of stars in mainstream blockbusters drastically enhances the recognition of the films, suggesting a shift in the discourse of mainstream propaganda.

The consummate attainment of *Founding* and *Beginning* lies in their intelligent and ingenious symmetry between the historical figures and film stars in terms of their outward appearance, personality and manner, which, on one hand, regenerates and remodels the historical figures into charming personae, and, on the other hand, adds an extra layer of gloss and glory on the stars. Audiences are fascinated by the stars' versions of the historical figures, and, further, they become riveted by their deeds in history as a result. As such, historical persons played by celebrities can create a more engaged film audience and bring more attention to the historical facts (Zeng 2010: 61). In effect, this imposes on the public a historical edification that is dogged by the Party's propaganda.

In *Founding*, the internationally famous and multi-award-winning Chinese Fifth Generation director Chen Kaige stars as the Nationalist Party general Feng Yuxiang. In the film, Feng Yuxiang, who is commonly accepted as a progressive officer with conscience and integrity in the Nationalist Party, censures the debased politics and flagging social reality under the rule of the Chiang family. Chen Kaige was invited to play the role of Feng not only because of their similar looks but also due to the respect that viewers have for him. Chen is a globally renowned director who has a substantial influence on the domestic and transnational film markets. The themes and focus of Chen's movies constantly revolve around historical and political narratives and serious topics. Gong and Yang (2010: 15) have described his works as "sublime allegorical cinema of the grand narrative." Chen rose to fame as a result of his internationally acclaimed film, *Farewell My Concubine* (*Bawang bieji* 1993), a film that touches on the sensitive and taboo subject of the Cultural Revolution and censures the soul-torturing nature of the movement through its splendid cinematic expression. It won the Palme d'Or award at the Cannes International Film Festival in 1993, and it was the first Chinese film to do so. As a result, Chen has habitually been dubbed a film poet and has earned a reputation for being a serious intellectual director with both a historical consciousness and an in-depth understanding of modern and contemporary Chinese history, politics and society. In this sense, Chen is similar to Feng in regard to their moral quality and human dignity.

Additionally, Chen Kaige has about him a military demeanour. When directing films, Chen is a domineering perfectionist and is very strict with the actors. In *Founding*, besides performing the Feng Yuxiang role, Chen was also invited to direct a scene and was exceptionally earnest and rigorous in selecting the shooting venue and arranging the extras and props. Again, these temperaments are similar to those of a military officer, further confirming Chen's aptness for the role. Chen's charisma and performance not only makes Feng's stories more convincing but also renders a distant historical figure more vivid and tangible to the contemporary film audience. For Chen, the Feng character also fortifies the audience's customary positive impression of him, which is an asset for the director's career progress.

Another notable figure in the history of modern China that is foregrounded in *Founding* is Du Yuesheng, who is played by Feng Xiaogang, the founder of present-day China's New Year Film (*hesuipian*). Du Yuesheng and Feng Xiaogang also have a similar appearance, and Du's daughter has indicated that Feng looks very much like her father in the film; in particular the expressions in their eyes are exactly the same (Yu 2009a: 27). Du, the almost mythical head of the Shanghai gangs prior to China's liberation, is a legendary character in the chronicle of modern China. It is widely agreed now that Du was prominent for his dexterous running of the Shanghai gangs and for his tactical synchronisation between gang factions and government officials and between business spheres and cultural circles. Previously, gang figures were unanimously defamed by the CCP propaganda machines; however, in *Founding*, the Du Yuesheng role has been given an affirmative reinterpretation with more human-like characteristics and emotion. Rather than painting Du as a ruthless, fraudulent and clever underworld leader, he is shown as a compassionate father who is not afraid to confront the power of the Chiang family in order to save his son. This personalized depiction of Du in *Founding* indicates the adaptability and development of mainstream propaganda discourse that endeavours to advance with the times.

Feng Xiaogang is like Du Yuesheng not only outwardly but also in character, specifically in terms of his talent and determination. Since the end of the 1990s, Feng's commercial films have repeatedly achieved good box-office returns and have enjoyed great regard among film viewers. In contrast to those more authoritative figures in the contemporary Chinese film circle such as Chen Kaige and Zhang Yimou, who trained at the Beijing Film Academy and attained global fame, and whose works mainly engage with historical and serious topics and themes, Feng is more a grass-roots hero. He never formally studied film directing, and his movies have been more concerned about familial issues and the daily life of ordinary people; consequently, his works are not recognized in mainstream film festivals in the West. However, in the equally prosperous domestic Chinese film market, especially in Beijing, Feng is the equal of Zhang and Chen. Feng Xiaogang's success is akin to Du Yuesheng's in many ways, as they both followed an informal or unconventional path before achieving fame, and they both became legendary characters in their respective fields. Viewers discuss how Feng precisely and perceptively interprets the Du Yuesheng role. Similar to Du Yuesheng, who enjoys a popularity that is even more revered than most of the orthodox figures in China's history, Feng Xiaogang's broadly acknowledged accomplishment and his heterodox status in the Chinese film industry is unmatched and enduring.

As already noted, in *Founding*, the Chiang Ching-kuo character is given a subversive revamp as a young and passionate political leader shouldering the future destiny of China, a person who shows fortitude and a sense of impartiality. Serving as a main historically negative-turned-positive character in the film, Chiang Ching-kuo is played by Chen Kun. Chen is one of the most eminent and skilled young actors of his generation on the mainland. In 2003, he starred in the TV serial *Song of Cloud and River* (*Jinfen shijia* 2003), an adaptation of the famous Republican-period fiction writer Zhang Henshui's novel of the same title, for which he was much admired. His role in *Painted Skin* (*Huapi* 2009) won him the best actor at the 2010 Hundred Flowers Awards. Chen is skilled at portraying young and rich elite types, and intellectual characters; thus, in *Founding*, this attribute helped him when approaching the very intricate situations and feelings involved in the interpretation of the Chiang character. Film critics and viewers alike have considered his representation of Chiang as the most effective rendering of a historical figure in the film. With his charming looks, fine acting skills and proven refined and upright on-screen image, Chen turns the young Chiang Ching-kuo into the most noteworthy figure in *Founding*. Chen's mature appearance and temperament adds positive elements to the role, while Chiang's strong identity, historical status and political achievements boost Chen's celebrity persona. In *Beginning*, Chen Kun adopts the Zhou Enlai role which again enchants the audience and broadens his flexibility of role as a professional actor.

In *Beginning*, the Hong Kong–based actor Andy Lau was allocated the role of Cai E, who was an outstanding army commander at the commencement of the Republic period. Based in the remote southern province of Yunnan, Cai E led the local military force in its overthrow of the Qing Dynasty. Besides his gallantry, Cai E is also celebrated for his romantic relationship with a legendary prostitute of the Republic time, Little Fengxian (Xiaofengxian), which has been adapted to numerous contemporary filmic and TV works. Andy Lau is a handsome man with much charisma, especially when he is dressed in the army uniform, and he is well suited to play the role of Cai E. Angela Baby, a Shanghai-born and Hong Kong–raised Chinese actress who is stunningly beautiful and very popular with the pan-Chinese audience, stars as Little Fengxian, the famous beauty and well-known prostitute. In *Beginning*, there is a scene where Cai E flees from China to Japan in order to cure his cancer, and as he parts from Little Fengxian he says to her: "I have dedicated myself to my country, therefore I am unable to make you any promises." Here, the general's awe-inspiring righteousness and his patriotic devotion not only touches Little Fengxian, but it also delivers a patriotic message to the film audience. In recent time, following his career expansion in the mainland region, Andy Lau has successfully reinvented himself as a pan-Chinese icon that suggests both Hong Kong's political allegiance to the PRC (Stenberg 2013) and the expected revival of the entire Chinese nation. Here, Lau's nationalist appeal collaborates with Cai's patriotic image, which makes his role in *Beginning* more poignant and stirring. Besides, Andy Lau's screen identity as a courageous, chivalrous and loyal fighter and gunman has long been recognized through his acting in a series of Hong Kong–produced gang films. In these films, the bravery and faith in the brotherhood of the characters starring Lau attracts the admiration of beautiful women, with whom they develop many touching love stories. In *Beginning*, Lau's striking appearance and courageous character not only add to the charm of the general in his amorous encounters with Little Fengxian, but they also project a captivating, adoring and patriot image for the filmgoers to worship. From another perspective, the heroic and romantic nature of the general confirms the proven aura of Lau held by his film fans.

Alongside Andy Lau's superb acting in the role of Cai E, Liu Yunlong's role as Jiang Baili provides another highlight of *Beginning*. Liu is a director-actor who stars in his successful self-directed TV drama serial, *Plotting* (*Ansuan* 2006). *Plotting* became a TV drama hit soon after its release in 2006, and it has been rerun numerous times by local satellite TV stations across China. Liu Yunlong has also established his screen image as a smart, versatile, cultured and fearless revolutionary. The storyline of *Plotting* is about the work and sacrifice of the CCP secret agents during the Chinese Civil War and the early stage of socialist China, through which the show upholds a collective and patriotic enthusiasm. In several interviews, Liu has expressed that he respects the spirit of dedication and loyalty of his father's generation and is keen to restore it for the contemporary audience. Thus, Liu Yunlong's customary celebrity identity, together with his personal characteristics, turn his portrayal of Jiang Baili, a patriotic scholar-general during the period of the Republic of China, into a credible and intriguing character. In his performance, Liu's highbrow and elegant image foregrounds Jiang's gift as both a military leader and an erudite scholar. Simultaneously, Jiang's nationalist concerns and commitments confirm Liu's proclivity to a collective and patriotic ethos.

Reconstructing historical figures: a "heretical" approach

In comparison with the orthodox illustration of historical characters in *Founding* and *Beginning*, an unorthodox illustration is also employed by the film directors to recreate influential and ordinary figures in the modern history of China. This unusual ploy chiefly follows a comedic allegorisation which is rarely used in the formerly produced mainstream cultural works. The archetypal propaganda artistic pieces that were turned out during the early decades of socialist China focussed on "lofty-noble-perfect" images (*gaodaquanxingxiang*) of heroes and true comrades who unavoidably lacked any individuality and charisma. This tradition continued into the new post-socialist period but had the unfortunate side effect of widening the gap between the viewing audience and mainstream propaganda. In order to overcome this negative trend, the current Shanghai municipal minister of propaganda Xu Lin instructed his staff to produce propaganda in such a way that the masses are eager to see and listen to it, and it must avoid any condescending manner, dull preaching and inflexible style (Shanghai xuanchuanbuzhang xulin: jianshou xuanchuansixiang zhendi jiuyao daihao xuanchuanduiwu 2013). Xu's directives indicate that the commercialization of mainstream cultural products is an inexorable trend in the present Chinese cultural marketplace. Another problem confronting the CCP propaganda institutions is how do they secure space for the official cultural discourse within the realms of commercial enterprises. In both *Founding* and *Beginning*, the Party propaganda apparatus experiments with comedic allegorisation by enlisting a group of A-list comedy actors and professional comedians such as *xiangsheng* (crosstalk) and *xiaopin* (witty skits) performers into the acting of the films, thus reducing the solemn tone and serious themes of the movies and increasing their popularity and entertainment value.

Ge You,[7] the most frequently used lead actor in Feng Xiaogang's New Year Film series, is also one of the most highly paid actors in contemporary Chinese cinema. In Feng's films, Ge plays kind-hearted, young layabouts. He is closely identified with the "leftover boy characters" that are garrulous, glib-tongued and articulate. Ge's Beijing style loquaciousness and humour that is conveyed by the Beijing dialect and accent has won him many die-hard fans, particularly in the northern cities of China. In *Founding*, Ge was employed to play a Red Army soldier who took part in the battle to liberate Beijing. Although dressed in the People's Liberation Army uniform, Ge's image seems to still lack any sense of honour and glory as his hilarious trouble-shooter identity in Feng's films has penetrated deeply into the viewers' minds. However, it is exactly this peculiar soldier image created by Ge that transforms the once-perfect CCP revolutionaries and heroes into more lively and realistic figures. In one scene from the film, when the soldiers arrive at the old city wall of Peking, Ge demonstrates his unique wit by remarking: "In front there is a landlord's courtyard, which is extremely solid, so we cannot bomb it using grenades. Therefore, we must request artillery aid." Here, by juxtaposing the Peking city with a landlord's courtyard, the simple logic of a peasant soldier is demonstrated and an ideological implication presented.

Feng Gong, an established *xiangsheng* performer, plays the Feng Guozhang role in *Beginning*. Feng Gong is actually the biological grandson of Feng Guozhang, who was once the president of the Republic of China. As a professional *xiangsheng* actor, Feng Gong's humorous lines and performance provide a light and jocular flavour to role as his grandfather. Likewise, in *Beginning*, Zhao Benshan, the most influential figure in the *xiaopin* circle of contemporary China, and a must-see face on the annual CCTV Spring Festival Gala, interprets well the Duan Qirui role. Duan is an accomplished strategist and politician who once served as the premier of Republican China. When Zhao Benshan appears in the film, the audience unconsciously relate Duan, to the ridiculous and comical characters Zhao created in his *xiaopin* works. The historical recount is thus imbued with a sense of hilarity and spoof, which is very entertaining.

Fan Wei, another leading *xiaopin* comedian, was employed in *Founding*. As one of the key performing partners of Zhao Benshan in his *xiaopin* works, Fan is another incredibly popular face on the stage of the yearly CCTV Spring Festival Gala.[8] In *Founding*, Fan plays Mao Zedong's cook, a frank and sincere peasant soldier who is extremely loyal to Mao. When Mao gives him a cigarette, he is reluctant to smoke it and instead stores it behind his ear. Fan has played the role of a simple and stubborn young man in Zhao's *xiaopin* series *Selling Crutches* (*Maiguai*) and *Selling Wheel Chairs* (*Maiche*), where he is always cheated by the character played by Zhao due to his kind-heartedness, naivety and honesty. The foolish and earnest image of Fan has taken root in the minds of most viewers, and this image coincidently concurs with the candid and faithful characteristics of Mao's cook in *Founding* (Li 2010: 63), which gives Fan's stage image a positive revamp. In *Beginning*, Fan Wei takes up the role of Li Yuanhong, the second president of Republican China. When depicted in his costume as a commander-in-chief, Fan's image projects a caricature of the dignified and prestigious president. In his conversation with Feng Guozhang, starring Feng Gong, Fan adopts a manner of speech that foregrounds the simplicity and idiocy of his *xiaopin* characters, which again creates a farcical effect.

Another comedian who stars in *Founding* is Guo Degang,[9] the exceedingly prolific *xiangsheng* master. *Xiangsheng*, a traditional Chinese performing arts form, had been losing status before Guo and his Deyun Club (*deyunshe*) began to put on *xiangsheng* performances in teahouses and theatres in Beijing from 1996. However, their fame did not come until 2005. From that year, Guo and his fellow *xiangsheng* performers were invited by TV channels across China to perform their works, and the Guo Degang phenomenon was widely reported in the media. Moreover, Guo's *xiangsheng* performances were uploaded onto different online entertainment websites, thus further expanding his recognition and reputation. In the film, Guo plays a photographer who takes photos for the representatives and committee members of the first National Chinese People's Political Consultative Conference (*zhengzhi xieshang huiyi*). Due to his popularity, Guo does not need to speak a word; he merely has to appear in a film, and the audience will begin to laugh. Besides Guo, his disciple Li Jing, a young *xiangsheng* performer who hosts (together with his performing partner He Yunwei) a comedy show at the Beijing Television Station, joins the acting cast in *Beginning*. Li plays the ambitious son of Yuan Shikai, who is eager to become the emperor of China. Li's wacky appearance adds an amusing touch to his role. In summary, the entertainment atmosphere created by the comedians converges with the joyful context of the founding of the People's Republic and the CCP, lifting the celebratory theme of the films to its zenith.

Conclusion

Founding and *Beginning*, as mainstream films, break through the barricade of commercial blockbusters and remodel official propaganda discourse into a mode which is much enjoyed by the viewing public. This breakthrough is achieved mainly by employing both established and unconventional approaches in their portrayal of characters in the early modern history of China. First, they illustrate historical figures in an empathetic humanist way by restoring the original characters and reaching a more realistic conclusion, as contemporary film viewers expect, which overcomes the inflexibility projected by a binary thinking that has long been steered by ideological antagonism and moral perfectionism. Although a humanist treatment of historical character in films of momentous subject does not commence with *Founding* and *Beginning* (as mainstream films such as *The Battle of Taierzhuang* [*Xuezhan Taierzhuang*], which was shot in 1986, had already experimented with this method), *Founding* and *Beginning*'s effort to carry on and improve this approach is unparalleled and commendable.

Second, the abundant deployment of stars in both big and small roles creates a fresh mode for casting mainstream blockbusters, which promoted the film and showed that the Chinese film market is steadily becoming more mature and agile. This kind of moulding has produced a meticulous type of "blockbuster with Chinese characteristics," which not only follows the Party line that requires it to accommodate public interest and taste but also makes the commercial elements and fashions (i.e. through the casting of celebrities and commercial production methods) serve the Party propaganda goals. Finally, the casting of comedians to play roles adds a humorous facet to *Founding* and *Beginning* in its reconfiguration of historical characters, revolutionary heroes and typically solemn events, which is original and avant-garde in comparison to earlier similar-themed productions, setting a new norm for the appraisal of mainstream films. These exclusive features are what make the two films groundbreaking and exceptional as Chinese mainstream film creations. As the arts are an embodiment of ideology, so *Founding* and *Beginning* provide "a great leap forward" in official discourse and propaganda.

Glossary

Ansuan 暗算
Bawangbieji 霸王别姬
Cai E 蔡锷
chaohaohua 超豪华
Chen Daoming 陈道明
Chen Duxiu 陈独秀
Chen Kaige 陈凯歌
Chen Kun 陈坤
Cheng Long 成龙
Dajuezhan 大决战
deyunshe 德云社
Dong Cunrui 董存瑞
Du Yuesheng 杜月笙
Duan Qirui 段祺瑞
Fan Bingbing 范冰冰
Fan Wei 范伟
Feng Gong 冯巩
Feng Guozhang 冯国璋
Feng Xiaogang 冯小刚
Feng Yuxiang 冯玉祥
gaodaquanxingxiang 高大全形象
Ge You 葛优
Guo Degang 郭德纲
Han Sanping 韩三平
He Yunwei 何云伟
hesuipian 贺岁片
Hu Shi 胡适
Huang Jianxin 黄建新
Huapi 画皮
Jiandangweiye 建党伟业
Jiang Baili 蒋百里
Jiang Jieshi 蒋介石
Jiang Jingguo 蒋经国

Jianguodaye 建国大业
Jinfenshijia 金粉世家
Kaiguodadian 开国大典
Kong Fansen 孔繁森
Lei Feng 雷锋
Li Dazhao 李大钊
Li Jing 李菁
Li Lianjie 李连杰
Li Yuanhong 黎元洪
Liehuojingang 烈火金刚
Liehuozhong de yongsheng 烈火中的永生
Likai Lei Feng de rizi 离开雷锋的日子
Liu Dehua 刘德华
Liu Yunlong 柳云龙
Lu Xun 鲁迅
Maiche 卖车
Maiguai 卖拐
Mao Zedong 毛泽东
Qingchunzhige 青春之歌
quanliangshangba 全梁上坝
Shangganling 上甘岭
Sun Zhongshan 孙中山
Wu Yanzu 吴彦祖
Wu Yusen 吴宇森
xiangsheng 相声
xianjingeren 先进个人
Xiaobing Zhang Ga 小兵张嘎
Xiaofengxian 小凤仙
xiaopin 小品
Xuezhan Taierzhuang 血战台儿庄
Yan'an 延安
Yang Ying 杨颖
Yongbuxiaoshi de dianbo 永不消逝的电波
Yuan Shikai 袁世凯
zhongguo dianying jituangongsi 中国电影集团公司
Zhao Benshan 赵本山
Zhou Enlai 周恩来
Zhou Ruifa 周润发
Zhou Xingchi 周星驰
Zhang Yimou 张艺谋
zhengshi xieshang huiyi 政治协商会议
zhengmianxuanchuan 正面宣传
Zhuliu 主流
zhuxuanlu 主旋律
Zouxianggonghe 走向共和

Notes

1 The "mainstream/main melody" (*zhuliu / zhuxuanlu*) discourse discussed in this chapter indicates the official, orthodox Party ideology of the CCP government, which carries on the revolutionary traditions of the Mao eras and promotes the rule of the CCP and the spiritual heritages of socialist revolutionary China. The mainstream cultural narrative of contemporary China has been undertaking a commercializing trend, which is best illustrated by *The Founding* (the film under investigation in this chapter) – a commercial mainstream movie/blockbuster. *The Founding* is the most representative of the mainstream film genre that is part of the varied forms of the mainstream artistic and cultural products of present-day China.
2 Mao's "Talks at the Yan'an Forum on Literature and Art" (1942) is most notable for its promotion of literature and art to serve political ends of the Party, which emphases that all art should reflect the life of the working class and should serve politics, in particular the advancement of socialism.
3 All the English translations of the Chinese quotes in this article are my own.
4 "Jianguodaye zhege dianying yidian dou bufuhe guilu" 2011, Sohu.com, http://yule.sohu.com/20090908/n266550240.shtml (accessed 6 Dec 2011).
5 Chow is a Hong Kong-based comedic actor-director who enjoys great popularity in mainland China. His performance in Jeffrey Lau's film series *A Chinese Odyssey* – part one, *Yueguang baohe / Pandora's Box* (1995), and part two, *Dasheng quqin / Cinderella* (1996) – familiarized mainland audiences with Chow's comedic style.
6 *The Founding* also became one of the most profitable domestic-produced Chinese movies that opened together with other domestic blockbusters such as *Yingxiong / Hero* (dir. Zhang 2002) and *The Promise* (Wuji), 2005. feature film, directed by Chen Kaige, produced by China Film Group Corporation.
7 Ge has played lead roles in several of Feng Xiaogang's films, including in *Jiafang yifang / Party A, Party B*, *Bujianbusan / Be There or Be Square*, *Meiwanmeiliao / Be Endless*, *Da waer / Big Shot's Funeral*, *Shouji / Cellphone*, *Tianxia wuzei /A World without a Thief*. In Feng's films, Ge plays layabout youths and is strongly identified with leftover boy characters who, while only commoners, have a kind heart. His portrayal of such characters has ensured mass audiences regard him with fondness and sympathy.
8 Zhao is recognized as being the best contemporary *xiaopin* comedian in China, and commoners look forward to his *xiaopin* performance on the annual CCTV Spring Festival Gala. As his appearance is one of the must-see performances of the gala, he is always scheduled to appear at the end to prolong viewers' interest. Fang Wei has been performing with Zhao in his *xiaopin* works over the past decade. Prior to this, Fan was a supporting character, but his good performing skills and personal charm led him to become a very popular *xiaopin* master who is as popular and welcomed as Zhao among Chinese audiences.
9 Guo achieved huge success with his 2005 *xiangsheng* works. In 2011, Guo and his club successfully gave the first commercial performance of *xiangsheng* overseas in two major Australian cities, Sydney and Melbourne, opening a new space for Guo and the performance of *xiangsheng*.

References

Brady, Anne-Marie. (2006) "Guiding Hand: The Role of the CCP Central Propaganda Department in the Current Era." *Westminster Papers in Communication and Culture* 3(1): 58–77.

Clark, Paul. (1987) *Chinese Cinema: Culture and Politics Since 1949*. New York: Cambridge University Press.

Cui, Shuqin. (2003) *Women Through the Lens: Gender and Nation in a Century of Chinese Cinema*. Honolulu: University of Hawaii Press.

Dal Lago, Francesca. (1999) "Personal Mao: Reshaping an Icon in Contemporary Chinese Art." *Art Journal* 58(2): 46–59.
Esarey, Ashley. (2005) "Cornering the Market: State Strategies in Controlling China's Commercial Media." *Asian Perspective* 29(4): 37–83.
Fang, Zhou. (2009) "Cong jianguo daye kan Han Sanping de jingji tuteng." (Reflection on the Economic Totem of Han Sanping, from *Found of a Republic*) *Zhongguo jun zhuan min* 10: 24–27.
The Founding of a Republic (Jianguodaye). (2009) Directed by Han, Sanping and Huang, Jianxin, Produced by: China Film Group Corporation, Beijing.
Gong, Haomin and Yang, Xin. (2010) "Digitized Parody: The Politics of Egao in Contemporary China." *China Information* 24(1): 3–26.
Guo, Xiao and Zhao, Zhengyang. (2009) "Cong jianguodaye kan dangqian guochan dianying fazhan xianzhuang de yixie tedian." (Reflection on Some Characteristics of the Development of Domestic Films from *Founding of a Republic*) *Yunnan yishu xueyuan xuebao* 4: 59–62.
Han, Chuanxi. (2009) "Jinru lishi de fangshi yu guojia xingxiang de yingxiang jiangou – yi jianguo daye wei zhongxin de kaocha." *Yishi guangjiao* 6: 9–11.
"Jianguodaye zhege dianying yidian dou bufuhe guilu." (*Founding of a Republic* Does Not Conform to Conventions) (2011) Sohu.com, http://yule.sohu.com/20090908/n266550240.shtml, viewed on 6 December 2013.
Lee, Leo Ou-fan. (1991) "The Tradition of Modern Chinese Cinema: Some Preliminary Explorations and Hypotheses," in Chris Berry (ed.) *Perspectives on Chinese Cinema*. London: BFI Pub: 6–20.
Li, Long. (2010) "90 hou guan jianguodaye zhigan." *Zhongguo jiaoyu fazhan yanjiu zazhi* 7(1): 63.
Li, Wenqiang. (2010) "Cong jianguodaye kan zhongguo xinzhuliu hongse dianying de tedian." *Dianying wenxue* 9: 60–61.
Lin, Feng. (2011) "Star Endorsement and Hong Kong Cinema: The Social Mobility of Chow Yun-Fat 1986–1995." *Journal of Chinese Cinemas* 5(3): 269–281.
Lu, Sheldon H. (1996) "Postmodernity, Popular Culture, and the Intellectual: A Report on Post-Tiananmen China." *Boundary 2* 23 (2): 139–169.
Lu, Sheldon H. (1997) "Global Post Modernization: The Intellectual, the Artist, and China's Condition." *Boundary 2* 24(3): 65–79.
Lu, Sheldon H. (2005) "Chinese Film Culture at the End of the Twentieth Century: The Case of *Not One Less* by Zhang Yimou," in Sheldon H. Lu and Emilie Yueh-yu Yeh (eds) *Chinese-Language Film: Historiography, Poetics, Politics*. Honolulu: University of Hawaii Press: 120–140.
Meng, Fanhua. (2003) *Chuan mei yu wenhua lingdaoquan: dangdai Zhongguo de wenhua shengchan yu wenhua ren tong* (Media and Cultural Leadership: The Cultural Production and Recognition of Contemporary China). Jinan: Shangdong Education Press.
The official website of the CFGC, available at: http://group.chinafilm.com/, viewed on 6 December 2013.
Rao, Shuguang and Pei, Yali. (1997) *Xinshiqi dianying wenhua sichao* (Reflection on Film Culture in the New Era). Beijing: China Radio and Television Press.
Shambaugh, David. (2007) "China's Propaganda System: Institutions, Processes and Efficacy." *China Journal* 57: 25–58.
"Shanghai xuanchuanbuzhang xulin: jianshou xuanchuansixiang zhendi jiuyao daihao xuanchuanduiwu." (Shanghai Municipal Minister of Propaganda Xu Lin: Maintaining That Propaganda Must Cultivate Good Propagandists) People's Daily, published

on 14 Oct 2013, accessed on 16 Sept 2015, available at: http://news.xinhuanet.com/politics/2013–10/14/c_117698428.htm.
"Shibada yilai Xi Jinping zongshuji guanyu 'sixiangxuanchuan gongzuo' huatide lunshuzhaibian." (The Summary of Xi Jinping's Speeches on Propaganda Since the 18th National Congress of the Communist Party of China) Milin Web, published on 15 Oct 2015, accessed on 18 Oct 2015, available at: http://www.xzml.gov.cn/zt_2563/201510/t20151015_863499.html.
Wang, Hui. (2009) "Jiedu Jianguodaye: zhuliu zhengzhipian de shidai meili." (Reading *Founding of a Republic*: The Charm of Mainstream Political Films) *Guancha yu sikao* 19: 58.
Wang, Xiaoyu. (ed.) (2003) *Zhongguo dianying shigang*. Shanghai: Shanghai Antique Books Press.
Williams, Raymond. (1980) *Problems in Materialism and Culture: Selected Essays*. London: Verso.
Wu, Xiaoli and Xu, Shenmin. (2005) *Jiushi niandai zhongguo dianying lun* (Reflection on 1990s Chinese Films). Beijing: Culture and Art Publishing House.
"Xi Jinping: xionghuaidaju bawodashi zhaoyandashi nuli ba xuanchuan sixianggongzuo zuodegenghao." (Xi Jinping: Having the Overall Situation in Mind, Seizing the Big Issues, and Making an Effort to Improve Propaganda Work) People's Daily Online, published on 21 Aug 2013, accessed on 6 Sept 2015, available at: http://cpc.people.com.cn/n/2013/0821/c64094–22636876.html
Xu, Jianfeng. (2010) "Zhuxuanlu dianying de yishu yu jishu ronghe." (The Merging of Techniques and Arts in Mainstream Films) *Wenyi pinglun: Xueshu Ban* 11: 47–48.
Xu, Yong. (2009) "Gongheguo dalishi yu liangge shidai liangzhong xushu: cong dianying jianguodaye kan xinzhongguo lishi hefaxing xushu de bianqian jiqi xiangzheng yiyi." (The History of the People's Republic and Two Eras and Two Narratives: Reflection on the Transformation of Historical Legitimacy Narratives of New China and Its Symbolic Meaning from *Founding of a Republic*) *Beijing dianying xueyuan xuebao* 6: 49–53.
Yin, Hong. (1998) *Jing xiang Yuedu: jiushi niandai yingshi wenhua suixiang* (Reading in the Mirror: Reflection on 1990s Film and Entertainment Culture). Shenzhen: Hainan chubanshe.
Yu, Nan. (2009a) "Dayegaocheng – jianguodaye: yichang zhongguo dianyingjie de baituandazhan." (The Completion of the Great Mission – Founding of a Republic: The Hundred-Regiment-Offensive in the Chinese Film Circle) *Xinshiji zhoukan* 27: 24–29.
Yu, Nan. (2009b) "Huang Jianxin: jianguodaye zhizao chule shehui huati." (Huang Jianxin: *Founding of a Republic* Generates Social Discussion) *Xinshiji zhoukan* 27: 36–39.
Zeng, Canyue. (2010) "Ping jianguodaye mingxinghua de xiju zhangle." (Comments on the Dramatic Effect of the "starization" of *Founding of a Republic*) *Dianying wenxue* 2: 61–62.
Zhang, Huiyu. (2010) "Cong jianguodaye yu fengsheng kan liangzhong geming lishi xushi." (Reflection on Two Historical Revolutionary Narratives from *Founding of a Republic* and *the Message*) *Shehui xuejia chazuo* 1: 97–104.
Zhang, Yingjin. (2003) "Industry and Ideology: A Centennial Review of Chinese Cinema." *World Literature Today* 77(3): 8–13.
Zhu, Ying. (2003) *Chinese Cinema During the Era of Reform: The Ingenuity of the System*. Westport, CT: Praeger Publishers.
Zhu Ying. (2008) *TV in Post-Reform China: Serial dramas, Confucian leadership and the global TV market*. London and New York: Routledge.
Zhu, Ying and Rosen, Stanley. (eds) (2010) *Art, Politics, and Commerce in Chinese Cinema*. Hong Kong: Hong Kong University Press.

3 The Cultural Revolution
How TV Drama Serials create collective amnesia

Introduction

Using the Cultural Revolution as a representative historical event, this chapter examines how the collective memory and popular history revolving around it are manufactured and interpreted via televisual media narratives. The collective memory of the Cultural Revolution, as I will show, is constructed and not preserved, and the collective framework of memory, as the predominant thoughts and the governing ideological rhetoric of society (which is the state/official/mainstream ideology promoted by the Chinese Communist Party [CCP]), configures people's memories of past events. A textual analysis of the TV dramas *A Place Where Dreams Start* (1998), *Bloom of Youth* (2006) and *Crimson Romance* (2004) (three typical revolutionary nostalgia texts) will expose the process of manufacturing collective memory concerning the Cultural Revolution for what it is – a cultural amnesia which caters to the current propaganda and ideological goals of the Chinese government.

In an earlier work, *On Collective Memory*, Halbwachs (1992 [1941]: 38–40) points out that

> in reality the past does not recur as such, that everything seems to indicate that the past is not preserved but is reconstructed on the basis of the present. [T]here exists a collective memory and social frameworks for memory; it is to the degree that our individual thought places itself in these frameworks and participates in this memory that it is capable of the act of recollection....
>
> Collective frameworks are ... precisely the instruments used by the collective memory to reconstruct an image of the past which is in accord, in each epoch, with the predominant thoughts of the society.

There are several frameworks of collective memory intersecting and competing with each other; however, at specific historical periods, only one of the many social frameworks of memory occupies the dominant position. Also, the prevailing collective memory must compromise with the prevalent ideological rhetoric of its times. In the political and social context after the founding of the People's Republic of China (PRC), collective memory and popular history have been exploited and manipulated by the ruling regime, the CCP, in order to serve its propaganda and political ends. During this reconstructing and reinterpreting process, some events and achievements of the CCP are amplified and exaggerated. Such embellishments included, for instance, the contribution of the CCP in the winning of the War of Resistance against Japan. However, and in contrast to these highlighted exploits, some events are intentionally neglected by the official propaganda narrative – for example, the human-made causes of the disaster that was the Great Leap Forward (*dayuejin*) and the subsequent agricultural and industrial catastrophes that led to the collapse of the national economy and the Great Famine (*dajihuang*); the socio-political disaster engendered by the Cultural Revolution; and the totalitarian crackdown of the 1989 Tiananmen Square student democratic protest.[1] In compliance with a general ethos of official "reconfiguration" and "misinterpretation" of collective memory and popular history in the trajectory of socialist China, the contemporary Chinese TV programs create and recount a visual historical narrative which not only falls in line with mainstream propaganda but also imaginatively reconstructs and resurrects the past memories in an entertaining and intriguing sense.

Television – whether it is prime-time entertainment programing, television documentaries, or TV news and public affairs programing – has become a medium which is productive and creative when it is used to recount, interpret and reinterpret history. Television serves as a principal means by which most people learn about history, and its nonfictional and fictional portrayals have similarly transformed the way viewers think about historical figures and events (Edgerton 2001: 1). "Television histories" or "media memories" have been extensively examined in order to illustrate and clarify how history is recorded and understood, and how collective memory is shaped in this age of media.

There are two distinct viewpoints on how collective memory is constructed in the contemporary media sphere: one is labelled *presentism*, and the other is *pastism*. Those scholars who hold a *pastism* position focus more on the role of television as a historian – consequently, "histories on TV are sometimes rejected out of hand for either being too biographical or quasi-biographical in approach, or too stylized and unrealistic in their plot structures and imagery" (Edgerton 2001: 7). On the other hand, scholars who advocate the *presentism* position consider that historiography is more concerned with recounting stories inspired by contemporary perspectives, rather than evoking and transporting any kind of unbiased truth about the past (White 1985; Hutcheon 1988; Ermarth 1992; Edgerton 2001). Fredric Jameson (1991) has noted a more unconventional approach of constructing history in the postmodern popular culture, in that TV and other visual media have nurtured a gradually "derealized" sense of presence, identity and history. According to Jameson, history has been replaced by an explosion of aesthetic replication and nostalgia that is indicative of a culture that still craves history but is eligible only of haphazardly cannibalizing varieties and imaginings from the past.

Besides these two antithetical viewpoints, there is a third perception that generates a more intricate rapport between *presentism* and *pastism*. It argues that objective history and collective memory formed on the TV media platform can be "complimentary, identical, oppositional, or antithetical at different times" (Zelizer 1995: 216). This more complicated way of thinking suggests that "more popular uses of memory have less to do with accuracy per se than using the past as a kind of communal, mythic response to current controversies, issues, and challenges" (Edgerton 2001: 5–6). In a reaction to current disputes, concerns, and confrontations, popular history and cultural memory cater to the requirement of dominant ideological forces and conform to established historical narratives within the particular societal being (Anderson 2001: 21). In so doing, the past becomes both malleable and adaptable, which allows us to create or invent another past via televisual media. Historical facts and social memories converge, mainly due to the practice whereby some events are underlined and others are camouflaged. We select components that fit our larger master-narratives, and we disregard or dismiss the importance of others (Schwarz 1982; Neiger, Meyers and Zanberg 2011). Collective memory makes compromise to, and is deployed by, dominant ideological thinking which directs public attention and distorts the viewer's knowledge about the past. Some historians and media critics argue against television's suitability for the construction of history, and television is considered as both disease and carrier in an epidemic of cultural amnesia in which television viewers are often characterized as victims. Television relies upon producing forgetfulness and the annihilation of memory, and it actually inhibits viewers' capacity to grasp and process the information about the past, with the result that history becomes opaque and distant (Doane 1990; Heath 1990; Anderson 2001).

In the case of present-day China, nostalgia TV serials set in the revolutionary eras, in particular during the decade of the Cultural Revolution, have become an established subgenre in the current Chinese media sphere. This chapter shows how the Cultural Revolution, as a conduit of collective memory dominated by ideological force, is represented and reflected in television media products that manufacture popular history and cultural memory. A textual analysis of a collection of some of these shows' plots and scenes will expose how some factual elements and moments of the past are used and emphasized, and how some others are neglected or concealed by the collective memory frameworks in order to be in accord with the master-narratives of this period and to cater to the predominant thoughts of the society. This chapter will also analyse how collective memory created by television media is employed as an allegorical response by ideological forces to current controversies, concerns and challenges. I will examine the collective memories as understood from the TV drama shows under examination in this chapter, and a version of the social memory and the popular history of the Cultural Revolution, one which is not preserved but reconstructed on the basis of the present, will be made clear. However, this version of the Cultural Revolution opens itself up to criticism as being a cultural propaganda tool which uses television narratives of history. In these reminiscences, a cultural amnesia victimizes the television audience and distorts the viewer's previous knowledge about the past. Moreover, the collective memory of the Cultural

Revolution is utilized to respond to the current political and social polemics of contemporary China.

TV-constructed collective memory of the Cultural Revolution

Immediately after the overthrow of the Gang of Four in 1976, an event that designated the end of the ten-year political and social turmoil that rampaged across socialist China, the Cultural Revolution was officially condemned as a conspiracy by a small group of opportunists. This group, headed by the Gang of Four, intended to usurp the Party and govern for themselves. In order to soothe the growing resentment of the Chinese people, the Cultural Revolution was overwhelmingly denounced in print and televisual media. Two examples of this political denouncement are the crosstalk works *Taking Photos* (*Ruci zhaoxiang* 1979) and *Hat Factory* (*Maozi gongchang* 1976), both of which targeted the Gang of Four and the Cultural Revolution, helped lessen the resentment felt by the Chinese people, and became immensely popular.[2] Afterwards, Deng Xiaoping made the courageous decision to redress the unjust and wrongful cases of many of those persecuted and falsely accused during the Cultural Revolution, which led to the rehabilitation of the victims' reputations. This move not only helped Deng's re-emergence into the political field but also helped to stabilize the precarious political situation in China at that time.

Over a decade later, during the comparatively free social and political atmosphere in China during the 1980s, a number of TV drama and film works about the Cultural Revolution emerged, showing a darker view of the Cultural Revolution. These visual recounts of the Cultural Revolution stem from, and collaborate with, the so-called Scar Literature (*shanghenwenxue*) that emerged soon after the end of the socio-political chaos.[3] Scar Literature was meant to be cathartic and to help the sent-down youths, marginalized Party cadres, and intellectuals heal the psychological wounds inflicted upon them during the tumultuous years of the Cultural Revolution and of the socialist revolutionary period in general. Scar Literature is introspective and melodramatic, and it is concerned above all else with the personal. It is mainly stories and individual accounts of sufferings, persecution and denunciations during the political and social movements and struggles in the heydays of Maoist China. In its account, Scar Literature examines personal losses that were caused by the political reasoning which underpinned those muddled times. Many of the films and TV drama serials that emerged during the post–Cultural Revolution era were adapted from Scar Literature novels, including the famous Fourth Generation director Xie Jin's movie *Hibiscus Town* (*Furongzhen* 1986) and the TV serials *Wasted Time* (*Cuotuo suiyue* 1982) and *Plain-Clothed Policeman* (*Bianyi jingcha* 1987). Although all these stories were written from different perspectives, they all depicted the Cultural Revolution as a dehumanizing and irrational time of political chaos and as a disaster which overwhelmed human nature by allowing politics and ideological correctness to become more important than the individual's humanity that they were intended to protect.

In 1988, a TV documentary called *River Elegy* (*Heshang*) was aired on China Central Television (CCTV).[4] *River Elegy* was a representative piece of a new enlightenment movement led by elite Chinese intellectuals who endeavoured to seek the truth about reviving the Chinese nation. They were particularly concerned about the aftermath of a series of the socio-political movements that reached their pinnacle during the Cultural Revolution. In *River Elegy*, the Cultural Revolution is exposed as symptomatic of the weaknesses engrained in traditional Chinese culture and in Chinese political structures (Chen 2011). According to Geremie Barme (1999: 23), the producers created a work which to a certain degree associated the Maoist-Stalinist political and economic canon with state Confucianism and traditional culture. The upshot of this admixture was a calamitous plan for the future of China. This introspection of the Cultural Revolution by *River Elegy* was, for many Chinese, deep and thought provoking.

However, the time of introspection was not to last, and the crackdown of the Tiananmen Square protests in 1989 marked a watershed between moderately liberal political and artistic regulation, and tight ideological surveillance and control. In 1990 several exiled writers and cultural critics made it clear that after the fourth of June, novel literary developments and progress in the mainland became impossible and "China had entered the equivalent of a cultural 'ice age'" (Barme 1999: 22). When the authority and legitimacy of the CCP rule was challenged again, the Cultural Revolution became a sensitive topic for the ruling regime, who wanted to distance the memory of the political mistakes from the public, and who also wanted to avoid any questions about the political validity of the CCP. Therefore, any inquiries or solipsism of the Cultural Revolution which yielded negative results were suspended and tightly censored by the dominant ideological institutions. Here, in the post-Tiananmen crackdown, a shift in ideological control occurred, one that would influence the formation of collective memory and popular history.

As a consequence of this shift, *River Elegy* was banned from being broadcast, as it did not convey an understanding of the history of socialist China that was in line with CCP thinking after the Tiananmen demonstration. The prohibition of *River Elegy* signifies the end of the history that promotes contemplation about the Cultural Revolution (Chen 2011). By the beginning of the 1990s, some works of the internationally awarded Chinese Fifth Generation directors Zhang Yimou and Chen Kaige were banned from showing in mainland China partly due to their criticism of the Cultural Revolution. Two pertinent examples of these works are *To Live* (Huozhe 1994) and *Farewell My Concubine* (Baiwang bieji 1993). Since then, negative memories of the Cultural Revolution have been gradually waning from the audience's televisual collective memory.

As China's market-based economy steadily matured and the public's attention shifted to consumption and recreation, the televisual collective memory of the Cultural Revolution re-emerged, depoliticized and commercialized as a revolutionary nostalgic cultural subgenre. Jiang Wen's movie *In the Heat of the Sun* (*Yangguang canlan de rizi* 1994),[5] Ye Jing's TV serials *A Place Where Dreams Start* (*Meng kaishi de defang* 1998) and *Bloom of Youth* (*Yu qingchun youguan de rizi* 2006), and Teng Wenji's TV drama *Crimson Romance* (*Xuese langman*

2004) all dramatize memories of the Cultural Revolution as romantic and passionate, abounding with courtships, love stories and the simple dramas of everyday life. According to Jameson's (1991) understanding of the construction of popular history, it is influenced by a postmodern cultural paradigm and in relation to the Cultural Revolution; this postmodern repackaging of the Cultural Revolutionary collective memory "derealized" the identity and history through erratically cannibalizing styles and images from the past.

Apart from the depoliticizing and romanticizing repackaging of the collective memory of the Cultural Revolution by commercial television (which occurred under the rubric of the collective framework and in accord with the governing ideology of China at the time), television was also used as a vehicle by official media institutions in the humanizing reconstruction of the popular history of the Cultural Revolution. The Beijing satellite TV station produced two cultural documentary programs named *Hundred Flowers* (*Baihua* 2009) and *Songs of Ages* (*Suiyue ruge* 2008), which commemorate the sixtieth anniversary of the founding of the PRC and the thirtieth anniversary of the Open Up reforms respectively. Both of the programs contain Cultural Revolution episodes, and, in sympathy with current concerns of official ideology, the two documentaries intentionally eschew the negative political and social repercussions of the revolutionary movements and instead trivialize the chaos and the disastrous outcomes by recounting interesting and poignant personal anecdotes of the witnesses (Chen 2011). Employing similar production frameworks and methods, a documentary titled *Educated Youth* (*zhishiqingnian*): *Born in the 1950s* (*Zhiqing: shengyu wushi niandai* 2012) also aired on CCTV's Channel One at prime time.[6] Not surprisingly, this show was also highlighted by the ubiquitous enthusiasm of the youths, who are depicted as being full of idealistic beliefs without a trace of introspection about the political chaos and human tragedy of those times.

Through the combined efforts of both official television and commercial television, the collective memory of the Cultural Revolution is once again reconstructed and reinterpreted, as being politically correct and as a reliable source of information. However, in this fictional version of the Cultural Revolution, the "real" history is concealed, and the TV audience is misled and cheated by a distorted and constructed collective memory which forgets and destroys the previous "real" history; a memory is fabricated in accordance with the dominant ideological discourses. This is especially true when it is formatted through a TV media that manufactures popular history and cultural commodity. If we take the Cultural Revolution as a typical example, we see that the evolutions of the collective memories revolving around it experienced different historical phases that reflect different ideological orientations and emphases.

Radical and social nostalgia: consuming the Cultural Revolution

Since the end of the 1980s, the Chinese TV drama market has been witnessing outstanding growth in both output and genres (Zhu 2008: 9), and, for Chinese audiences, TV drama ranked third among the top ten TV genres (Zhang 2009: 172). A revolutionary nostalgia sub-pattern is a hybrid TV drama subgenre combining elements and formulas from youth idol drama, family ethics drama, and revolutionary drama set in the early decades of socialist China. As an established pattern in the current Chinese TV drama scene, the revolutionary nostalgia serials replace the brutal political class-struggle plots with intrigues of romance, courtships, love and marriage. There exists a "depoliticizing" and "humanizing" trend that is infiltrating socialist memory and the revolutionary history of the CCP (Lu 2007: 133).

Although revolutionary nostalgia TV serials appear more as a cultural commodity than as a tool of political propaganda, they have an obvious official flavour about them. This subgenre uses the appeal of the Red classics (in a broader sense), marketing to a nostalgia trend prevalent in the contemporary Chinese cultural environment (Qian 2008: 164). In particular, by beautifying, reviving and rehabilitating the Cultural Revolutionary spirit, they serve the current political agenda of the CCP regime by promoting socialist China's revolutionary heritage and combatting the negative consequences brought about by the economic reforms.

Within the current economic, political and social conditions of China, there are some critical reasons that contribute to the manufacturing of nostalgia using the memories and icons from the early stage of socialist China. For example, nostalgia is used to counterbalance the negative consequences of the combination of political and economic patterns in post-socialist, post-revolutionary China (Lu 2007: 131). Nostalgia is culturally fabricated to cater to the emotions of the contemporary Chinese audience, who harbour a longing for the revolutionary past and spirit that are embedded in their totalitarian nostalgic imagery. In post-socialist, post-revolutionary China, economic reforms, together with social and cultural changes, have created social upheavals that challenge the leadership, authority and legitimacy of the CCP regime, and it is political reasoning that has triggered the recent trend of nostalgia in popular culture and especially on TV. According to Zhu (2008: 34),

> Natural disasters, economic uncertainty, mass protests against corruption, and the subsequent Tiananmen Square crackdown, as well as the fall of Communism in Eastern Europe, propelled the paranoid Chinese state to revive old cultural symbols, cults, and practices in the early 1990s, including the myth of Mao.

Zhu is correct in observing a top-down state-led nostalgia trend; however, there also exists a bottom-up version: the totalitarian nostalgia phenomenon evident in the revival of Mao's Little Red Books, his images, and other symbolic items of the Cultural Revolution. "A 'Red wave' of commercially packaged revolutionary songs, plays, and films not only floods the market, but also feeds a certain nostalgia for the totalitarian past" (Cui 2003: 51). This phenomenon is considered "a roundabout way of protesting the social stratification caused by the economic reforms which were initiated by Deng Xiaoping and his followers at the end of the Cultural Revolution" (Honig 2003: 175).

Under the influence of both the top-down official nostalgia trend and the bottom-up grass-roots totalitarian nostalgia tendency, the production of nostalgia in contemporary China takes a postmodern shift to recollect revolutionary memories and to create revolutionary fantasies in order to toe the line with the dominant ideology and to satisfy consumers' sentimentalities. In doing so, the new subgenre of revolutionary nostalgia TV drama aggrandises the Chinese Revolutions, in particular the Cultural Revolution's "good old days." Embedded in the TV serials are the historical "facts" and the ideals of the Revolution which are labelled by Jameson (1991: 66) as "stereotypes of historical realities," "spectacle" or "simulacrum." These so-called cultural and historical "facts" do not adhere to their historical period and lack continuity. They lack historical veracity and are manipulated for the contemporary Chinese consumer-led cultural market with the sole purpose of exploiting their charm and appeal. Jameson's (1991: 67) discussion about popular American nostalgia films also applies to the contemporary Chinese nostalgia revolutionary TV drama serials:

> [O]ur social, historical and existential present, and the past as "referent" – the incompatibility of a postmodernist "nostalgia" art language with genuine historicity becomes dramatically apparent. The contraction propels this model, however, into complex and interesting new formal inventiveness: it being understood that the nostalgia film was never a matter of some old-fashioned "representation" of historical content, but approached the "past" through stylistic connotation, conveying "pastness" by the glossy qualities of the image, and "1930s-ness" or "1950s-ness" by the attributes of fashion.

In contemporary Chinese nostalgia revolutionary TV serials, the "stereotypes of historical realities" are not the metaphors of revolutionary irrationality and chaos. On the contrary, these cultural "facts" and emblems are imbued with fashions, affections and revolutionary passions. Nostalgia, revolutionary popular history and collective memory purposely ignore the main historical truth, and that is that the Cultural Revolution was a colossal political and human catastrophe. Instead, these manufactured memories and histories highlight its romantic and idealist features, which then reinvigorate the Cultural Revolution in its collaboration with the present political imperatives of the dominant official ideology of the CCP. These political imperatives are to revive what they see as the more positive legacies of the Cultural Revolution, while simultaneously manufacturing cultural spectacles and delusions for the audience.

However, this distortion of important facts about the Cultural Revolution generates images and narratives that "derealize" the sense of authenticity and integrity. The intentional reconstruction of the collective memory of the Cultural Revolution causes cultural amnesia that victimizes the TV audience. Based on engendering obliviousness and the eradication of memory, TV actually impedes viewers' competence to grasp and process the material about the past, and this clouds and disassociates the history of the event. In particular, the younger generation, who do not have first-hand experiences of the Cultural Revolution, are misled about their understanding of it and of its political and social ramifications.

A trendy history and the popular postmodern recollection of the Cultural Revolution: *A Place Where Dreams Start, Bloom of Youth* and *Crimson Romance*

A Place Where Dreams Start aired in 1998 on the CCTV channel at prime time, and its popularity triggered the production of more revolutionary nostalgia TV dramas such as *Crimson Romance, Bloom of Youth* and so on. In all these postmodern revolutionary nostalgia televisual works, the Cultural Revolution serves wholly or partly as the historical and socio-political narrative background. As reflected in the plots and storylines of these TV shows, the collective framework employed to reconstruct the cultural memory and popular history of the Cultural Revolution is a complex, postmodern nostalgia rhetoric that is exploited by both official ideology and the populist sentimentalities of the audience, both of which target imagery of the totalitarian past that is resplendent with revolutionary faith and passion.

In the process of depoliticizing, romanticizing and making fashionable a new understanding of the Cultural Revolution, and of weaving individual emotions with political enthusiasm in this political movement, market forces adroitly utilize revolutionary discourse through manufacturing spectacles, simulacrums and stereotypes of historical realities. As a result, the TV audience lose their independent perspective to perceive historical facts, and their reminiscences are incorporated into the collective framework that is in accord with the established narrative of the governing ideological power.

A Place Where Dreams Start, Crimson Romance and *Bloom of Youth* all, in a similar way, recount the stories of a group of youths who were born in the 1950s and grew up during the heydays of the Cultural Revolution. The plots of these three dramas trace the maturation process of these protagonists from the Cultural Revolution period to the Opening Up era. Instead of focusing on their struggles and life trajectories during the reform days as exhibited in the shows, this chapter engages with their adolescent experiences and "the good old days" during the Cultural Revolution which are foregrounded by the TV plays. One of the characters in *Bloom of Youth* confesses: "We are all very grateful to those days which granted us unprecedented freedom." The "good old days" for these youths refers particularly to those days during which they were "left behind" in Beijing, before they were sent to the country or joined the army. Most of these teenage characters in the three shows, who were aged between fifteen and twenty, were children of the cadres' class, who were mostly bureaucrats, public servants or army generals. These sons and daughters of cadres figure prominently as a particular fashionable set in the culture of the city.

In all three shows, most of the plots depicting the youths during their Cultural Revolution days focus on their passionate and very personal experiences, which are intended to epitomise the revolutionary nostalgia drama as being romantic and idealistic, as opposed to the obedient stereotype of the communist revolution era. These stories are of the carefree lifestyles of ordinary teenagers of the Mao era. Although the youths are politically aligned, they usually spend their days playing, socializing and trouble-making, as the uncertainty of those turbulent times prevents them from continuing their studies. Their stories revisit and mourn the passing of this generation's "glory" days. In this way, the memory of the Cultural Revolution is represented in a postmodern jamboree full of casual romances, love affairs and brutal fights among a group of friends and like-minded peers, and this representation reflects an idiosyncratic revolutionary enthusiasm and fervour.

These left-behind youths in the shows bear an uncanny resemblance to the trouble(d)-shooter characters in the works of Wang Shuo, the famous Beijing-based Hooligan Literature (*piziwenxue*) writer. At the end of the 1980s, Wang Shuo's Hooligan Literature enjoyed high esteem among Chinese readers. He was especially appreciated by those chic and cynical youths living in big cities, for his "shun loftiness" (*duobichonggao*) themes (Wang 1993) and semantic features which are full of witty remarks and sharp satire as conveyed by the Beijing dialect. Geremie Barme (1999: 63) has noted:

> Wang Shuo was not a doomsayer or a pessimist but a playful writer of serious intent who availed himself of the contemporary Chinese cultural order to depict a fictional world of great humor, perception, and release. In his work, we are dealing not only with entertainment fiction or coded political writing but also with a far more compelling form of art: a literature of escape and sublimation.

Those trouble(d)-shooters (*wanzhu*) that constitute the majority of Wang Shuo's novel characters are a group of youths who adopt a playful and cynical stance where "troubleshooting" is understood as a spirit, a force and a kind of action art. These trouble(d)-shooter youths spent their formative years in Maoist China, where their individuality and freedom were exploited by the collective and its politics-driven ideology. The ideological brainwashing of the socialist collective and revolutionary dogmas left an imprint on the youth's persona. Their altruism and optimistic brashness towards life are inflated and "eulogised." These banished youths both under Wang Shuo's pen and under the portrayal of the revolutionary nostalgic dramas adopt a more playful and blindly optimistic outlook on life in terms of their experiments with unconventional behaviour and unusual or even avant-garde lifestyles. For example, some use all their spare time flirting, and some engage in immoral or illegal conduct such as stealing and gang fighting. However, in both Wang Shuo's writing and the storylines of the nostalgic revolutionary dramas, all these "abnormal" acts of these trouble(d)-shooter characters do not harbour any evil intent. They intend only to be playful, which reflects the absurd social reality of China during the Cultural Revolution era, one that is full of paradox, puzzlement and uncertainty. Further, the trouble(d)-shooters also talk passionately about saving the world and helping those in need, a desire driven by their revolutionary enthusiasm and idealism.

In the three shows under examination of this chapter, the days of the carefree youths are restored as a repertoire of revolutionary passion and fashion during the Cultural Revolution era. Their lifestyle is repackaged and romanticized: from the standardization of their clothes (army uniform), to their places of congregation, such as the Moscow Restaurant, Beijing Xinqiao Hotel (*Beijing xinqiaofandian*) (which specialises in Western-style cuisine) and Shicha River skating rink (*Shichahai bingchang*), all fashionable places where trendy Beijing youths gathered. Their behaviour in each environment is glamorized in order to portray untroubled youths of the Mao era. Their natures are portrayed as undisciplined and cheerful, and their main concerns are fun making, talking love, flirting and infighting. In many scenes of the shows, the characters are trendy, relaxed and carefree and are able to enjoy their leisure. The shared themes of the three shows are innocence, friendship, romance and brotherhood.

Among the youths of the Cultural Revolution era, a discourse of love and pre-marital sex was not something unusual; it was normal, and it constituted a major part of their young lives. During the chaos of revolution, when adults were busy with political matters (or to be distained by the revolutionary committee or working groups) and unable to devote much time to their children, the children, and especially the teenagers, enjoyed enormous freedom, for the most part doing whatever they wanted to do. Often this included things – that under normal circumstances – they would never consider, and talking about romance, once shunned, was now routine. The boys nicknamed it hooking up with girls (*paipozi*), and they nicknamed girls who were willing to "flirt" with them as prostitutes (*quanzi*). When a group of boys and girls spent a night together, it is referred to as staying out the whole night (*shuaye*), which, in the Beijing dialect, takes on a cavalier like "devil-may-care" understanding.

In an opening scene of *Crimson Romance*, when a group of boys try to engage with two pretty girls they meet in a park, they are shunned by the girls who initially see them as just a group of hooligans. The girls try to disengage from their banter and insinuations, and, when the girls refer to the boys as "rogues," the boys reply: "How come you know my name?" And when the girls further label them as "bastards," they shamelessly respond: "How come you know my nickname?" This short dialogue demonstrates the semantic features of the Wang Shuo–style loquaciousness and humour that is conveyed by the Beijing dialect. During their continuing harassment of the girls, one of the boys offers to shake hands with the girls; however, again he is refused. Without giving up, he quotes the lyrics of "The Internationale": "So come brothers and sisters, for the struggle carries on. The Internationale, unites the world in song! So comrades come really." In another scene, the conversation between a girl and a boy reads:

BOY: How come you have not been coming to the skating rink lately? If you only work by fits and starts, how can you take over the revolutionary missions in the future?
GIRL: You haven't been to the skating rink much either. What are you busy doing?
BOY: Recently I have been busy attending meetings. I am immersed in matters of world revolutions in Paris, America and Czechoslovakia.

Another scene of the drama shows the boys quarrelling with each other over trivial personal matters, and, when the dispute escalates and their chosen positions seem intractable, one of the boys steps up and tries to quell the anger of his friends: "I now understand why the Chinese revolutions always encounter setbacks; it is because there is too much internal fighting among fellow comrades."

In a similar scene in *A Place Where Dreams Start*, the youths are seen gathering at the Moscow restaurant, dressed in army uniforms, and imitating the speech and gestures of the Communist leaders of the Soviet Union. Later in the show, when two youths bid farewell to each other as they head to their respective army brigades, one of them says, "Down with the Fascists!" and the other replies, "Victory belongs to the people!" In these scenes, not only is the carefree lifestyle and the revolutionised logic of the youths exhibited, but also the misaligned nexus between the communist cause and ideals of socialist China, which deeply impact upon the outlook on life and life values of the youths growing up in those times.

In *Crimson Romance*, when the group of youths become angered and then enraged by a street hooligan who is from Beijing's rougher side of town and whom they believe killed one of their peers, they confront the "street punk," and one youth addresses the others and says: "Our current revolutionary mission is to destroy this bastard, and later we should do something that is in the interest of the people." In addition, when the boys discuss the urgency of their "revolutionary tasks," they cite Chairman Mao's poems, such as "Ten thousand years are too long; seize the day, seize the hour!"[7] In their final discussion about how to settle with the object of their revenge, three leaders of the youths, who each have their own followers, gather at the Moscow restaurant.

YOUTH ONE: It is time to eliminate a public scourge. Debts of blood must be paid in blood.
YOUTH TWO: Now different corps of the Red Army have joined together, what is the right time to fight with this street punk.
YOUTH THREE: Chair Mao has taught us that thousands of revolutionary martyrs have given up their life heroically for the interest of the people. So let us hold high their banners and go forward down the path made by their blood!
YOUTH ONE: The strong pass of the enemy is like a wall of iron, yet with firm strides, we are conquering its summit.[8]
YOUTH ONE, TWO AND THREE TOGETHER: We are conquering its summit, the rolling hills sea-blue.

After reciting the poem, the youths sing "The Internationale" to boost their morale and to give them courage to fight with the street punk. In another scene of *Crimson Romance*, one of the boys returns to his home, which has previously had its access blocked by the revolutionary committee, as the boy's father was under isolated examination by the Party. The boy steals his father's antique vase and sells it to a stranger for three hundred Yuan, a tidy sum at the time. He then purchases a large barrel of ice cream for himself and his friends to share, but this leads to him to getting diarrhoea. When his friends persuade him to stop eating, he replies: "Once I have started a revolution I must go all the way. Just think about The Long

March of the Red Army, my current hardship does not count for anything. . . . [W]hat I am practicing is my revolutionary will."

In *Bloom of Youth*, when the youths talk about their friendship, they relate it with the friendship between China and Albania and between China and North Korea. In these scenes, the revolutionary slogans and passions intermingle well with personal emotions and relationships. The personal actions and thoughts that are driven by revolutionary ideals create an affected sacred atmosphere, which makes for a comical reading of the revolutionary discourse through postmodern parody. In the shows, people's over-politicized behaviours during the Cultural Revolution era seem not to be viewed as unreasonable, and, on the contrary, they are made humorous, idolized and sublimed. In doing so, the Cultural Revolution is transformed from a disorderly political farce to a sacred battle led by the revolutionaries and their followers: a battle that calls for equality, emancipation and sacrifice.

Apart from appropriating and making acceptable the "light-hearted" revolutionary passions and idealism into daily routines and personal life, the three TV drama shows also romanticize the brutal fighting among youths during the Cultural Revolution era and weaves it into the revolutionary context. During the confusion of revolutionary China, the troubled, yet optimistic, youths are involved in street skirmishes, which range from small-scale confrontations to large-scale urban warfare. There are numerous scenes in the three shows that display hostile youth groups jostling for a dominant position over various disputes, and always willing and ready to spill each other's blood.

In *A Place Where Dreams Start*, one scene shows two groups of youths fighting for dominance in front of the Wu Gate (*wumen*) of the Forbidden City, and, in *Crimson Romance*, two groups of youths gather at the Xiannong Temple of Beijing for a large melee. The fighting arenas chosen for the fight scenes, such as the Forbidden City and the Xiannong Temple (*xiannongtan*), add to the quasi-epic atmosphere, which, however, also contains a hint of cynicism. In one scene, hundreds of youths dressed in army uniforms and riding bicycles are shown "advancing towards the enemy" and the designated "battle field." They are laughing and excited and talk valiantly and spiritedly to each other. Some girls sit on the crossbeams of their boyfriends' bikes, flirting with them. The stimulating music creates a farcical-cum-sacred atmosphere which transforms the violent and militant fighting and occasion into a sham, where foolhardiness and blind gallantry reign supreme. The youths are ready to spill each other's blood in the upcoming struggle. Upbeat and full of bravado, they would use whatever they could as weapons (iron bars, knives, wooden clubs and big-buckled belts) to inflict often deadly force on the enemy – other youths. The detailed fighting scenes, the close-up filming of the moments before death, the ear-piercing screaming of the injured – it all evokes curiosity, horror, fantasy and visual ecstasy among the audience.

The brutal fight scenes amongst the youth groups signify the mode of how disagreements were settled and how revenge was taken during the Cultural Revolution. The social violence reflects the unscrupulous and outrageous conduct and reactions to "enemies" which was motivated and promoted by the political and social movements and struggles during the socialist revolutionary times. In the shows, the youths are portrayed as passionate and heroic fighters as they all blindly followed the revolutionary dogmas and optimism because of their worship of Mao, whose directives dominated their behaviour and thinking during their formative years. The resurrection and the reverence of the icon that is Mao are reflected in contemporary Chinese popular culture products. It reveals the interesting cultural phenomenon that is embedded in totalitarian nostalgia. The cruelty and malevolence of the fight scenes are depicted as something sacred, solemn and stirring. From the audience's perspective, the fighting is not the actions of felonious, misguided, unscrupulous or muddle-minded youths but gallant actions that deserve to be cherished and admired. These chivalrous behaviours and carefree lifestyles of the revolutionary youths during the Cultural Revolution era have great appeal to the contemporary TV viewer. This chaotic period is given a positive revamp by the shows, which laments the passing of such a glorious and epic era, an era that blends the bold with romance. In addition to replicating and following Mao's thoughts and directives, the youths also imitate and engage with the revolutionary speech and rhetoric when fighting. In one episode of *Bloom of Youth*, when several youths are put into the detention house after taking part in brutal street combat, one of them asks his friend:

YOUTH ONE: Where am I?
YOUTH TWO: Zhazidong [a prison run by the secret service of the Nationalist Party to house communist revolutionaries].
YOUTH ONE: Please tell our comrades to continue the struggle, and the Party will think of a way to rescue us.
YOUTH TWO: Down with the Fascists!
YOUTH ONE: Freedom belongs to people!

Later, the two youths start to talk about their girlfriends, and one warns the other: "Under these special circumstances [in the detention house], it would better do not think about our girlfriends, as it will distract and crumble our revolutionary will." Here, when the speeches and behaviour of the youths are interwoven with revolutionary routines, customs, and rhetoric, the positive and chivalrous images of the carefree youths are emphasized, while at the same time a postmodern caricature is also impressed upon the audience. The voiceover of the youths in *Bloom of Youths* reflects: "At that time, we all dreamt of the start of war between China and the Soviet Union, therefore we could all become war heroes." In the three shows, when the youths bid farewell to each other before heading to their respective army brigades or to their designated countryside to receive education from the farmers, they salute military style and say to those who bid farewell to them at the platform of the railway station: "Folks, [when our forces expand in the future] we will certainly come back."

In these passages and scenes from the TV plays, the revolutionary slogans and official rhetoric coalesce well with personal sensations and practices of the troubled youths during the Cultural Revolution era. The actions and affairs occur during the youths maturation years and are driven by revolutionary ideals and ideology, which creates a feeling of artificial sacredness in harmony with irony and playfulness. The over-politicized behaviours that are inherited from the revolutionary traditions seem not to be viewed as excessive, and, on the contrary, they are exalted and sublimated. However, from a different perspective, these postmodern burlesques of the revolutionary practices, mores and magniloquence used by the youths also bear a canon-mocking imprint (Tao 2007). As the revolutionary slogans are articulated by the carefree youths, and as the revolutionary ideology is made real by the street fights, the ideational socialist revolutionary discourse is parodied and depoliticized. The audiences easily detect the misalignment and discordance between the orthodox and sacred official tutelage and the heterodox and dissident actions of the unscrupulous youths, which generates a humorous effect that caters to fun-seeking contemporary viewers.[9]

In these three shows, through randomly choosing the spectacles and simulacrums of the Cultural Revolution, social memories and historical genuineness are reconfigured via the process by which some events are emphasized and reimagined, and others are intentionally avoided and concealed in order to conform with the established ideological orientation. For example, the romance and street fights are stressed, rather than scenes of class struggle or scenes of criticism and denunciation at public meetings. Furthermore, the picture presented about friendship, family matters and relationships does not mesh with the actual distorted interpersonal relationships during the Cultural Revolution era – for instance, sons and daughters reporting, criticising and denouncing their parents for their anti-revolutionary behaviour; the suspicious relationships between friends and colleagues; and the divorces caused by strict class delineations. The shows largely ignore the negative impacts on the lives of the common Chinese people caused by the Cultural Revolution. Further, by replacing the scarred historical memories, sensitive social and personal issues such as love triangles and pre-marital affairs become the new focal points of the televisual narratives, thus greatly enhancing the correlation between the drama and the reality of contemporary Chinese society. In this way, the negative political and social influences and implications of the Cultural Revolution are diluted and neutralized, and the audience identifies more with the superficial romances and love stories that constitute the majority of the collective memory of the Cultural Revolution.

Moreover, revolutionary nostalgic TV drama texts, such as the three shows under discussion of this chapter, also experiment with sensualizing and sexualizing the Cultural Revolution. By foregrounding the female body and sensuality during the Cultural Revolution, the plays give emphasis to the impression that the Cultural Revolution was an unconventional era of freedom and idealism. During the Cultural Revolution, "traces of femininity and sexuality were sanitised and nearly erased" (Qian 2010: 297), and "both the state and the cinematic apparatus suppress female sexuality for the ideological constitution of revolutionary histories" (Cui 2003: 90). Contrary to the historical picture of the suppression of female sensuality, in the shows, women's deferential nature is not utterly rejected and obscured but fermented by revolutionary passion and fanaticism.

Sex, sexuality and femininity are given a new dynamic by defining the progressive and avant-garde nature of a previously asexual historical and political period. The Luo Dongna character constitutes the core of feminine and sensual discourse in *A Place Where Dreams Start*. This discourse has its beginning in the vague and surreal representation of Luo's body. Her physique is graceful and is presented tightly wrapped in her army uniform, which she re-tailored to fit her slim body. With her hair down to her shoulders, Luo "cat walks" in the army compound, attracting many voyeuristic leers from the male soldiers. Revolutionary China is well known for its promotion and use of simple, quasi-military, almost peasant-styled dress. "The media always encouraged Chinese citizens to struggle for political correctness and to put aside the pursuit of self-adornment" (Ip 2003: 350); thus, they helped develop the ideal of the female form as an androgynous iron girl (Chen 2003). Obviously, Luo's over-attentive focus on her appearance provides an unprecedented and unconventional figure for Maoist China.

In another scene the audacious Luo is shown as an elegant silhouette standing by the window of her bedroom playing the violin. This charming image of Luo seduces Song (her boyfriend) and ultimately leads to their illegitimate pre-marital sex. The camera zooms in for just a fleeting moment to catch this erotic scene between Luo and Song, which occurs in Luo's bedroom with simple and typical settings and decorations of the revolutionary era. With the classic Chinese music *Butterfly Lovers* (*Liangzhu*) playing in the background, Song appears to hallucinate as he sees the beautiful vision of Luo's body. Luo's alluring image is constructed to highlight the romance and even erotic features of Cultural Revolution memories. In Luo and Song's case, Luo is the fearless and tempting Eve of biblical legend. Her conspicuously sexual body enchants Song, causing him to break his obligations to the revolution. From the voyeuristic male point of view, the camera's focus accentuates the contours of her sensuous body and the enchanting expression in her eyes. Luo is transformed from an innocent proletarian soldier to a sensual pleasure source and siren-like female evildoer.

Likewise, in *Crimson Romance*, Zhou Xiaobai always takes the initiative to have body contact with Zhong Yuemin (her boyfriend) by (for example) sitting on his legs and hugging and kissing him. In *Bloom of Youth*, in the case of Fang Yan and his girlfriend Li Bailing, one night, when Fang plans to stay the whole night at Li's home, he can barely restrain his sexual impulse and nearly forces Li to have sex with him. After some heavy petting on Li's bed, Fang intends to undress Li before he finally restores his rationality and lets go of Li. However, after Fang gives up his passionate but reckless behaviour, it is Li whose desire has been ignited by Fang, and she wants to make love with him. Here, both Luo Dongna, Zhou Xiaobai and Li Bailing's roles created in the three shows successfully grasp the conjuncture of revolutionary fervour and sensual desires that are expected by contemporary Chinese audiences. While the main purpose of characters in orthodox revolutionary literature is to portray revolutionary mass suffering, these woman characters, and the contemporary television viewer, enjoy the simultaneous pursuit of emotional orgasm, which in turn generates a positive impression of Cultural Revolution on the contemporary TV audience. These TV shows depict the female body as an embodiment of freedom and passion, which also implies that there was such an ethos during the Cultural Revolution. This foregrounding of the female body and desire in the Cultural Revolution context emphasizes the audience's impression that the Cultural Revolution was an unconventional era of freedom and enthusiasm, when in reality it was something else.[10]

In summary, revolutionary nostalgia dramas share many features with contemporary idol dramas in terms of shaping fashions and featuring trendy lifestyles and of focussing on relationships and female desires, albeit in a special Cultural Revolution socio-political context. They stimulate the imagination and evoke admiration among the contemporary Chinese TV audiences. However, this free manufacturing of the collective memory of the Cultural Revolution risks misleading the viewer and clouding the understanding, judgement and retrospection of the younger generation about this important and recent era; it is a regressive approach to the popular history and cultural recollection.

Conclusion

The evolution of representations and interpretations of the Cultural Revolution reflected in contemporary Chinese TV programs provides a means by which we can examine the motives and determinants of the construction of the collective memory and popular history as they parallel the predominant thoughts and ideas of a specific epoch. When we analyse historical events and phenomena via televisual texts concerning the Cultural Revolution, it becomes clear that the relationship between TV and historiography is complex and could be at times antithetical. *A Place Where Dreams Start*, *Crimson Romance*, and *Bloom of Youth* serve as typical examples where the televisual media devices manufacture a series of postmodern spectacles and simulacrums to form fictional historical realities. These manufactured realities cater to the demands of the dominant ideological discourse in terms of highlighting certain historical anecdotes and events and intentionally neglecting and concealing others, which consequently victimizes the viewers and distances them from genuine history.

In contemporary China, the dominant collective framework within which the popular memory of the Cultural Revolution is constructed is the official one that is upheld by ideological inclination and popular nostalgic sentimentality, both of which indicate an imagery of delusion about the totalitarian past of revolutionary socialist China. Under these circumstances, the once thought-provoking and in-depth reflections about the cause and repercussions of the Cultural Revolution have been negated. For the Chinese people, in particular those who did not experience the political chaos and catastrophe themselves, their memory is filled with passionate and idealistic narratives and images, which allows nostalgia to be a strategy that helps to avoid and reconfigure the historical wounds. The audience immerses itself in an atmosphere created by romance, courtship and sexual freedom where it is assimilated into and identifies with the collective memory built by the TV programs under the surveillance and monitoring of the governing political rhetoric.

Televisual programs are often hijacked by the predominant thoughts of society and form an intriguing nexus with it in terms of obscuring real history and manipulating a conjured past. Therefore, in the three shows under examination of this chapter, televisual narratives should be recognized as unsuitable and misleading as a reliable media for presenting and exposing history. As a result, they present a factitious and romanticized Cultural Revolution to the contemporary TV audience. This radical and regressive rewriting of the Cultural Revolution reduces the critical and retrospective power given to it by Scar Literature and Films, and furthermore it disturbs the objective judgement towards the Cultural Revolution and the younger generations' understanding about it. Thus, in order to retrieve a better understanding of recent historical events, marginalized frameworks of memory should be encouraged. The re-emergence of the Scar Literature reflected in the America-based Chinese writer Yan Geling's novels such as *The Criminal Lu Yanshi* (*Lufan yanshi*) (2011) and *A Woman's Epic* (*Yige nuren de shishi*) (2006)[11] are examples of these marginalized frameworks of memory. They are not merely deteriorating or vanishing, for, in some circumstances, they are evolving, interfering and challenging the leading framework in terms of offering alternative and even antithetical historical narratives in opposition to the established mainstream narratives. The attacks and challenges launched by the relegated and subordinate memory frameworks to the controlling frameworks are meaningful in that they provide opportunity for the historical facts and truths to re-emerge from the amnesia and stasis of people's memory. Therefore, the historical truth is restored and people are able to give history a more contemplative consideration and learn lessons from their past experiences and setbacks.

Glossary

Ba Jin 巴金
Baihua 百花
Banzhuren《班主任》
Bejing xinqiaofandian 北京新桥饭店
Bianyijingcha 便衣警察
Chen Kaige 陈凯歌
Cuotuosuiyue 蹉跎岁月
dajihuang 大饥荒
dayuejin 大跃进
Du Daozheng riji: Zhao Ziyang haishuolexie shenmo《杜导正日记：赵紫阳还说了些什么》
duobichonggao 躲避崇高
Furongzhen 芙蓉镇
Gaigelicheng《改革历程》
Ganxiaoliuji《干校六记》
Gao Xingjian 高行键
Hai Yan 海岩
Heshang 河殇

Jiabiangou jishi《夹边沟纪事》
Jiang Wen 姜文
Liangzhu 梁祝
Liu Xinwu 刘心武
Lufan Yanshi《陆犯焉识》
Manjianghong: he Guo Moruo tongzhi 满江红：和郭沫若同志
Mao, buweirenzhi de gushi《毛，不为人知的故事》
Maozigongchang 帽子工厂
Mengkaishi de defang 梦开始的地方
Mubei: zhongguo liushiniandai dajihuang jishi《墓碑：中国六十年代大饥荒纪实》
paipozi 拍婆子
piziwenxue 痞子文学
qiuanzi 圈子
Rucizhaoxiang 如此照相
shanghenwenxue 伤痕文学
Shichahai bingchang 什刹海冰场
shuaye 刷夜
Suixianglu《随想录》
Suiyueruge 岁月如歌
Teng Wenji 滕文骥
Wang Shuo 王朔
Wangshibingburuyan《往事并不如烟》
wanzhu 顽主
wumen 午门
xiannongtan 先农坛
Xie Jin 谢晋
Xueselangman 血色浪漫
Yan Geling 严歌苓
Yang Jiang 杨绛
Ye Jing 叶京
Ye Xin 叶辛
Yige nuren de shishi《一个女人的史诗》
Yiqine: Loushanguan 忆秦娥：娄山关
Yuqingchun youguande rizi 与青春有关的日子
Zhang Yimou 张艺谋
Zhiqing: shengyu wushiniandai 知青：生于五十年代
zhishiqingnian 知识青年

Notes

1 Since communist rule, the predominant causal agent of collective memory has been CCP ideology; however, some alternative accounts of collective reminiscence have still managed to be published or released both in and outside China. Some examples of these alternative collective memory texts are the reportage literature about the Anti-rightist Movement; *The Chronicles of Jiabiangou* (*Jiabiangou jishi*), which was

published in 2003 by the Flower City Publishing House; *The Past Is Not Like Smoke* (*Wangshi bingbu ruyan*), which was published in 2004 by the People's Literature Press; and the documentary film *The Ditch* (*Jiabiangou* 2010, directed by Wang Bing), which was shot with financial support from France and was shown at the Venice Film Festival. There are also several oral and diary texts and feature films published or released in Hong Kong, Taiwan and France about the Tiananmen demonstration, such as *The Secret Journal of Zhao Ziyang* (*Gaige licheng* 2009; and its English version, *Prisoner of the State: The Secret Journal of Premier Zhao Ziyang*, which was published in the United States in the same year); *Diary of Du Daozheng: What Else Did Zhao Ziyang Say* (*Du Daozheng riji: Zhao Ziyang hai shuoguo xie shenmo* 2010); and the film *Summer Palace* (*Yiheyuan* 2006, directed by Lou Ye). There are also numerous other texts published in America and Great Britain that provide unofficial narrative about the history of Mao's China, such as *Mao, the Unknown Story* (*Mao, buwei renzhi de gushi* 2005) and *Tombstone: The Untold Story of Mao's Great Famine* (*Mubei: zhongguo liushiniandai dajihuang jishi* 2012).

2 On *xiangsheng*'s role in criticising the Cultural Revolution after the overthrow of the Gang of Four, Link (1984: 84) comments that "it is *xiangsheng* above everything else that people say, 'vents one's gall (*jiehen*).'"

3 Scar Literature (*shanghenwenxue*) emerged in the late 1970s, not long after the end of the Cultural Revolution (1966–1976). According to Zhang Yinde, it did not hesitate to attack the Cultural Revolution once it was over, together with the tragic events of the People's Republic. Scar Literature carried with it a cascade of narratives that remained unabated throughout the 1980s. The denunciation of violated humanism by Ba Jin (*Random Thoughts / Suixiangliu*), Yang Jiang (*A Cadre School Life: Six Chapters / Ganxiaoliuji*), Liu Xinwu (*Head Teacher / Banzhuren*), Ye Xin (*Wasted Time*) and Hai Yan (*Plain-Clothed Policeman*) gave rise to a literature of emotional testimony, which was hugely popular with the Chinese audience as it threw a retrospective and thought-provoking light on the personal encounters and setbacks experienced by Chinese intellectuals and commoners during socialist revolutionary China. See Zhang 2010: 28.

4 According to Geremie Barme (1999: 23), *River Elegy* is the most widely viewed and debated documentary ever produced on the mainland of China. This multipart documentary series was the outcome of a collaborated endeavour involving scholars, writers, and TV directors. The documentary conducted a mass audience discussion about politics, culture, and economic reform that had formerly been limited to intellectual circles. The producers of the documentary "suggested that the solution to the nation's problems was to abandon the traditional inland, earth-bound worldview (as symbolized in particular by the Great Wall and agrarian culture) for a revolutionary orientation linked to the sea, commerce, and contact with the outside world."

5 Jiang Wen's *In the Heat of the Sun* is a pioneer movie which romanticizes the revolutionary fever which is found in a group of teenagers and their life experiences during the Cultural Revolution. By amplifying and exaggerating their impulsive sexual exploits, which according to Larson is a "revolutionary eroticism" (1999: 422), this film foregrounds the revolutionary passions and fanaticism of the times.

6 During the Cultural Revolution, educated youth (*zhishiqingnian*) – unlike those carefree youths portrayed in *In the Heat of the Sun*, *A Place Where Dreams Start*, *Crimson Romance*, and *Bloom of Youth* – did not have the good fortune to experiment with the "luxurious," sensational and wild lifestyles created by the unique political atmosphere. Instead, they were sent to rural areas and often to the remotest regions of the country such as the Northeast and Inner Mongolia to receive education from the farmers. They were forced to cope with a callous and difficult natural and alien environment. After the initial revolutionary fervour and ecstasies receded, the educated youth soon become conscious of their situation. They were isolated and felt abandoned. They were doubly harmed, for apart from the arduous work allocated to them by the production

brigade of the villages, they also had to find ways to bring some hope and enjoyment to their dreary lives. Most importantly, however, they needed to find some influential connections and valid reasons to return to the cities from where they had come. In *Educated Youth: Born in the 1950s*, these harsh memories and the psychological "scars" inflicted by the "exile" of the educated youth are overshadowed and replaced by "treasurable" and "meaningful" experiences generated by their sent-down days. For more discussion, see Rene 2013; Honig and Zhao 2015.

7 This sentence is an excerpt from Mao Zedong's poem "The Whole River Red: Reply to Comrade Guo Moruo" (*Manjianghong: he guomoruo tongzhi*) in which he has written the famous and widely quoted sentence: "So many deeds cry out to be down, and always urgently; the world rolls on, time presses. Ten thousand years are too long; seize the day, seize the hour!"
8 Here, the youth chants a well-known line from Mao Zedong's poem "Recalls Qin E: Loushan Pass" (Yiqine: loushanguan).
9 For more discussion about this postmodern parody of the orthodox revolutionary discourse, which is a popular topic within China's contemporary media landscape, see Cai 2016.
10 For more discussion, see Larson 1999; Cai 2014.
11 *The Criminal Lu Yanshi* and *A Woman's Epic* further the tradition of Scar Literature and probe into the political and cultural catalysts that contribute to the authoritarian rule of Mao and the subsequent social and human catastrophes of this traumatic period in the history of China. Yan's novels display a unique perspective in showing the conspiratorial nature and rapport between the defects of the Chinese persona and the disturbing features of the political campaigns, which together fabricated social and human mishaps.

References

A Place Where Dream Starts (Meng kaishi de defang). (1999) Directed by Ye Jing, Produced by China International Television Corporation, Beijing.
Anderson, Steve. (2001) "History TV and Popular Memory," in Gary Richard Edgerton and Peter C. Rollins (eds) *Television Histories: Shaping Collective Memory in the Media Age*. Lexington: The University Press of Kentucky: 19–36.
Ba, Jin. (2009) *Random Thoughts* (Suixianglu). Beijing: China Writers Publishing House.
Barme, Geremie. (1999) *In the Red: On Contemporary Chinese Culture*. New York: Columbia University Press.
Bloom of Youth (Yu qingchun youguan de rizi). (2006) Directed by Ye Jing, Produced by Beijing Banghe Film & Culture Co., Ltd., China.
Cai, Shenshen. (2014) "Rhetoric and Politics of the Female Body and Sex in Two Contemporary Chinese TV Drama Serials: A Dream Starts and Blow the North Wind." *Journal of International Women's Studies* 15(1): 151–166.
Cai, Shenshen. (2016) "*Past Events of the Northeast: Twenty Years of the Mafia Gang* – Readings of the Nature of a Trouble(d)Shooter, a Postmodern Parody and a Revived Spirit of Chivalry." *Asian Studies Review* 40(1): 106–119.
Chen, Tina Mai. (2003) "Female Icons, Feminist Iconography? Socialist Rhetoric and Womens' Agency in 1950s China." *Gender & History* 15(2): 268–295.
Chen, Yu. (2011) "Cong xianlipian 'Baihua' he 'Suiyue ruge' kan wenge lishi jiyi de jiange." (The Construction of Collective Memory of the Cultural Revolution Reflected in Greeting Documentaries *Hundred Flowers* and *Songs of Ages*) *Wenhuayanjiu* 11, available at: http://www.culstudies.com/html/wenhuayanjiu/cmspath}/html/wenhuayanjiu/wenhu/2011/1025/9695.html

Crimson Romance (Xuese langman). (2003) Directed by Teng Wenji, Produced by Runya Entertainment Co., Ltd., China.

Cui, Shuqin. (2003) *Women Through the Lens: Gender and Nation in a Century of Chinese Cinema*. Honolulu: University of Hawaii Press.

The Ditch (Jiabiangou). (2010) Feature Film, Directed by Wang Bing, Co-Produced in Hong Kong, France and Belgium by Wang Bing, K Lihong, Hui Mao, Philippe Avril, Francisco Ville-Lobos, Sebastien Delloye and dianba Elbaum.

Doane, Mary Ann. (1990) "Information, Crisis, Catastrophe," in Patricia Mellencamp (ed.) *Logics of Television*. Bloomington: Indiana University Press: 222–239.

Du, Daozheng. (2010) *Diary of Du Daozheng: What Else did Zhao Ziyang Say* (Du Daozheng riji: Zhao Ziyang hai shuoguo xie shenmo). Hong Kong: Cosmos Books Ltd.

Edgerton, Gary R. (2001) "Introduction: Television as Historian: A Different Kind of History Altogether," in Gary R. Edgerton and Peter C. Rollins (eds) *Television Histories: Shaping Collective Memory in the Media Age*. Lexington: The University Press of Kentucky: p. 1–16.

Edgerton, Gary R. and Rollins, Peter C. (eds) (2001) *Television Histories: Shaping Collective Memory in the Media Age*. Lexington: The University Press of Kentucky.

Educated Youth: Born in the 1950s (Zhiqing: shengyu wushi niandai). (2012) TV Documentary, Directed by Zeng Hairuo, Produced by Beijing Five Star Legend Culture Media Co., Ltd., China.

Ermarth, Elizabeth. (1992) *Sequel to History: Postmodernism and the Crisis of Representational Time*. Princeton, NJ: Princeton University Press.

Farewell My Concubine (Baiwang bieji). (1993) Directed by Chen Kaige, Produced by Beijing Film Studio & Hong Kong Tomson Film Corporation, China.

Hai, Yan. (1985) *Plain-Clothed Policeman* (Bianyijingcha). Beijing: People's Literature Press.

Halbwachs, Maurice and Lewis, A. Coser (eds and trans) (1992) *On Collective Memory*. Chicago: The University of Chicago Press.

Hat Factory (Maozi gongchang). (1976) Crosstalk, performed by Chang Guitian & Chang Baohua.

Hibiscus Town (Furong zhen). (1986) Directed by Xie Jin, produced by Shanghai Film Studio, China.

Honig, Emily. (2003) "Socialist Sex: The Cultural Revolution Revisited." *Modern China* 29(2): 143–175.

Honig, Emily and Zhao, Xiaojian. (2015) "Sent-down Youth and Rural Economic Development in Maoist China." *China Quarterly* 222: 499–521.

Heath, Stephen. (1990) "Representing Television," in Patricia Mellencamp (ed.) *Logics of Television: Essays in Cultural Criticism*. Bloomington: Indiana University Press: 267–302.

Hundred Flowers (Baihua). (2009) TV Documentary, Directed by Wang Chunhua, Produced by Beijing Yangguangjiangtong Culture and Entertainment Co., Ltd., China.

Hutcheon, Linda. (1988) *A Poetic of Postmodernism: History, Theory, Fiction*. New York: Routledge.

In the Heat of the Sun (Yangguang canlan de rizi). (1994) Directed by Jiang Wen, produced by China Film Co-Production Corporation, China.

Ip, Hung-Yok. (2003) "Fashioning Appearances: Feminine Beauty in Chinese Communist Revolutionary Culture." *Modern China* 29(3): 329–361.

Jameson, Fredric. (1991) *Postmodernism: The Cultural Logic of Late Capitalism*. Durham: Duke University Press.

Larson, Wendy. (1999) "Never This Wild: Sexing the Cultural Revolution." *Modern China* 25(4): 423–450.
Link, Perry. (1984) "The Genie and the Lamp: Revolutionary *Xiangsheng*," in Bonnie S. McDougall (ed.) *Popular Chinese Literature and Performing Arts in the People's Republic of China 1949–1979*. Berkeley: University of California Press: 83–111.
Liu, Xinwu. (1979) *Collection of Liu Xinwu's Novellas* (Liu Xinwu duanpian xiaoshuoji). Beijing: China Youth Publishing House.
Lu, H. Sheldon. (2007) *Chinese Modernity and Global Biopolitics: Studies in Literature and Visual Culture*. Honolulu: University of Hawaii Press.
Neiger, Motti, Meyers, Oren and Zanberg, Eyal. (2011) "On Media Memory: Editors' Introduction," in Motti Neiger, Oren Meyers and Eyal Zanberg (eds) *On Media Memory: Collective Memory in a New Media Age*. Houndmills, Basingstoke, Hampshire; New York: Palgrave Macmillan: 1–24.
Plain-Clothed Policeman (Bianyi jingcha). (1987) Directed by Lin Ruwei, produced by Beijing TV Art Centre, China.
Qian, Gong. (2008) "A Trip Down Memory Lane: Remaking and Rereading the Red Classics," in Ying Zhu, Keane Michael and Ruoyun Bai (eds) *TV Drama in China*. Hong Kong: Hong Kong University Press: 157–172.
Qian, Gong. (2010) "Red Woman and TV Drama," in Christopher Crouch (ed.) *Contemporary Chinese Visual Culture: Tradition, Modernity and Globalization*. New York: Cambria Press: 295–316.
Rene, Helena. (2013) *China's Sent-Down Generation: Public Administration and the Legacies of Mao's Rustication Program*. Washington, DC: Georgetown University Press.
River Elegy (Heshang). (1988) TV Documentary. Directed by Xia Jun, produced by China Central Television, China.
Schwarz, Barry. (1982) "The Social Context of Commemoration: A Study in Collective Memory." *Social Forces* 61: 374–402.
Songs of Ages (Suiyue ruge). (2008) TV Documentary. Directed by Wang Chunhua, produced by Beijing Jingshi Culture Media Co., Ltd., China.
Summer Palace (Yiheyuan). (2006). Directed by Lou Ye. produced by Dream Factory, Laurel Films, Fantasy Pictures and Sylvain Bursztejn's Rosem Films.
Tao Dongfeng. (2007) "Making fun of the canon in contemporary China: Literature and cynicism in a post-totalitarian society. *Cultural Politics* 3(2): 203–221.
Taking Photos (Ruci zhaoxiang). (1979) Crosstalk, Performed by Jiang Kun and Li Wenhua.
To Live (Huozhe). (1994) Directed by Zhang Yimou, Produced by Era International (Hong Kong) Ltd., China.
Wang, Meng. (1993) "Shun of Loftiness." (Duobi conggao) *Dushu* 1: 1–14.
Wasted Time (Cuotuo suiyue). (1982) Directed by Cai Xiaoqing, produced by China Central Television, China.
White, Hayden. (1985) *Tropics of Discourse: Essays in Cultural Criticism*. Baltimore: Johns Hopkins University Press.
Yan, Geling. (2006) *A Women's Epic* (Yige nuren de shishi). Hunan: Hunan Literature and Art Press.
Yan, Geling. (2011) *Criminal Lu Yanshi* (Lufan Yanshi). Beijing: Writers Publishing House.
Yang, Jiang. (2010) *A Cadre School Life: Six Chapters* (Ganxiaoliuji). Beijing: Life Bookstore.
Yang, Jisheng and Mosher, Stacy (trans). (2012) *Tombstone: The Untold Story of Mao's Great Famine*. London: Allen Lane.

Yang, Xianhui. (2003) *Chronicles of Jiabiangou* (Jiabiangou jishi). Guangdong: Flower City Publishing House.

Ye, Xin. (1982) *Wasted Time* (Cuotuosuiyue). Tianjin: Baihua Literature & Art Publishing House.

Yearning (Kewang). (1990) Directed by Lu Xiaowei, produced by Beijing TV Art Centre, China.

Zelizer, Barbie. (1995) "Reading the Past Against the Grain: The Shape of Memory Studies." *Critical Studies in Mass Communication* 12(2): 215–239.

Zhang, Rong and Halliday, Jon. (2005) *Mao, the Unknown Story*. UK: Random House.

Zhang, Tongdao. (2009) "Chinese Television Audience Research," in Ying Zhu and Chris Berry (eds) *TV China*. Bloomington: Indiana University Press: 168–179.

Zhang, Yihe. (2004) *The Past Is Not Like Smoke* (Wangshi bingbu ruyan). Beijing: People's Literature Press.

Zhang, Yinde. (2010) "Gao Xingjian: Fiction and Forbidden Memory." *China Perspectives* 2: 25–33.

Zhao, Ziyang. (2009) *The Secret Journal of Zhao Ziyang* (Gaige lichen). Hong Kong: The New Century Press.

Zhu, Ying. (2008) *Television in Post-Reform China: Serial Dramas, Confucian Leadership and the Global Television Market*. London and New York: Routledge.

4 *The Search for Modern China* and *The Pillar Standing in Midstream*

Two examples of the nationalist genre of Chinese commercial media

Introduction

Apart from employing traditional media platforms, the commercial online media portals are also employed as one of the most efficient, wide-reaching and prevailing media channels used by the Chinese Communist Party (CCP) propaganda institutions to disseminate its official ideology. This chapter will examine two web documentary programs which were released by Sohu Web (*souhuwang*), a large and popular online media portal in China. These two online documentaries are titled *The Search for Modern China: Looking Back at Historical Moments* (*zhuixun xiandai zhaongguo: huiwang lishi shuijian* 2009) and *The Pillar Standing in Midstream: The Great Backstage Battlefield of the War of Resistance against Japan* (*dizhuzhongliu: weida de dihoukangzhan* 2015). An in-depth textual analysis of these two online documentaries shows how the commercial online media websites collaborate with the official propaganda rhetoric in promoting nationalist sentiment and in creating an image or a re-imagination of the CCP as being the decisive factor in terms of leading the Chinese people to victory in the war against Japan, and also in its efforts in prevailing against the West's strategy in trying to weaken China through isolation and trade embargoes. In other words, this chapter discusses how commercial media takes into consideration the influence of the state nationalism discourse in their narration of historical events and their program designing in order to find a living space in a market economy which is partly dominated by ideological force. This correlation of official ideology and commercial media programs, combined with the distinctive features of modern media (such as timeliness, commercialization, popularity and its ability to be incisive), enables patriotic and nationalist emotions to be more appealing, more natural and more entertaining. This chapter will also deliberate on the pragmatic consequences of the predominant nationalist mood in sustaining the legitimacy of the CCP government, and it confirms that compromises have been made by the commercial media in response to the official ideological control where an objective perspective of history has been abandoned.

In the history of socialist China, the media – be it in traditional forms such as print, broadcasting and television, or be it in modern patterns including film, internet and social networking systems – has never been a wholly free domain for conveying news, conducting public debates and discussing social topics and concerns. The media, as a mass public communication tool and arena, has been constantly employed and hijacked by the CCP to disseminate its ideology and, as propaganda, to manufacture consensus across the entire society.

> Consent is something that is won; ruling groups in a society actively seek to have their worldview accepted by all members of society as the universal way of thinking. Institutions such as schools, religion, and the media help the powerful exercise this cultural leadership because they are the sites where we produce and reproduce ways of thinking about society.
> (Croteau, William and Stefania 2012: 160)

In China, the CCP government has a tradition of manipulating the media to provide "cultural leadership." The practice of utilizing media to achieve socio-cultural and, moreover, political accord can be traced back to the days of Mao when the CCP realized that harnessing the media is a prerequisite for starting a revolution and for maintaining a government (Chan 2003: 159). Throughout the history of socialist China, the media has been considered a crucial element of the ideological apparatus in China's political system. It is indispensable for legitimating the Party-state, indoctrinating the public and coordinating campaigns (Chan 2003).

Since the founding of the People's Republic of China (PRC), the media has been owned and/or controlled by the central government, and it is tightly monitored by the CCP government at all levels. However, since the Opening Up reform period of the 1980s, China's media industry has been going slowly through a marketization and decentralization process which has given birth to non-state and commercial media players in the contemporary Chinese media landscape. "Media marketization is a relatively slow process, taking twists and turns that reflect the CCP's disjunctive approach to development – maintaining ideological control on the one hand and embracing marketization on the other" (Chan 1993, 2003: 160). This twin function of the media in the post-socialist period follows former Party secretary-general Jiang Zemin's idea that, within a market economy, the media needs to shoulder the responsibility of propagating, while at the same time it also needs to survive (Zhang 2002: 7). This transformation of duty and role has led to a situation where the Chinese media is no longer regarded as "equivalent to communist propaganda," and there is now a more balanced view of it as a combination of the "creative industries" and "architect state model" (Donald and Keane 2001; Keane 2006). The development of media and communication tools has empowered non-state competitors to evolve creatively with the state, where a "contesting but also conjunctive" relationship between the state and non-state media players has formed (Yu 2009).

While the emergence of non-state commercial media challenges the official-state monopoly over the Chinese media industry, the overall grip of the Party over media content has never waned. In particular, in the post-1989 era, the CCP set out to reaffirm media control and renovate its ruling technologies (Zhao 2008: 22). The Party has made it clear that media reform does not contradict the media's role as a mouthpiece of the Party (Zhao 2008: 24; Hong, Lu and Zou 2009: 47). At a national conference on propaganda and ideology in 1994, the former Party secretary-general Jiang Zemin called on the media to act as a tool to control public opinion. He also emphasized that speaking for the Party should continuously be the paramount purpose of all media institutions (Cheng 2001: 28). The Chinese media has been converted from a "brainwashing state apparatus" to a "Party publicity Inc.," and it has become an entity which is "a capitalist body wearing a socialist face" (Lee 2003: 18). Despite many changes that have occurred in China's media landscape, it is still incapable of reflecting social attitude and instead reflects the political requirements of the Party (Hong et al. 2009: 52–53).

Under the overall guidance of the Party, the newly formed relationship between state and non-state media players is conjoined and collaborative. Within the parameter of the state-market complex, the Chinese party-state apparatus maintains its control over the media in terms of implementing political means directly or by monitoring via the rule of the market (Ma 2000; cited in Hu 2001: 193). As an emerging but important player in the media, the "internet is a means of advancing China's stake in the new information economy while utilizing the architecture of the Net as a means to reassert central surveillance and administration" (Hu 2001: 194) through a group of government institutions, including the State Council Information Office (SCIO), which is moulded after the press offices of Western governments and directs government communication with the outside world; the Ministry of Information Industry (MII), which both orders the technological and industrial arrangements of China's internet system and is responsible for authorising internet service and content providers; together with the Internet Information Management Bureau, which is charged with the liability of censoring internet news and Bulletin Board Services (BBS) and directing Party-state propaganda on the internet (Zhao 2008: 23).

Sina Web (*xinlangwang*) is one of the most popular commercial online news portals in China; however, its domestic political news is sourced from *The People's Daily* (*renminribao*) or *Xinhua News Agency* (*xinhuashe*), two of the main official news outlets on the Chinese mainland. Although Sina Web achieved instant success through its news content component, it has been cautious of being converted into an objective of regulation or periodic crackdowns (Hu 2001: 195). On 7 November 2000, new rules were enacted by the State Council which forced commercial websites to distribute only news that had been checked by traditional media. In September 2005, SCIO and MII issued the "Regulations on the Management of Internet News and Information Services," which strengthened and polished this regime of government clout over internet news and informational and BBS content (Zhao 2008: 28). Sina's chief manager, Jiang Fengnian, said in an interview that they were engaged in entertainment and sports and were attempting to avoid sensitive topics and that they hope the government understands their intentions and efforts (Fang, Li and Wang 2000). According to Hu (2002: 198), China's young dot-com millionaires do not want to turn themselves into "political revolutionaries," and they want only to retain their harmonious relationship with the government. In the current Chinese cultural market, only those who are dexterous both in business and in politics will survive. The internet may not be able to be as rebellious or play the role of a saviour as the mass media did in China in the past (Hu 2001: 199).

In addition to issuing rules to oversee commercial online media performance, the state regulators also engage with the non-state online media players in terms of advising them about official ideology and policy. In 2001, the Association of Chinese Journalists, a government-sponsored professional organization, established the China Online Media Forum. This forum is guided and directed by the State Council's News Office, which is China's primary information monitoring organ. China's major state-owned and privately owned online news websites participated in the convention and actively engaged in consultations with policy makers. This quasi-governmental forum seized the role of explaining Party policy, monitoring and enforcing internal discipline, and synchronizing interactions among its members (Wu 2007: 138). Consequently, the forum serves as a conjunction and conduit between the dominant ideological discourse and the commercial online media, through which the commercial online media is regulated and disciplined, which keeps them in line with the Party-state ideology and instructs them how to read and understand the official discourse. In summary, the world's largest online community "is governed, and in the foreseeable future will still be governed, by the CCP government, which regards, the cyber sphere as another component of its gigantic propaganda machine" (Wu 2007: 135).

Patriotism and nationalism as propaganda in the new post-socialist era

Patriotism and nationalism are two constant themes in the propaganda rhetoric of the CCP government, and these two discourses are inseparable, interdependent and interactive in the political and cultural trajectory of contemporary China. During the War of Resistance with Japan, patriotism and nationalism become dual political causes of the CCP in their endeavours to win support from the Chinese people and to consolidate its legitimacy and popularity as it competed with the Nationalist Party. After winning the War of Resistance against Japan, winning the civil war with the Nationalists, and then establishing the CCP government enlisted patriotism as a dominate political propaganda agenda. It has been the most powerful means available for the CCP to unite the Chinese people and to strengthen its authority and legality. After the Opening Up reforms and the subsequent 1989 Tiananmen demonstration, the CCP saw the need to launch another round of patriotic education in order to create an atmosphere in which the Chinese people could be influenced by patriotic rhetoric and the beliefs and spirit of nationalism (Beijing Review 1994: 4). This new round of patriotic propaganda was achieved by a multitude of means, which included major state projects such as the "hundred books program," the "hundred films program" and the establishment of "bases for patriotic education" in terms of mobilizing schools, families and society. In this strategy they included newspapers, radio, TV, cinemas, theatres, publications, national days, anniversaries and festivals (He and Guo 2000: 27).

However, by the 1990s, the situation had altered moderately as patriotic emotion was no longer the single preference of the Party and its mouthpieces, and nationalism progressively became the core for an agreement beyond the boundaries of official culture (Barme 1999: 256). Nationalism in China was reborn as a practical political apparatus (Guo 2004: 24), a new ideology and an ideological basis used to replace Marxism and Maoism, which were fading from the contemporary China political landscape (Zheng 1999: 2). A nationalism discourse was revived by the CCP, most notably after the 1989 Tiananmen demonstration, to educate and unite the Chinese people and to stabilize its rule and legitimacy (Zhao 2004: 8). Furthermore, nationalism was, and still is, considered to be a useful way in which to solve the contemporary Chinese problems which centre on the decline of central power, the weakening of national identity, and actual or perceived external threats (Zheng 1999: 17). The CCP's focus on nationalism is also a distraction from any attention given to internal problems and is a means for gaining influence in the diplomatic world (Zhao 2005: 76). Thus, nationalism has been the most serviceable contrivance of state ideology (Xu 2001; Cui 2003: 74), and it is used successfully to assist with domestic socio-political stability and in the diplomatic field to present a picture of national solidarity.

The Search for Modern China: *Looking Back at Historical Moments*

The Search for Modern China was a special web video documentary program made for the celebrations of the sixtieth anniversary of PRC by Sohu Web in 2009, and it commemorates the anniversary by revisiting file coverage of significant historical moments. Sohu Web was established in February 1998 by Zhang Chaoyang, a MIT doctoral student who used the money he raised from the United States to launch a website with an odd Chinese name: *Souhu*, literally meaning "the searching fox" (www.sohu.com) (Wu 2007: 36). Sohu grew very quickly and was extremely successful, and, in 2000, Sohu.com was effectively listed on the Wall Street Nasdaq stock market. Three years after, in 2003, Sohu.com became one of the Nasdaq's best-performing stocks (Wu 2007: 59). As one of the most successful and influential commercial websites in contemporary China, Sohu Web's contribution to the huge memorial celebration was the presentation of a gift to the nation.[1] *The Search for Modern China* comprises of a series of web-based audiovisual documentaries recording the most striking and sensational moments in the history of modern China. The thematic sections of the series include *Fragments of My Memory, Looking Back at Historical Moments, They Changed China, In Search of Modern Wealth,* and *In Search of Modern Character*. These fragments of *The Search for Modern China* highlight key people and issues, crucial historical moments, and opportunities of change in the development of modern China. The focal point of this discussion is one section of the entire series – *Looking Back at Historical Moments* – which is representative of the theme and ethos of the whole sequence of the program.

The sixtieth anniversary of the PRC was routinely used by the CCP for patriotic and nationalist education, to lift the morale of Chinese people, to strengthen their pride in their nation, and to confirm the people's confidence and loyalty to the Party. In order to achieve these goals, the CCP organized an official address from the former Party secretary-general Hu Jintao, a military parade, and a celebratory party at Tiananmen Square to commemorate the day. Most of the official and commercial media conducted live relays of the celebration. In addition to reporting the official celebrations, and in order to fulfil its responsibility in terms of faithfully following the Party line, Sohu Web produces *The Search for Modern China* documentary series, through which it places its lens behind the veil of history to discover those haunting and exhilarating moments that happened in the course of socialist and post-socialist China. These documentaries can be considered a historical memoir of modern China under the rule of the CCP. The dominant tone of the program, plus its thematic design and production devices, reveals the conjunctive bond between the discourse of official ideology and the discourse of commercial media, and the surviving rudiments of commercial media in an ideologically controlled cultural and entertainment landscape.

Looking Back at Historical Moments is a collection of filmed annals which trace historical moments from 1919 to 2008. The chronicle spanning the 1919–1948 period, Red Spreads, acts as the overture of the annals, which foreground and amalgamate the contribution made by the CCP to the founding of the New China and signify the political allegiance of Sohu Web to the official ideology of the Party. Except for the simple handling of the prologue years, every episode of *Looking Back at Historical Moments* deals with a specific year in chronological order from 1949. Focusing on one of the most momentous or controversial issues of the particular year, each segment lasts for six to seven minutes, unfolding historical instants with the help of photographic and video files, comments of a mixture of actual recordings and overlaid, and background music. The topics range from Land Reformation, the Three-anti (*sanfanyundong*) and Five-anti Campaigns (*wufangyundong*),[2] the Great Leap Forward (*dayuejin*),[3] and the Cultural Revolution, to the Misty Poems (*menglongshi*),[4] the Tangshan Earthquake, the Opening Up policy, Chinese soccer, the internet, and the Beijing Olympic Games, all of which reflect the challenges overcome by the people and the progression of modern China. During these retrospections, there is applause and eulogy for great achievements; there are comments on history and particular people; there are also extolments of the impregnable nationalist spirit and longing for a more prosperous future. However, it is not difficult to discern that behind the annals is a fermenting patriotic and nationalist sentiment, which strikes a chord with the Chinese people at a time when China is emerging in the international arena as a world superpower.

While responding to the call of the official propaganda discourse, the online media is also highly commercialized, producing a fashionable web documentary commodity that is rich in selling points and caters to the needs and sentimentality of the netizens. Commercial online media provides a functional conduit where state and popular interests merge, and it is both a political asset and a source of commercial profit for itself. Dal Lago, commenting on contemporary Chinese art, notes "the transition of propagandistic models from ideological dissemination to mass consumption creates an unexpected correspondence between socialist and consumerist systems of mass communication" (Dal Lago 1999: 47; cited in Cui 2003: 73). Although Dal Lago may well have been referring to contemporary Chinese art generally, his comments are also true of commercial online media and the Sohu Web documentary. The background layout of the documentary page screen is rich in nostalgic flavour, from the sepia photos of the Great Wall to the Beijing Railway Station embedded in antique style frames. There is a sense of agelessness that permeates through the screen and reaches out to the viewer as the nostalgic mood is heightened. Nostalgia is a trendy fashion in the contemporary Chinese cultural market: Confucius, the classics of traditional Chinese philosophy and culture, history-themed TV dramas, and renovated historical sites are becoming a most popular commodity in the contemporary cultural marketplace of China.

In addition to the use of nostalgia, background music is another commercial feature employed by online documentary production. In order to make the program more entertaining, *Looking Back at Historical Moments* employs a range of Chinese and foreign classical music, pop music, jazz, rock and roll, rap, and film soundtracks – for example, "Ballade" from *Braveheart*; "That's Why I Like It"; "I Believe"; "Scarborough Fair"; "For My Fallen Angel"; "May It Be"; Beethoven's symphonies; Chinese pop music including "I Am a Little Bird," "A Thousand Asking," "Life Like the Summer Flower" and "Chess"; and Japanese pop music including "Pure Love" and "Summer." This eclectic selection of music adds a frivolous and romantic flavour to the narratives of history, which tend to make the patriotic and nationalist coaching seem more natural and less calculated and intrusive. The clever use of such visual and audio effects points to the accuracy of commercial online media's estimation of the taste and expectations of contemporary Chinese audiences. By its employment of commercial online media, the official propaganda is converted into recreational and leisure material and is more amenable to public consumption.

Throughout the instalments of *Looking Back at Historical Moments*, there is a conspicuous and recurring theme – sport. Sporting games and events serve as an ideal means to mix and camouflage patriotic and nationalist sentiment with entertainment. In so doing, the documentary reviewed a number of the most stirring moments in Chinese sporting history and embedded them with patriotic and nationalist passion. In the opinion of Dayan and Katz (1992: viii; cited in Lee 2003: 5), sports, as a media event, could be taken as ceremonial politics, which illustrates the craving for togetherness and fusion, which will consequently enhance the status of the authorities and integrate social groups. The 1961 instalment of *Looking Back at Historical Moments* is named *Win Honour: To Conquer the Enemy with Twelve Smashes of the Ball*. This instalment shows the glorious moments when Chinese table tennis athletes defeated their foreign rivals, winning great honour for China. At the twenty-sixth session of the World Table Tennis

Games, which was held in Beijing in 1961, the Chinese athletes beat their foreign competitors at a critical moment and lifted the national morale. A Chinese voiceover enhances the patriotic fervour:

> Beijing undertook this session of the World Table Tennis Games because China needed to fight a great battle in front of the world. Beijing witnessed the confidence and determination of China in a carnival atmosphere. Xu Yunsheng's twelve hits turned confidence and determination into action and displayed them to the whole world. After dividing from Russia, China fell into an unprecedented diplomatic predicament. Enmity from the West was as strong as before, and China was enduring the most difficult times since the founding of the PRC. However, China is still able to show its strength through sporting competitions and give loneliness a heavy hit.[5]

Sport conveys a definitive and unique meaning in the political and diplomatic arena for the Chinese government and for the Chinese people alike. "The overdetermination lies in the linking of the achievement of individual Chinese athletes with that of the nation, and a collective desire to read the sports events as both metaphors and metonyms of China's greatness in an international context" (Sun 2001: 123). These voiceover comments – above, and throughout the instalments – bear a strong resemblance to Maoist propaganda and have a tone of Maoist passion, thus merging sporting enthusiasm with revolutionary zealousness. This intentional combination precisely blurs the boundary between political preaching and the entertainment value engendered by the competitive spirit of sporting events. Moreover, the comments reveal that communist China was blockaded by the West and secluded by Russia during its infancy, and it was the CCP that had arduously and resolutely led the Chinese nation and its people to break out and survive the blockade, which prioritises the contribution made by the CCP in its defence of the country in both the economic and the political domains. The voiceover continues:

> For the first time the Chinese feel national pride and esteem, and the political meaning of national glory is confirmed with the hits into the ideology of Chinese people. After twelve smashes, the Chinese, during the hardest of times, find a new medium and force to convey and implement their patriotic emotion.

Here, the web documentary highlights the explicit connection between sports glory and national pride, and it shows the political implications of this correlation. The national honour brought about by sports competition is juxtaposed with the emergence of China as a political power on the international stage. Although different from the military invasion by Japan, the economic and political block and animosity from the West and Russia during the nascent years of socialist China is resurrected by the documentary. The memories of those national challenges serve a new situation; they stimulate and awaken the patriotic and nationalist feelings of the viewers. Thus, this instalment could be read as slightly coded political coaching that serves the ideological goal of the CCP.

The 1985 instalment – *Soccer: A Game and a Dream* – is given similar interpretation by Sohu Web as the voiceover starts:

> No matter which country people come from, they treat soccer games as battles. This group of young Chinese men led by Zeng Xuelin are regarded as brave soldiers. When they walk onto the ground, they represent China, and when they defeat their rivals, it's a success for the whole nation.

There is no difference between Chinese soccer fans and their counterparts elsewhere in the world, because for them the game of soccer is not only a sporting competition but also a symbol of national pride. However, in terms of propaganda usefulness, talking about soccer has greater mass appeal than talking about politics or ideology; therefore, soccer serves as a good medium in terms of triggering patriotic fervour. The 1985 instalment further illustrates how media reporting influences people's feelings. When a soccer riot broke out in Beijing on 19 May 1985, after the visiting Hong Kong team crushed the host side, the voiceover comments:

> The shameful loss, the huge psychological dissatisfaction, and the heavily wounded national emotion, drive the young soccer fans insane. They began to destroy anything they could find: cars, telephone booths and the glass panes of store fronts . . . a group of young fans grabbed a Reuter's reporter and shouted: "Tell me which team is better – The Chinese team or the Hong Kongese team? I will kill you if you pick the wrong one."

Soccer has long been given different symbolic meanings by people of different countries. For China in particular, soccer has been symbolically described as a castrated man, given that the Chinese national soccer team almost never performs to the expectations of the people and never wins any important games in the international arena; therefore, even the Chinese national morale, esteem and pride have also been castrated. This castrated-man image of China is identifiable with the sick man of East Asia complex, which was coined when the young modern China endured continuing military and economic bullying from the other nations. The international wire service news reports compared the above-mentioned soccer riots with the anti-foreign Boxer rebels active in Beijing at the turn of the century (cited in Barme 1999: 236). Barme (1999) has also observed that this sort of revengeful and irrational behaviour by the young soccer fans resembles the Wang Qiming style of Chinese masculinity in *Beijingers in New York*,[6] and the "screw you foreigners" (Barme 1995) impulse embodies the retrieved and restored national pride and spirit of the Chinese people. In the 1985 episode of the documentary, by orchestrating the juxtaposition between soccer and the wounded national esteem and glory, the show constructs and evokes an instant and intense nationalist sentimentality among the online viewers, especially with young audiences. According to Wu (2007: 117), nationalism is a super ideology that exceeds other forms of philosophical notions, political principles and religious beliefs. Once it comes into being, it survives as its own reason and obeys only its own logic. Wu's argument helps explain the irrational and uncontrollable emotion of the soccer fans when a nationalist sentiment is sparked. Promoting populist nationalism is seen as a harmless and beneficial enterprise for the market-driven media, and this understanding goes a long way in explaining why dramatized and bellicose nationalist discourses are produced (Lee 2003: 4) and why the conformist attitude adopted by commercial online media portals towards the official propaganda apparatus is justification for Sohu Web's motive in picking this particular event to underline the emotional nationalist discourse.

In the 1986 instalment (*Rafting – The Yangzi River Flows East*), when a foreigner is granted the right to first raft the Yangzi River, sacred and solemn nationalistic emotions are promoted:

> Why was the Chinese mother river first rafted by foreigners? Are we Chinese not brave enough to conquer the Yangzi River? The Chinese people were all irritated. Back then, the navigators all had families and their most valuable youth had already withered away. However, their youthful hearts are still alive; they did not want to mourn for the past, especially in these Opening Up days. They felt suppressed after being enclosed for so long. When the world shows itself to them, with an unprecedented impact, they are engulfed by an impulse to catch up, to be the best, to win glory for the country and to resurrect the Chinese nation.

Here, an overwhelming feeling of a collective victimhood and a national crisis emerge out of a competition for the right to be the first to raft the Yangzi River. By portraying the navigators as martyr-like figures, the narrative of this instalment creates a perilous milieu as if China is surrounded by some latent nemeses. Guo (2004: 34) has pointed out that "the image of China-as-victim serves a domestic political purpose . . . [and] the inculcation of a sense of victimhood is designed to enhance an awareness that past humiliations can be repeated if China remains technologically backward and becomes politically divided." It is easy to detect here a hidden political message which confirms the CCP's authority and legitimacy in keeping the Chinese nation united and the Chinese society stable and prosperous. In this instalment, the Opening Up reforms are heightened and serve as a watershed moment in the history of socialist China, which again endorses the "wise" and "bold" decisions of the Party and ratifies the unmatched opportunity and promising prospect it brings about for the Chinese people. As the commentary goes:

> On September 21, 1986, when Yao Maoshu and his team conquered the Tiger Leaping Gorge [*hutiaoxia*], people standing on both sides of the river sang the national anthem spontaneously. . . . People were lost in revelry, and this revelry beckoned for more youths to embark on a journey in search of the national honour. In addition, their American rivals, who only consider rafting to be an ultimate sports activity, could not understand this celebration.

Singing of the national anthem connects an audience with national pride. Compared to the actual audiences standing on the riverbank, the cyber audiences of the online documentary are much larger and probably younger as well. Mass participation is considered an important feature of China's cyber nationalism and contributes greatly in promoting the patriotic and nationalist sentiment among the Chinese mass of netizens. While the population of Chinese netizens keeps climbing, the coaching dispersed through the profitmaking online media will reach larger audiences. The open criticism of the American athletes' understanding of river rafting indirectly indicates that sports activity has some political meaning in China. As shown in the Sohu Web documentary, a normal sports game can be highly politicized and idealised in China. This situation highlights the role played by commercial online media in promoting official propaganda and reveals the intimacy between the ruling ideology and the lucrative media institution.

The 1997 instalment is titled *Flying Over: Annotation to the Year of Return*. "Flying over" refers to the Hong Kongese celebrity Blackie Ko's[7] (Ke Shouliang) feat of driving over the Tiger's Mouth of the Yellow River, which symbolizes the return of sovereignty of Hong Kong to the PRC in 1997. Ko's venture is similar to the Yangzi River rafting endeavour of Yao Maoshu and his peers, which shouldered the burden of boosting national morale and pride. Conducted by a Hong Kongese star, as a representative of the whole population of Hong Kong, this exertion metaphorically portrays the Hong Kong people's elation of returning to Chinese sovereignty, which concludes with the celebrity's symbolic venture. Sohu Web comments:

> In the heart of those people who have received a hundred of years of education about Hong Kong as a colony, it is probable that only the courageous flying over the roaring Yellow River is capable of abating humiliation. As the attention of the world is drawn to this event, a flying over becomes a sign of reunification and resurgence of a nation.

In this instalment, the end of the colonized history of Hong Kong is used as a symbol which points to the termination of China's bad times and its humiliating past. The unification of the Chinese nation is a principal strategy employed by the CCP to form its united front in the new period, which is of critical importance in settling its legitimacy. Sohu Web, as a commercial online portal, shows that it is very good at understanding the reasoning behind the official discourse in terms of choosing and underscoring this risk-taking event. Its move to retell and emphasize Chinese unification by way of an adventurous sports event conducted by a Hong Kongese icon reveals how it creatively engages with dominant ideology.

The 2001 instalment, *Bid for the Olympic Games: Current Roaring in the Carnival*, raises the nationalist sentiment and emotion embedded in *Looking Back at Historical Moments* to its zenith. The voiceover continues:

> When the news that China had won the Olympic bid arrived in Beijing ... what flashed through the minds of the people was ... that hosting the

Olympic Games in China is the most powerful reply to those who bombed our embassy and crashed our planes.

In the above voiceover, the 1999 Chinese embassy incident is mentioned, and the memories and humiliation of isolation and enmity from the West are redeemed as motivation to serve the cause of reviving the great Chinese nation, which is embodied by China's winning of the staging of the Olympic Games. Honours obtained by the Chinese athletes during the previous sessions of Olympic Games had created many moments of glory and triumph, which could be easily made into political spectacles for audiences at home and abroad. This, in turn, would accumulate political capital for the Chinese government for its various strategic needs, including promoting patriotism and increasing its political legitimacy (Sun 2001: 126). The CCP is determined to use the resurrection of the Chinese nation for political purposes. They hope that it will overcome domestic malaises, retrieve its fading influence and validity, and enable it to maintain a stable and harmonious society. It may be that their intention in winning the right to stage the games was to make all other problems fade into the background, and that all other social problems and national missions including building democracy, combating social injustice and promoting individual rights would be cast aside by a rising nationalism.

The Sohu Web commentary continues and points China in only one direction:

We must unite together, and put all our efforts into building a more powerful and confident nation. We should stop entangling ourselves with the trivial concerns of life and the gain and loss of individuals. We should make sacrifices and contribute in order to maintain long-term stability and continuous prosperity of our nation. When the year 2008 comes, we will be able to show the world the most excellent achievements and the greatest power of our nation.

Here, the status of the individual is sublimed by the nation, and individuals should be prepared to sacrifice themselves for the nation. On a platform provided by China's commercial online media, the traditional propaganda discourse of Chinese state nationalism, illustrated by classic slogans, finally re-emerges at an imperative historical moment. Observably, it is hard to find a more suitable occasion to articulate and accentuate the patriotic and nationalist sentiment than when the Chinese Olympic dream came true. The CCP thus accurately grasps this unique historical instant to spread its ideology in collaboration with the profit-seeking media players, which witnesses the changeover of propagandistic patterns from political distribution to mass consumption via the internet.

The Pillar Standing in Midstream: *The Great Backstage Battlefield of the War of Resistance against Japan*

The Pillar Standing in Midstream is a ten-episode TV documentary co-produced by the Beijing Municipal Publicity Department and Beijing TV Station's (BTV). It was released via BTV's signature program *Archives* (*Dangan*)

Two examples of the nationalist genre 95

commemorating the seventieth anniversary of the Global War against Fascism in general and the Chinese People's War of Resistance against Japanese Aggression. In order to make this program available to a wider audience, BTV collaborated with Sohu Web to release the documentary via the military channel of the portal.[8] By the middle of the 2000s, China had "leapfrogged" in a decade from "a pre-telephone" state to the second-largest online nation in the world, with a 100 million online population (Wu 2007: 11); and by July 2010, China had the world's largest web population – 420 million (Berg 2011: 149). However, the world's largest online population is under the rule of the CCP and will be for the predictable future (Wu 2007: 11). In order to more effectively spread the mainstream ideology, the official propaganda machine enlists the commercial media platform due to its huge potential audience, and the young people, who comprise the majority of China's online population (Berg 2011: 149), are particularly targeted by the CCP for patriotic and nationalist education.

BTV's show *Archives* is a national high-end documentary brand which has been granted many top professional awards in the field. *The Pillar Standing in Midstream* was first aired via BTV in 2014, and it is the first documentary which concerns itself with the non-conventional warfare of the Chinese People's War of Resistance against Japan. In so doing, the documentary shifts the focus from portraying the frontline battlefield (*zhengmianzhanchang*) – which in the early stages of the war was largely managed by the Nationalist Party – to depicting the backstage battlefield (*dihouzhanchang*) and construction of the anti-Japanese bases (*kangrigenjudi*) led by the CCP during the fourteen years (1931–1945) national war. The program sifts through and focusses on the CCP's contribution to the war, including the establishment of an anti-Japanese national united front of the Nationalist Party and the CCP against Japanese aggression. It shows the creative military thoughts and strategies of the CCP such as guerrilla warfare, establishment of the anti-Japanese bases, and garnering support of the Chinese people, especially rural peasants. *The Pillar Standing in Midstream* utilizes many valuable video files, archives and historical photos as materials and evidence, and it includes on-site visits to all of the nineteen anti-Japanese bases across the country, plus the more than thirty historical sites of the War of Resistance against Japan. Moreover, the show's producers collected many historical files from the Central Committee of the Communist Party History Research Office (*zhongyangdangshi yanjiushi*), the Central Committee of the Communist Party Archives Bureau (*zhongyang danganguan*), local governments and memorial halls, and they consulted extensively with the experts from these institutions, in order to make every picture and every comment reliable and convincing.

In order to enable this elaborate documentary to reach a broader audience, BTV teamed up with Sohu Web. According to the director of the military channel of Sohu Web, their cooperation with the BTV was not merely a simple composition in contents but making use of the military channel of the Sohu Web as a venue and taking advantage of the new techniques of the internet to make the brilliant and meaningful content of *The Pillar Standing in Midstream* available and enticing to more netizens. The intent was that the netizens would become more familiar with

96 *Two examples of the nationalist genre*

the War of Resistance against Japan and with the major role played by the CCP in the outcome of the war. It was presumed that the show would help disseminate a patriotic ethos, aid in the remembering of history, and enable viewers to cherish the memory of the martyrs. Sohu Web's deputy editor-in-chief and director of the news centre, Wang Xing, stated that, in order to achieve these goals, Sohu Web would use the recommended video position (*shipintuijianwei*) on its home page and relevant channel homepages to promote the documentary; it would advertise the images, texts and short videos of the program on its site's special topics section (*wangzhanzhuanti*); and it would employ new internet techniques and devices to expand the impact of the documentary. The Beijing Internet Information Office praised the cooperation between BTV and Sohu Web as innovative and inspirational in terms of utilizing the distinctive features of modern media (such as timeliness, commercialization, popularity) to foster the substances and to magnify the effect of traditional media means (Bitiwei qianshou souhu kaiqi jinian kangzhan jiemu hulianwangjia shidai 2015).

After broadcasting at prime time via the BTV channel and online via the Sohu Web, *Pillar Standing in Midstream* not only received acclaim from media and cultural scholars and critics but also won favourable comments from netizens, which were posted and transmitted via social media networks, such as microblogs and WeChat. One netizen comments: "I sincerely suggest that domestic TV producers make less farcical anti-Japanese TV series [*kangrishenju*] and more programs like *The Pillar Standing in Midstream*, as in my opinion, this is true patriotic education!" Another netizen expresses: "I am very much impressed by BTV's *Pillar Standing in Midstream*, and I recommend this documentary to every contemporary Chinese person!" Another netizen comments: "This program is truly moving! It is really necessary to let everyone know, remember and engrave in their mind the historical events and details as many of us are totally ignorant about them." Another netizen remarks: "Young people should no longer watch the brainwashing entertainment programs, let's watch *The Pillar Standing in Midstream*. Our happy life today is made possible by the martyr's blood and life, therefore China's peace does not permit any other nation's damage and could not be trampled by any organizations!" (Dizhuzhongliu – weida de dihoukangzhan bochu wangyou reyi lishi, 2014). These positive feedbacks to *The Pillar Standing in Midstream* from many passionate netizens is indicative of a surge in patriotic and nationalist sentimentality, and they suggests that the combined efforts of traditional and modern media practitioners in their spreading of official ideological discourse was a success.

The first two instalments of *The Pillar Standing in Midstream* are *The North-Eastern Resistance against Japan Memorial Hall: Witness of Japan's Invasion into China* and *Resisting Foreign Aggression: The Establishment of the Chinese United Front against Japanese Invasion*. They emphasize that it was the CCP which first raised the banner of the War of Resistance to Japan, and they underline the non-resistance policy upheld by the Nationalist Party government during the early stage of Japan's incursion into the north-eastern provinces of China (*dongbeisansheng*). According to these two episodes, and in contrast to the passive choice of the Nationalist Party, the CCP publicised an announcement to cultivate and stimulate national spirit where the CCP made it clear that it would support vigorously the Chinese people in their fight to end Japan's invasion. In this quest, the CCP sent Party members to coordinate and guide an army of volunteers from North-east China (*dongbeikangriyiyongjun*) to combat the Japanese troops, and they also formed a guerrilla force to fight alongside the volunteer army. The famous North-East Anti-Japanese United Army of the CCP and one of its generals, Yang Jingyu, which were known by every household in China due to previous patriotic films and propaganda programs, are routinely highlighted in the documentary, further enhancing the CCP's role in the national independence struggles of modern China.

The third episode, *The Famous General Comes to Jinchaji Which Makes the Japanese Troops Feel Terrified*, is about the building of the first anti-Japanese base in the Shanxi, Hebei and Chahar regions. These areas were considered by the Nationalist officers as lacking military importance and value; therefore, they were abandoned by the Nationalist army. After the Xi'an Incident (*Xianshibian* [1936]),[9] the Nationalist Party and the CCP formed the Chinese united front against Japanese aggression, according to which the Nationalist army was in charge of the frontline and main battlefield, and the CCP army was mainly tasked to attack the Japanese behind the enemy lines. This particular episode makes it clear that because that the Nationalist government failed to mobilize the people to take part in the War of Resistance against Japan, their army encountered continuing setbacks and failures. However, the CCP – in particular Mao Zedong's military wisdom and strategy of mobilizing the people to support their troops in combat with the Japanese invaders, which is best exemplified by the construction of anti-Japanese bases – proved extremely effective and far-sighted. In those anti-Japanese bases, the CCP organized the peasants to cultivate previously wild land to plant different crops to support the farmers themselves and the CCP soldiers, and the peasants also volunteered to transport the military supplies (such as rations and weapons) to the frontline of the battlefield. Moreover, the farmers also assisted the CCP army in their military operations against the Japanese troops, which included transferring secret messages and hiding CCP soldiers in their houses. The narrative of the documentary highlights Mao's clever military strategies which supported the frontline battlefield dominated by the Nationalist Party forces. The narrative did however fail to comment on Mao's other strategies, which were to use the war against Japan as a diversion for the Nationalist Party and also to build and nurture a strong army and a strong military position for the CCP.

Before the united Chinese front against Japan was established, the CCP troops were brought under considerable military pressure by the Nationalist Party military forces; however, during the War of Resistance against Japan, due to the CCP troops' absence at the frontline battlefield, and relying on the economic support provided by their anti-Japanese bases, the CCP troops expanded extensively, and the legitimacy of the CCP as an advanced political power was strengthened. This was a decisive factor in its final defeat of the Nationalist forces during the subsequent Chinese Civil War (1945–1949). According to the documentary, by the end of the war, the CCP had built up nineteen anti-Japanese bases. Taking the Jinchaji base as a typical example, we see that within the first three years of its establishment, the CCP increased troop numbers to two hundred thousand soldiers, and it created around eighty new counties in the Jinchaji base where none had existed before and populated them with over twelve million people. Across its anti-Japanese bases, the CCP further established democratic electoral systems and implemented the movement of reducing rent and interest, which greatly lessened the burden of the farmers on the bases. Accordingly, the CCP's main and local military forces increased to 1.32 million by the end of the war from 0.11 million at the beginning of the war. Moreover, the CCP gained huge popularity and support among the Chinese population.

In the sixth instalment of the documentary, other unique military strategies engaged by the CCP troops during the War of Resistance against Japan, including tunnel warfare (*didaozhan*) and mine warfare (*dileizhan*), are also emphasized.[10] As the host of the documentary explains, in their encounter with the Nationalist army on the battlefield, the Japanese forces occupied an absolute dominant position; however, behind enemy lines, the CCP had mobilized the Chinese people to wage a guerrilla war against the invaders, which mainly took the form of tunnel and mine warfare. The documentary acclaims the tunnel and mine warfare as a pioneering and effective undertaking which caused terror among the Japanese troops, which once again eulogised the military mind of Mao and his followers while implicitly satirising the incompetency of the Nationalist army and its commanders.

Besides underscoring the input of the CCP anti-Japanese bases in the victory of the national war, the documentary also elevates the battles fought by the CCP to a pivotal and superior position when compared to those military encounters where Nationalist forces engaged the enemy. The Battle of Pingxingguan (*pingxingguanzhanyi*) is one of the biggest and well-known military engagements fought and won by the CCP troops during the entire War of Resistance against Japan. As the host of the documentary comments:

> The Battle of Pingxingguan lifted greatly the morale of the CCP army, and many major media organizations were very active in covering the battle. This is the first victorious battle since we [the CCP] sent the army to North China. It broke the myth that the Japanese army is invincible, and it boosted the morale of the whole nation.

In the same instalment, the Battle of Taierzhuang (*taierzhuangzhanyi*), a major battle fought by the Nationalist force, was the only conventional frontline battle covered in the document. In this fierce battle, which lasted for almost twenty days, a desperate Nationalist army fought the enemy and inflicted more than ten thousand fatalities to soldiers of the Japanese elite corp. Compared to the Battle of Pingxingguan, where around one thousand Japanese combatants were killed, the Battle of Taierzhuang, together with other important battles fought by the Nationalist militias during the War of Resistance against Japan, was obviously given a downgraded and skewed historical revamp by the documentary. For example, the human and economic losses of the Nationalist Party forces (which were much larger than that of the CCP) are intentionally avoided in the documentary.

In addition to prioritizing the military achievements of the CCP and its army in China's war against Japan, *The Pillar Standing in Midstream* also attempts to strengthen the bonds between the Chinese people and the CCP. These efforts are reflected in the documentary's narrative as it highlights the support of the people to the Party during the war and vice versa the Party's faith in serving the people:

> Even during the dangerous and difficult times of saving the nation, the CCP still puts the interests of the people first, and the people have become the faith of the CCP members that is bone deep. . . . On the eve of the day when Zeng Huai is about to flee from his village, he spent a night together with the CCP members, which changed his mind to staying. Perhaps Zeng is moved by the sincere attitude adopted by the Party members when they engage with the people, or he is convinced of the CCP army's spirit when in combat with the Japanese invaders, or he just finds the long-gone feeling of safety during those chaotic and risky times. And for the CCP members, only when the people have this kind of sense of security, will they progress more firmly in the further road and in their resistance to the national enemy.

This commentary by the host of the documentary bears a remarkable resemblance to the rhetoric used in official propaganda, and it aims to recover the waning trust and legitimacy of the CCP among the Chinese people. Extensive corruption among its Party members and an inequitable social reality of modern-day China, as seen and exemplified by the widening gap between the nouveau riche and the poor, has been the main cause of doubts about the CCP's trust and legitimacy. By the end of the concluding instalment of *The Pillar Standing in Midstream*, the legitimacy of the CCP is again self-endorsed through the title of a revolutionary song – "Without the Communist Party There Would Be No New China" (*meiyou gongchandang jiumeiyou xinzhangguo*) – confirming the idea that it was the CCP who saved the Chinese nation at the most precarious and challenging time, and that it will be the CCP that can be trusted to do it again. The song is labelled by the documentary as "the song of truth of the Chinese revolutions." In its closing section, the documentary points out that, by 1941, the guerrilla war fought by the CCP had become the main shield of the resistance against Japan, and the CCP forces had become China's focal strength of the anti-Japanese forces. It was, they claimed, the CCP troops that had launched a big military counter-offensive against the Japanese army which led to the final victory of China's War of Resistance against Japan. In other words, the CCP troops, the CCP anti-Japanese bases, and the intelligent and far-sighted military strategies adopted by Mao and his commanders, including guerrilla war with its tunnel and mine tactics, led to the path of success. The CCP had led the Chinese people's War of Resistance against

100 *Two examples of the nationalist genre*

Japan and had moved from strategic defence to stalemate, and then to the counter-offensive stage, finally achieving outright victory. In the concluding remarks of the documentary, the great and many sacrifices made by the CCP towards victory in the national war are summarised:

> During the great War of Resistance against Japan, the CCP army fought bravely in more than 125 battles, killed more than 1.71 million Japanese and puppet army soldiers (among which there were 520,000 Japanese combatants) with the loss of 610,000 of its own troops. The CCP army seized more than 680,000 guns, more than 11,000 machine guns and 1.8 thousand artillery pieces. The CCP forces recovered more than 104 million square meters of national land and emancipated 0.1255 billion Chinese people.

However, corresponding data relating to Nationalist Party troops is wholly ignored and forgotten, and so a slanted and biased recount of history is presented.

Conclusion

Through the combined case studies of the Sohu Web documentary *The Search for Modern China: Looking Back at Historical Moments* and the BTV Sohu Web–collaborated documentary *The Pillar Standing in Midstream: The Great Backstage Battlefield of the War of Resistance against Japan*, a nexus between the Chinese state propaganda discourse and China's non-state commercial media practitioners is exposed by the concerted campaign of patriotism and nationalism with the Chinese people, in particular the online population. China's domestic private internet industry depends on fostering close ties with government in order to achieve its business goals. It is not in any position to confront Party authority so it must accept the monitoring and discipline applied by the state apparatus. Thus, Chinese mainland media, be it state or non-state institutions, has shown that it is incapable of becoming an independent and impartial organization, either in theory or in practice.

The CCP is determined to manipulate media in order to uphold and propagate its policies and beliefs, and the commercial media sector is unable to challenge the official rhetoric and ideology. Instead, commercial media adopt a compromising attitude towards the regulations and control wielded by the state propaganda machine. Although the political thawing of past decades has witnessed many brave attempts by the media to reveal the corrupt and damaging culture of officialdom, such as the efforts of investigative news reporting programs and the TV serials, the Party propaganda apparatus has not loosened its control, and the Party hardliners habitually punish any non-conformist media. Under this situation, the commercial media needs to carve out a space which will accommodate both the political polity and the market rules. They consider nationalism a safe contact point which guarantees both the sanction of the State and the participatory passion of the ordinary people. Consequently, state and popular nationalist discourse merge on the platform provided by commercial media productions.

Although nationalism has been resurrected by the Party-state as a replacement for the outdated Marxist ideology as a means to restore and maintain cohesiveness and harmony within a sometimes-fractious society, the CCP has also recognized that nationalism can be unstable and hard to control and that out-of-control nationalism can lead to domestic upheavals and external disharmony. Therefore, the CCP government adopts a very cautious stance in employing nationalist sentimentality within China and in solving the exterior disputes in the international arena. In other words, the discourse of nationalism is a double-edged sword which must be dealt with carefully and judiciously when it is enlisted to tackle domestic and diplomatic issues. In this sense, media institutions, be they state-owned or privately owned, play a critical and indispensable role in echoing the appeal of the official rhetoric in order to make use of the nationalism discourse to serve the political purpose of the Party.

Glossary

Bei Dao 北岛
Beijingren zai niuyue 北京人在纽约
Chahar 察哈尔
dajihuang 大饥荒
Dangan 档案
dayuejin 大跃进
didaozhan 地道战
dihouzhanchang 敌后战场
dileizhan 地雷战
dizhuzhongliu: weida de dihoukangzhan 砥柱中流：伟大的敌后抗战
dongbeikangriyiyongjun 东北抗日义勇军
dongbeisansheng 东北三省
Gu 顾城
Hebei 河北
Hu Jintao 胡锦涛
hutiaoxia 虎跳峡
jinchaji 晋察冀
kangrigenjudi 抗日根据地
kangrishenju 抗日神剧
Mang Ke 芒克
Mao Zedong 毛泽东
meiyou gongchandang jiumeiyou xinzhongguo 没有共产党就没有新中国
menglongshi 朦胧诗
pingxingguanzhanyi 平型关战役
Qiqihar 齐齐哈尔
renminribao 人民日报
sanfanyundong 三反运动
Shanxi 山西
shipintuijianwei 视频推荐位

Shu Ting 舒婷
souhuwang 搜狐网
taierzhuangzhanyi 台儿庄战役
Wang Qiming 王启明
wangzhanzhuanti 网站专题
wufanyundong 五反运动
Xianshibian 西安事变
xinhuashe 新华社
xinlangwang 新浪网
Yang Jingyu 杨靖宇
Zhang Chaoyang 张朝阳
Zhang Xueliang 张学良
zhengmianzhanchang 正面战场
zhongyang danganguan 中央档案馆
zhongyangdangshi yanjiushi 中央党史研究室
zhuixun bainian zhongguo: huiwang lishi shunjian 追寻百年中国: 回望历史瞬间

Notes

1 There are previous examples of Sohu Web's attempts in agitating patriotic and nationalist feelings among the Chinese netizens, which could be verified by its participation in China's cyber nationalist activities. China's cyber nationalism is a bottom-up nationalism which is in contrast to the top-down state nationalist discourse. China's cyber nationalism, according to Wu (2007: 2), is a nongovernment-sponsored nationalism that originated in China's online sphere from 1994 until the present. It was ignited and reinforced by a series of international events, which include the 1998 Indonesia anti-Chinese riots, the 1999 U.S. bombing of the Chinese embassy, the 2008 Beijing Olympics torch relay and the 2012 London Olympics. After the 1999 embassy incident, Sohu Web conducted an instant online survey, and the result of the survey indicated that 94 per cent of respondents did not accept the United States' explanation, and there followed an emotional patriotic and nationalist outpouring of sentiment among the Chinese netizens (Wu 2007: 48). In 2003, when the chemical weapons left over by Japanese troops at a construction site in Qiqihar (a north-eastern Chinese city) resulted in casualties to Chinese workers, Sohu Web co-sponsored an online petition urging the Japanese government to apologize to the dead and wounded workers and to make compensations (Wu 2007: 77). In so doing, Sohu Web gained both political trust and popularity among the online population. For more information, see Wu 2007.
2 The Three-anti Campaign (1951) and Five-anti Campaign (1952) (*san fan wu fan yundong*) were reform movements launched by Mao Zedong right after the founding of the PRC which aimed to get rid of corruption and "enemies of the state." The result turned into a series of campaigns that strengthened Mao's power base by attacking political opponents and capitalists. The three antis imposed were corruption, waste and bureaucracy. The five antis imposed were bribery, theft of state property, tax evasion, cheating on government contracts and stealing state economic information.
3 The Great Leap Forward Movement (1958), which is the main cause of the Great Famine (*dajihuang*, 1960–1963), resulted from collective and political radicalism, policy failure and government mismanagement (Kung and Lin 2003: 67; Zhao and Reimondos 2012). The subsequent Great Famine caused millions of fatalities, and the official propaganda machine shuns it and also puts a ban on any literary and media works about it. For more information, see Kung and Lin 2003; Zhao and Reimondos 2012.

4 Misty Poems denote a group of poetry works which have been officially denounced as "ambiguous" or "vague." The Misty Poem genre signifies the boycott of a group of young twentieth-century Chinese poets to the constraints on art during the Cultural Revolution. The magazine *Today* (*Jintian*) is the burgeoning place of this particular Chinese modern poetry style and Bei Dao, Mang Ke, Gu Cheng and Shuting are its main initiators and contributors.
5 All translations from English to Chinese of the original voiceover are the author's.
6 *Beijingers in New York* (Beijingren zai niuyue 1994) is the TV drama adaptation of America based Chinese writer Cao Guilin's bestselling novel of the same title, which was published in 1991. The storyline of the TV show tells the story about Wang Qiming and his wife, Guo Yan, as they realize their American dream that revolves around their migration to the United States and their struggles, achievements and misfortunes in a foreign land. The Wang Qiming character (starring Jiang Wen) created by the show is much loved by the Chinese audience as it represents a kind of Chinese, or oriental-style, wisdom, toughness, masculinity and pride.
7 Blackie Ko (1953–2003) was a Taiwan-based movie producer and director, singer, actor and stuntman. Ko was recognized as the superlative automotive stunt choreographer in Asia.
8 Sohu Web's military channel focuses on reporting military-related information and development in the history of China and the world. Along with the escalation of China's economic and military power, military reformation and progress of contemporary Chinese army and weapons are of enormous interest to netizens.
9 The Xi'an Incident of December 1936 (*Xianshibian*), which serves as an important turning point in Chinese modern history, took place in the city of Xi'an during the Chinese national war against Japanese invasion. On 12 December 1936, Chiang Kai-shek, the leader of the Nationalist Party, was detained by Marshal Zhang Xueliang, who was a former warlord of Manchuria and commander of the north-eastern army. Zhang was unwilling to implement the policy enacted by Chiang which was not to resist the Japanese invasion in the north-eastern provinces. The incident led to a compromise between the Nationalists and the Communists and led to a united front against the threat posed by Japan.
10 Tunnel and mine warfare are the unique invention of the CCP-led troops and anti-Japanese masses which constitute a certain part of the backstage battlefield combats. The old-generation Chinese viewers are familiar with this special warfare as patriotic films produced by the CCP movie studios at the early stage of socialist China, such as *The Tunnel Warfare* (Didaozhan 1965) and *The Mine Warfare* (Dileizhan 1962), have been viewed dozens of times by them. Also, in 2010, a recently made TV drama serial *The Tunnel Warfare* (*Didaozhan*) revamped the popularity of this unique warfare among the contemporary Chinese audience.

References

Barme, Geremie. (1995) "To Screw Foreigners Is Patriotic: China's Avant-Garde Nationalist." *The China Journal* 34: 209–234.
Barme, Geremie. (1999) *In the Red: On Contemporary Chinese Culture*. New York: Columbia University Press.
Beijingers in New York (Beijingren zai niuyue). (1994) Directed by Zheng Xiaolong and Feng Xiaogang, Produced by TV Art Center and China: TV Production Center, Beijing.
Berg, Daria. (2011) "A New Spectacle in China's Mediasphere: A Cultural Reading of a Web-Based Reality Show from Shanghai." *The China Quarterly* 205: 133–151.
"Bitiwei qianshou souhu kaiqi jinian kangzhan jiemu hulianwangjia shidai" (BTV Teams up with Sohu Web to Open up the Internet + Era of Commemorating Programs of the

War of Resistance against Japan 2015), available at: http://news.sohu.com/20150818/n419164907.shtml, viewed on 7 Nov 2015.

Chan, Joseph. (1993) "Commercialization Without Independence: Trends and Tensions of Media Development in China," in Joseph Cheng and Maurice Brosseau (eds) *China Review 1993*. Hong Kong: Chinese University Press: 1–21.

Chan, Joseph. (2003) "Administrative Boundaries and Media Marketization: A Comparative Analysis of the Newspaper, TV and Internet Markets in China," in Chin-Chuan Lee (ed.) *Chinese Media, Global Contexts*. London: Routledge: 159–176.

Cheng, Manli. (2001) "Analysis of the Chinese Communist Party's Thought of News." *Journalism and Communication Studies* 3: 24–30.

Croteau, David, Hoynes, William and Milan, Stefania. (2012) (fourth edition), *Media/Society*. Thousand Oaks, CA: Sage.

Cui, Shuqin. (2003) *Women Through the Lens: Gender and Nation in a Century of Chinese Cinema*. Honolulu: University of Hawaii Press.

Dal Lago, Francesca. (1999) "Personal Mao: Reshaping an Icon in Contemporary Chinese Art." *Art Journal* 58: 46–59.

Dayan, Daniel and Katz, Elihu. (1992) *Media Events: The Live Broadcasting of History*. Cambridge, MA: Harvard University Press.

"Dizhuzhongliu – weida de dihoukangzhan bochu wangyou reyi lishi" (The Broadcasting of *Pillar Standing in Midstream: The Great Backstage Battlefield of the War of Resistance to Japan Stirs Up Heated Debate on History Among the Neitizens*). (2014) Available at: http://www.wyzxwk.com/Article/shidai/2014/09/327900.html, viewed on 7 Nov 2015.

Donald, Stephanie and Keane, Michael. (2001) "Media in China: New Convergences, New Approaches," in Stephanie Donald, Michael Keane and Yin Hong (eds) *Media in China: Consumption, Content and Crisis*. Richmond: Curzon: 3–17.

Fang, Xiangmin, Li, Peng and Wang, Xin. (2000) "Scrutinising Sina [in Chinese]." *Sanlian Life Weekly* [in Chinese], March 2000.

Guo, Yingjie. (2004) *Cultural Nationalism in Contemporary China: The Search for National Identity Under Reform*. New York: Routledge, Curzon.

He, Baogang and Guo, Yingjie. (2000) *Nationalism, National Identity and Democratization in China*. Aldershot: Ashgate.

Hong, Junhao, Lu, Yanmei and Zou, William. (2009) "CCTV in the Reform Years: A New Model for China's Television?" in Ying Zhu and Chris Berry (eds) *TV China*. Bloomington: Indiana University Press: 40–55.

Hu, Xin. (2002) "The Surfer-in-Chief and the Would-be Kings of Content: A Short Study of Sina.com and Netease.com," in Stephanie Donald, Michael Keane and Yin Hong (eds) *Media in China: Consumption, Content and Crisis*. Richmond: Curzon: 192–199.

Keane, Michael. (2006) "From Made in China to Created in China." *International Journal of Cultural Studies* 9(3): 285–296.

Kung, James Kai-sing and Lin, Justin Yifu. (2003) "The Causes of China's Great Leap Famine, 1959–1961." *Economic Development & Cultural Change* 52(1): 51–73.

Lee, Chin-Chuan. (2003) "The Global and the National of the Chinese Media: Discourses, Market, Technology, and Ideology," in Chin-Chuan Lee (ed.) *Chinese Media, Global Contexts*. London: Routledge: 1–31.

Ma, Eric. (2000) "Rethinking Media Studies: The Case of China," in James Curran and Myung-Jin Park (eds) *De-Westernizing Media Studies*. London: Routledge: 21–34.

The Mine Warfare (Dileizhan). (1962) Co-directed by Tang Yingqi, Xu Da and Wu Jianhai, Produced by August First Film Studio, Beijing.

The Pillar Standing in Midstream: the Great Backstage Battlefield of the War of Resistance to Japan (Dizhuzhongliu: weida de dihoukangzhan). (2015) Co-Produced by Beijing Municipal Publicity Department and Beijing TV Station, available at: http://mil.sohu.com/s2015/dzzl/index.shtml, accessed 7 Nov 2015.

The Search for Modern China: Looking Back at Historical Moments (Zhuixun xiandai zhaongguo: huiwang lishi shuijian). (2009) Produced by Sohu History Channel, available at: http://news.sohu.com/s2009/guoqing60/, viewed on 7 Nov 2015.

Sun, Wanning. (2001) "Semiotic Over-Determination or 'indoctritainment': Television, Citizenship, and the Olympic Games," in Stephanie Donald, Michael Keane and Yin Hong (eds) *Media in China: Consumption, Content and Crisis*. Richmond: Curzon: 116–127.

The Tunnel Warfare (Didaozhan). (1965) Directed by Ren Xudong, produced by August First Film Studio, Beijing.

Wu, Xu. (2007) *Chinese Cyber Nationalism: Evolution, Characteristics, and Implications*. Lanham, MD: Lexington Books.

Xu, Ben. (2001) "Chinese Populist nationalism: Its Intellectual Politics and Moral Dilemma." *Representations* 76(1): 120–140.

Yu, Haiqing. (2009) *Media and Cultural Transformation in China*. London and New York: Routledge.

Zhang, Tongdao. (2002) *Meijie chunqiu: Observation on TV in China*. Beijing: China Film Press.

Zhao, Suisheng. (2004) *A Nation-State by Construction: Dynamics of Modern Chinese Nationalism*. Stanford, CA: Stanford University Press.

Zhao, Suisheng. (2005) "Nationalism's Double Edge." *The Wilson Quarterly* 29(4): 76–82.

Zhao, Yuezhi. (2008) *Communication in China: Political Economy, Power, and Conflict*. Lanham, MD: Rowman & Littlefield Publishers.

Zhao, Zhongwei and Reimondos, Annal. (2012) "The Demography of China's 1958–61 Famine: A Closer Examination." *Population* 67(2): 281–308.

Zheng, Yongnian. (1999) *Discovering Chinese Nationalism in China: Modernization, Identity, and International Relations*. Cambridge; Melbourne: Cambridge University Press.

5 A rising star professor
Yu Dan and her interpretation of the *Analects*

Introduction

Chinese professor Yu Dan (b. 1965) has become an immediate cultural success with her book *Yu Dan lunyu xinde* (2006; published in the West with the English title *Confucius from the Heart: Ancient Wisdom for Today's World* [2009] – hereafter *Confucius*), which helps promote people's interest in the Chinese classics and national studies. As a work which bears the marks of both Confucian ideology and popular Confucianism, the Yu Dan phenomenon captures the development of the national studies craze, in particular those areas relevant to Confucian ideas and principles in contemporary China. Yu Dan's recognition indicates a recent revival of ancient Chinese cultural, philosophical and moral traditions which are in line with the propaganda agenda of the CCP administration. This chapter analyses the Yu Dan sensation and the intense debate it has stimulated, and reviews its subtle collaboration with official discourse and proselytization and its achievement as a popular-cum-serious (lowbrow/highbrow) cultural product. It also analyses the role the Yu Dan spectacle plays in changing the social status and functions of intellectuals in the contemporary Chinese political-social-cultural milieu.

Yu Dan is a professor and associate dean of the School of Arts and Media at Beijing Normal University. Yu and her well-known book *Confucius* are controversial topics in cultural discussions of modern-day China. James Leibold notes that in mainland China today, "one cannot enter a bookstore without encountering Professor Yu Dan's depoliticized, self-help musings on the *Analects*, which has sold ten million legitimate and another six million pirated copies, inviting comparisons with Mao's little red book" (Leibold 2010, 18). Recently, *Confucius* was published in the West, and Yu's total royalties for the book have reached 2.6 million RMB. *Confucius* is a collection of the transcript of Yu's lectures about the *Analects*, which were broadcast via the CCTV's prime-time science and education show *Lecture Room* (*Baijia jiangtan*) in October 2006.[1] Due to its popularity, transcripts of Yu's talks on the program were composed into a book in November of the same year. With the combined success of her TV shows and texts, Yu Dan is known across China, both in academic circles and as a celebrity among the general public. Yu has become the most famous woman in China and has been nicknamed an "academic super girl," a "female Zhang Yimou" (one of China's most famed Fifth Generation film directors) and a "female Dale Carnegie."

The Yu Dan phenomenon is illustrative of the changing contemporary Chinese cultural landscape, while it also reveals new trends in government propaganda. In recent times, under both the Hu Jintao and the Xi Jinping administrations, items of exceptional national cultural heritage that are embedded in philosophical ideas, aesthetic interest, moral ideals and life attitudes that constitute the spiritual home of the Chinese nation are being emphasized as part of the propaganda policy of the CCP. Under this overall strategic direction, Confucius and his principles comprise one of the more important traditional cultural elements to be embraced and cherished by the Chinese cultural academics, critics and commoners alike. Among a plethora of Confucian discourses, Yu Dan's presentation of a therapeutic stoicism wrapped in Confucian fabric to a Chinese public that is weary of cultural self-doubt, economic dislocation and political disempowerment has been proved to be good timing and astute judgement. However, from another perspective, Yu's personalised and haphazard deliberations on the *Analects* confront and challenge the social duties of intellectuals who are supposed to shoulder the responsibility of providing honest research data to the public, criticising social injustice and questioning any government mismanagement. Through an analysis of the Yu Dan phenomena, the following discussions consider the reasons for the intense debate *Confucius* has caused; its elusive partnership with official discourse and ideology; its feat as an exemplary cultural product; and its utility in shifting the roles and social status of intellectuals in current China.

Confucian ideas and the national studies craze in modern and post-Mao China

During most of Chinese history, Confucian ideas, in one form or another, have been a dominant force in China. From the turn of the twentieth century, these ideas, the issue of China's traditional culture, and the "national studies craze" have become matters of continuous and intense controversy (Chen 2011: 22). Over the past century, Confucian thought has been judged and re-evaluated, usually negatively, by the ruling powers and cultural elites. In the May Fourth Movement (1919), progressive and innovative Chinese intellectuals, such as Chen Duxiu and Hu Shi, adopted a critical attitude toward traditional thought and culture. "Down with official Confucianism!" was the slogan that symbolized this intellectual trend (Chen 2011: 22). Thus, Confucianism was condemned as the custodian of feudal thought and behaviour, preventing the emancipation of people's thinking and shackling their spiritual freedom.

For us to better understand the trajectory of the Confucian discourse and the "national studies craze," it might be helpful to mention the "national essence campaign," which was initiated in the early 1900s by conservative elite thinkers and literati and continued in earnest into the Republican period. As the product of the concerns of elite intellectuals such as Liang Qichao, who worried about the military and cultural invasion from the West and the potential replacement of Chinese traditional culture by Western culture (although he did support the selective adoption of Western culture), this campaign sought to protect China's "national essence" (*guocui*) (Ding 1995: 2). This led to the appeal to revive not only national learning (*guoxue*) but also national painting, national theatre, national language, national medicine, national martial arts, national dress and so forth. These endeavours to recoup and convalesce the cultural essence of the Chinese nation was due not only to the sense of pride the intellectuals had in their own civilization but also to the national crisis that besieged a China facing subjugation by Western imperialism forces and the force of cultural imperialism. The political ends of the "national essence campaign" render both race and patriotism, which had the implication of contesting not only the "alien" rule of the Qing dynasty but also "Europeanization."

The "national essence campaign" revealed a paradox and a conundrum. On one hand there was a belief in "perpetuating a national essence that is crucial to national existence and well-being," whereas, on the other hand, there seemed to be a requirement to "eradicate and rewrite the past that produced that essence, because it had become an obstacle to national progress" (Dirlik 2011: 6). One focus of the "national essence campaign" in its early stage was its criticism of Confucian learning (*ruxue*), a position that contrasts sharply with the present-day national studies craze that privileges learning and texts associated with Confucianism (Makeham 2011: 16; Ding 1995: 10).

However, during the period of the Nationalist Party's rule on the mainland, in particular in the 1930s, a re-identification and reunion of national essence and *guoxue* with Confucian discourse took place through state patronage of Confucianism (Dirlik 2011: 10). Conversely, at the time the CCP took control of the mainland region and launched the Cultural Revolution (1966–1976), Confucian thought was again labelled as being "feudalistic, conservative thought, an impediment that Mao had to demolish in order to push forward his own revolutionary thought, and it was subjected to organised, widespread criticism throughout the country" (Chen 2011: 22). Up until the era of the Opening Up reforms, which began at the end of the 1970s when a new process of modernization was implemented by Deng Xiaoping and his colleagues, China's traditional culture was once again side-lined and rebutted. China's liberal intellectuals led the way in the total repudiation of Eastern civilisation in favour of Western civilisation, and the popular 1988 documentary series *River Elegy* (*Heshang*) serves as a good example of this phenomenon.[2] Confucius and his doctrines, as the most established emblem of Chinese thought and civilisation, were thought to be too archaic and impractical to serve China's new situation.

Nonetheless, the situation altered with the steady economic transformation of China and the ensuing escalation in national economic strength, which together ushered in a cultural and psychological awareness among the Chinese people and government. One facet of this alteration was the hunt for an enhanced national self-confidence, which resulted in a heightened regard for traditional cultural legacy, embodied in the revitalization of Confucian thought, ideology and practice. There were diverse catalysts behind this reconfiguration and renaissance of national culture, including government support and promotion, elite intellectuals' enthusiasm and input in the so-called New Confucianism studies (both domestically and overseas), and an emerging popular fashion for Confucianism among the general public. Gradually, the conjoining of these incentives led to the arrival of a "national studies craze."

The Chinese government soon appropriated the Confucian discourse, making it a part of a top-down instrumentalization of Confucian principles and cultural relics which appealed to the ordinary citizens' affinity with their ethnic identity, their country and their government. In 1984, a government-funded "Chinese Confucian Foundation" was established, with the then State Council member Gu Mu serving as honorary president. In 1986, in the context of the seventh five-year plan, the government sanctioned the foundation of a large research group on contemporary Confucianism directed by Fang Keli, a professor at Nankai University in Tianjin. A key motivating dynamic for the government's support of this research program was the imperative of modernizing the country by implanting the Confucian discourse back into Chinese culture, which had proven to be central to the economic modernization and expansion of the four "Asian Tigers" (Billioud 2007: 52) and the related "Asian economic miracle." Moreover, around this time, numerous festivals and ceremonies honouring Confucius were ordered and sponsored by the government. These were held at the temples of the sage's hometown Qufu in Shandong Province and other localities and were broadcast live by CCTV (Chen 2011: 23; Billioud 2007: 52; Billioud and Thoraval 2009: 82–100). In these cautious appropriations of Confucian cultural customs, the government made use of Confucian ideas such as harmony (*hexie*) and the rule of virtue (*yidezhiguo*) to back up and reinforce its rule and legitimacy (Billioud 2007: 50). This was particularly evident after the crackdown on the fourth of June democratic protest in 1989, when the political leadership mobilized traditional concepts to retrieve its dwindling validity. Following this, in the 1990s, Confucianism served a dual role for the government: first, its "authoritarian" traits contributed to a "socialist spiritual civilization"; and second, it aided social unity and postulated a cultural antidote to the peril of Westernization and the deleterious upshots of economic modifications on Chinese social and political life (Meissner 2006: 48).

Likewise, Confucian discourse was invigorated within academic circles. In 1985, the founding of the Academy of Chinese Culture (*Zhongguo wenhua shuyuan*) and the Chinese Confucius Research Institute (*Zhonghua Kongzi yanjiusuo*) marked the "genuine burgeoning of enlisting Confucianism in the ongoing cultural debates over tradition and Westernization" (Song 2003: 85). Besides this, a number of Hong Kong and Taiwan New Confucianists – including illustrious authors such as Mou Zongsan, Tu Weiming (Du Weiming) and Yu Yingshih – had their works recommended for publication on the mainland. The core theme of these New Confucianist scholars' research relates to the "saviour" role that Confucianism could play in the modern world (Song 2003: 93). In addition, from the early 1990s, national studies institutes were created in many of the top universities in mainland China (Chen 2011: 23; Makeham 2011: 14). For example, in 1992, the Research Centre for Traditional Chinese Culture at Beijing University was established, followed by the publication of the journal *Research on Guoxue* (*Guoxue yanjiu*) in the middle of 1993 (Makeham 2011: 15).

The national studies craze has remained a cultural sensation in the twenty-first century and has evolved into many popular forms, predominantly in the rebirth of Confucian principles and manners, which cannot be simply comprehended under the rubric of top-down instrumentalization led by the government, as it instead reflects "a much larger popular aspiration" (Billioud and Thoraval 2007: 5). This noteworthy movement in the appropriation of tradition from the bottom up exhibits a "progressive transition from the imaginary to the real," during which "empty, incantatory references to tradition make way for actual appropriation of ancient cultural heritage [where] [t]raditional values were no longer merely invoked; an effort was made to actually live according to them in various ways" (Billioud and Thoraval 2007: 5). For instance, popular books relating to Confucianism and conventional culture became bestsellers.[3] The Confucius MBA (master of business administration) programs, which are purposely tailored for business people and run by prestigious universities, have become trendy among the commercial elites. Also, the international Confucius Institutes sponsored by the Chinese government triggered a resuscitated interest in Confucius, time-honoured classics, and national essence in both the domestic and the international spheres. Further, the popular national studies craze fuels the culture industry as national studies can provide cultural content for business, and the national studies craze has become a renewable resource of cultural trade that has "undergone an appropriate process of creative conversion" (Makeham 2011: 15).

At the grass-roots level, popular Confucian practices can be found in the rapid dissemination of a campaign to encourage children to read classical literature (*xiaoer dujing*)[4] and in the spread of private schools where students study classics of ancient cultural heritage and imitate Confucian living routines and manners (Billioud 2007: 58; Billioud and Thoraval 2007: 4; Billioud and Thoraval 2009: 82–100). An example of the Confucian-style private schools can be found in Yidan School (*Yidan xuetang*), where children read ancient classics and act within Confucian rules of etiquette. The school's curriculum focusses on the training of Confucian protocols, and the motto of the school is "less talk, more action," which mirrors Confucian codes and elucidates that self-transformation is not a simple intellectual practice (Billioud and Thoraval 2007: 14).

Another model of popular Confucianism in practice is the Lujiang Cultural Education Centre (*Lujiang wenhua jiaoyu zhongxin*) located in rural Anhui Province. Every six months, the Lujiang Centre admits a group of thirty students from a local village to receive coaching based on traditional culture. During their learning and schooling periods, all the trainees must submit to ascetic Confucian rituals and practice Confucian comportments, such as using the suitable and codified words when greeting someone and asking after their well-being. The Lujiang Centre aligns its pedagogy to the doctrinal pillars of Confucian virtues such as filial piety, loyalty and honesty (Billioud and Thoraval 2007: 14). The education and behavioural principles of the Lujiang Centre are that "Confucius is alive and is with you, me, him, and the mentality of the Chinese people." "Confucianism is no longer an ideology of a certain class; it has become a major part of the Chinese national character or a 'psycho-cultural construct [*wenhua xinli jiegou*]'"

(Song 2003: 88). After graduation, the students teach other people of the village what they have studied at the centre, thus postulating the potential for a positive makeover of the whole village, and, in order to maximize this potential, the centre and the program received support from the local government. The centre is still a "relatively isolated case, but it is indicative of the potential for the insertion of Confucianist themes into new political-cultural constructions," and it is "inventing, somewhere between political control and moral proselytism, a new form of governmentality that could gain widespread acceptance" (Detournier and Ji 2009: 73).

While the national studies phenomenon continues to gain favour from both the government and civil society, some activist intellectuals have gone a step further and recommend a "Confucian fundamentalism." Jiang Qing, the main promoter of this concept, suggests that Confucianism should be turned into the "state religion" and "state ideology." China could achieve this by "implementing a political system allying religion (Confucianism) and state in which the state would take on the responsibility of moral education . . . by establishing a system of 'Confucian constitutional government' and making Confucianism the foundation of the state's legitimacy" (Chen 2011: 26). This idea of Confucian fundamentalism has been attacked, with one critic charging that it is "reactionary to modern democratic government and tramples on the concept of 'equality.'" In their arguments against Jiang Qing's proposal and its unsuitability for the Chinese situation, scholars point out that basic modern values – such as human rights, as well as the notions of democracy and rule of law – are lacking in Confucianism (Chen 2011: 26).

The Confucian revival trend of the national studies craze has caused concern and criticism from many contemporary Chinese intellectuals. One leading argument is that the national studies craze is truly just a marginalized position in China's modernization process and that the present phenomenon is surely just the last whimper of traditional culture as it becomes assimilated in the modern era of a new Chinese dawn (Chen 2011: 25). Other scholars hold that "Confucian doctrine was negated back during the May Fourth movement, and that to restore it now to such high esteem is historical revisionism" (Chen 2011: 25). The 2010 Nobel Peace Prize winner, Chinese writer and political dissident Liu Xiaobo also protested that "[t]he ideal Confucian personality amounts to nothing more than a 'self-enslaving personality [*zijue de nuxing renge*]'" (Song 2003: 90). Further, he remarked that the submission of Chinese intellectuals – with their great sense of duty and responsibility – to their rulers indicates "the ultimate level of enslavement [*nuhua jijing*], [which] has not only prevented the Chinese people from developing analytical skills, but has also stunted individuality and creativity" (Song 2003: 90).

In summary, the overall trend of the national studies craze is understood and reasoned by most scholars as either a top-down government instrumentalization or a bottom-up popular Confucianism. Yu Dan stands apart from these scholars through her "middle-ground" position between the top-down and bottom-up paradigms. It is therefore significant to examine what makes Yu Dan, a once-unknown female professor, so exceptional and different from other academics and what makes her so attractive to both academic attention and public debate.

Yu Dan's explanation of the *Analects*

The success of Yu Dan's interpretation of the *Analects* owes much to the CCTV prime-time show *Lecture Room*. *Lecture Room* is a very popular education and science program, and one that is prominent within a field of other entertainment-focused shows – such as talk shows, game shows and talent contests – that are many and widespread in China's cultural landscape. The official media platform provided by CCTV enabled Yu to transform the *Analects* – an intricate and, for some Chinese, little-read Chinese classic – into a vivid *duanzi* (piece of storytelling). The delivery style of *Lecture Room* is similar to that of the traditional Chinese *pingshu* (storytelling) performance, which is a folk art form. In *pingshu* recital, normally, the storytellers stand behind a prop desk and relate a fragment of a novel or historical legend from memory. During the performance, the performers can adjust and stimulate the mood of the audience and control the storytelling through employing body language, such as gestures and facial expressions, and through modifying their speaking voice and tone.

As a genuine storyteller in *Lecture Room*, Yu Dan did not present a lecture revolving around focal topics and themes but instead offered a combination of stories and anecdotes (Li 2010: 159; Li 2007: 54). This method transforms the classics into collections of interesting tales, and it was this mode of presentation which led to her popularity with the audience. Yu's exposition, training and eloquence enabled her to explain profound classical phrases in simple terms and allowed her to insert Chinese and foreign fables, historical stories, anecdotes of famous people, unofficial histories and personal life stories circulated on the internet into her recounting of the *Analects*. Yu Dan deftly adopted these tales and sketches to clarify her ideas and arguments and to add flavour and interest to her talk, leaving her audience with the impression that she is erudite yet also modest and unassuming. For example, as evidence to substantiate her viewpoints, Yu referred to the Eastern Jin dynasty poet Tao Yuanming's experiences as an official and to anecdotes of the famous Northern Song dynasty poet Su Dongpo. Yu used any materials that were useful to her and her views of Confucian teachings. These would include a range of resources from allusions to Buddhism to Tolstoy's allegories to stories about a British tennis player.

Yu Dan's interpretations of the *Analects* are what I would call "*xishuo*" (playful narrative).[5] *Xishuo* adopts a casual and relaxed manner when discussing historical, official and serious topics or events in novels, films and TV shows. Further, the organization of the contents of Yu Dan's broadcasts and writings about Confucius and the *Analects* aligns with the popular books that often are categorised as "self-improvement," with themes such as achieving personal goals, improving personal relations and generating wealth, and with tips on how to become successful, such as *Chicken Soup for the Unsinkable Soul* (*Xinling jitang*); *Rich Dad, Poor Dad* (*Fubaba, qiong baba*);[6] and so forth.

To readers who are familiar with these volumes, it is clear that these books use anecdotes, reports of famous people, unofficial histories and fables to fuel and boost the interest of the audience. Using a cordial and inconspicuous tone, which is similar to that used when speaking, these bestselling books claim to offer an immediate, practical approach to achieving instant results – an expected outcome that is usually hinted at by the book titles. It is suggested that whoever reads *Chicken Soup for the Unsinkable Soul* will directly become wiser and whoever reads *Rich Dad, Poor Dad* will immediately become a smart investor. Attracted by these promises of prompt and effective solutions to their needs, readers who want to become rich and successful overnight have great expectations from these popular texts.

According to this logic, if wisdom and fortune can be duplicated, why not attitude? Yu Dan's talk on the *Analects* and her *Confucius* are dedicated to providing an omnipotent "prescription" that can give each person a more optimistic outlook (Wu 2008: 8); thus, the "[Chinese] should buy her book, if they mean to be happy, orderly and content to stay in their places" (Nylan and Thomas 2010: 222). The selling point of Yu's interpretation is that it tries to offer a comprehensive answer to the perplexities and bewilderments confronting contemporary Chinese people. Accordingly, an essential theme of Yu's explanation is its emphasis on one's attitude towards life. Yu (2006) states:

> Every person has their difficult times and regrets and we can do nothing about it. However, what we can do is to change our attitude and mood toward them. One of the essences of the *Analects* is that it tells us how to deal with these misgivings and difficulties with a positive attitude.

Here, Yu Dan proposes that a positive attitude and a placid mood will defeat all life's misfortunes. Yu's reading thus resurrects and renews the principal ideas of Confucian thought in relation to their current utility and value in remoulding the personality and comforting the temper of the Chinese people. In doing so, Yu's personal perceptions and revelations of the *Analects* rejuvenate the values of the timeworn text and shorten the distance between the audience and the classic. Speaking in a humble manner, Yu seeks to share with others what she has learned from reading the *Analects*, which drives her to believe that the book's philosophically inspirational ideas and advices about human life have jumped the barrier of time and space and shed new light for the future of every human being. In other words, Yu's lectures and her *Confucius* are attempts to convert her own comprehension of the classics into "serving the people."

Yu Dan's lectures and book are scheduled to release in an "ideal" historical moment. The policy of openness has been in place for around thirty years, and now, when the repercussions of the reform are becoming clear (including political corruption, social injustice and the collapse of morality), many Chinese people have been left behind in the rapidly changing economic times and feel confused, discriminated against, disgruntled and uneasy about the future. As Yu (2006) observes, we often hear people complaining that society is not just, that their lives are hard. Actually, instead of accusing everyone but yourself, why not examine yourself? Based on Yu Dan's opinion, people without a peaceful mind feel continually dissatisfied, jealous, cynical and melancholy. Conversely, people with a positive mentality examine themselves and engage in self-reflection, as Confucius did. As a follower of Confucian ideas, Yu Dan trusts that "a thoughtful citizenry with 'settled hearts' makes for a more secure society that eventually will achieve the greatest good for the greatest number" (Nylan and Thomas 2010: 221). Here, Yu's deliberation of the spiritual core of Confucianism appears very orthodox, as there is "a consensus amongst Confucians that the path best manifests itself as a spiritual ideal that is embodied in a system of values and attitudes of mind" (Guo 2004: 82), and she projects moral engagement, which is labelled *de*, or "moral power," by classical Confucians (Bell 2008: 164).

However, the premise that an upbeat outlook and moral self-discipline will lead to encouraging renovation and eliminate social disproportion is not confirmed, as for many Chinese it is merely a self-pleasing and self-deceiving anaesthetic. A recent human-interest news feature depicted the day's work of a manual labourer in Beijing. Forty-year-old Lao Nie came from Henan Province and works as an express delivery worker. The feature showed his harsh living conditions: his six-square-meter windowless temporary living quarters, his three-yuan (around 0.5 USD) lunch, and a close-up of his bent back and the tears rolling down his wrinkled face. Despite his hard work, Lao Nie could not afford his daughter's university tuition fees, and he was also worried about losing his job in the near future. According to Yu Dan's reasoning, Lao Nie should examine himself and contemplate how his behaviour may have led to his difficult living conditions. Nevertheless, it is dubious whether such an examination is justified, as it is unlikely that Lao Nie himself is responsible for his complications. Additionally, if Lao Nie finds nothing wrong with himself, should he pretend that he is living a satisfying life? Or should the government take obligation to improve his situation? Clearly, Yu Dan advocates using the Confucian "wisdom" to remodel the Chinese mind-set, in particular that of those victimized by the brisk socio-economic vicissitudes, and therefore a solicitous public of matured mind will be cultivated. Yu Dan's lookouts espouse an imagined harmonious society that echoes the propaganda rhetoric of the CCP government in which China's "haves" and "have-nots" cohabit congenially as the operation of moral clout would overcome all the social malaises and prejudice. Observably, instead of dealing with the origins of social inequality, the Chinese government places the burden of reform on common people through admonishing them to behave in a more ethical and harmonious manner, which has been the "main thrust of the CCP's propaganda campaigns in recent year" (Kong and Hawes 2015: 48–49).

There is an obvious flaw in Yu Dan's rationale, and her construct of the *Analects* may be seen in two opposing ways. While her work abets ordinary people to relax and accept the reality of their lives, and "detoxes" and "purifies" the minds of the people,[7] it can also be held as stifling people's critical thinking. If Lao Nie could mimic Ah Q's behaviour and copy his spiritual victories, his life would be easier, at least mentally. Yu's interpretation of the *Analects* is essentially a revamped version of Ah Q's blind optimism, which is lampooned and criticised by China's most famous modern writer, Lu Xun, in his novella *The True Story of Ah Q* (*A Q zhengzhuan*) (Wu 2008: 9; Yan and Yang 2009: 65). Lu Xun's story traces the "adventures" of Ah Q, a rural farmer with little education and no fixed vocation. Ah Q is notorious for his "spiritual victories," which is Lu Xun's euphemism for self-delusion even when encountered with tremendous defeat or shame. Ah Q emboldens himself psychologically to be spiritually "superior" to his opponents even as he surrenders to their attacks. Lu Xun exposes Ah Q's extreme delusions as characteristic of China's own delusion at his time. Ah Q's transcendent triumph is branded as one of the most idiosyncratic features of the deep-rooted bad habits of the Chinese people, which are judged and condemned by Lu Xun as the true problem of a backward China of his time. The literary figure Ah Q, it might be noted with a small degree of sarcasm, does, to some degree, epitomise the "idealised gentleman" with a "modest" stance imagined by Yu Dan. The correlation between the two characters therefore leads to a re-evaluation of the classic, of Confucius's teachings, and of Yu's explication of it.

It is clear that what Yu Dan has reclaimed is precisely that which Lu Xun and his May Fourth peers were dedicated to removing, the habitual ways of thought and behaviour of the Chinese people as predisposed by Confucian ideas and connoted by a meek and compliant mentality. A central problem in Chinese culture has been the suppressing force that impedes people's faculty to think against the grain and that limits their scepticism and criticism. This sceptical and unruly ethos called for by Lu Xun almost hundred years ago is left behind by Yu Dan, as such passion and excess are not exhilarated and esteemed in Confucian thought. Here, Yu Dan's clarification of a Confucian mentality and personality denotes a regression of history. The critical thinking and rebellious spirit that Lu Xun hoped that the Chinese people would acquire are still necessary for today's China, which needs a democratic turn in its social and political domain.

Although China's current economic and political transformation is occurring under the rubric of "socialism with Chinese characteristics," it may also be succinctly summarised by two phrases – "economically modernised" and "politically stalled." China needs a restyling of its political system if it is to become more democratic, rather than merely waiting for a humane government managed by a group of competent and compassionate "gentlemen" that is propositioned by Confucius's political ideals. Thus, from this point of view, the Yu Dan style of spiritual victories may temporarily contribute to the building of a "harmonious" society, while, in the long run, it will be a leg-iron fitted to the Chinese people and impeding them from achieving political enlightenment.

Yu Dan's interpretation of the *Analects* and the debates it stimulates

As an instant success, Yu Dan's lectures and writings about Confucius and the *Analects* have attracted considerable attention and have sparked stimulating debate. Some critics consider Yu a contemporary preacher of traditional Chinese classical culture and a leading light of this form of scholarship. However, others, including the distinguished scholar Li Zehou, believe that Yu has just popularised the classics via the conduit of modern media, rather than conducting serious research on Confucius (Li cited in Wu 2008: 5). Yet Yi Zhongtian, a professor of literature at Xiamen University and another celebrity academic from *Lecture Room*, offers positive feedback about Yu's TV show: "This programme aroused the common people's interest, and rekindled their enthusiasm to learn about Chinese history and traditional Chinese culture, and any in-depth analysis should be left to the historians" (Yu Dan zhizheng: wenhua fuhao haishi liyi boyi 2007). Daniel Bell (2008: 166) also comments on Yu Dan's effort:

> Yu Dan is addressing a popular audience, not experts. Let me be more positive. There's a kind of division of labor between experts and popularizers, and the division can be mutually beneficial. Popularizers can learn from and incorporate the insights of experts, and experts can learn from attempts to show the value of the classics for the contemporary world. We, meaning those of us teaching and writing on the classics, should be grateful for Yu Dan's contribution. She shows that our work can and should have relevance beyond academic circles.

In addition, Sun Yuanming (cited in Yan and Yang 2009: 65), the director of the Centre for Psychology Studies at Chongqing Institute of Social Sciences, states:

> Star professors such as Yi Zhongtian and Yu Dan proficiently combine knowledge and mass communication media to offer a series of popular feasts of Chinese national studies. These modern scholars have special expertise and are skilled at expressing thoughts and feelings. Their dissemination of the national essence and traditional Chinese cultures has positive effects.

Despite these scholars acknowledging Yu Dan's efforts in spreading traditional Chinese culture and teaching its ancient classics, there are others who take a critical standpoint towards this cultural sensation. Some researchers state that Yu's exploration of the *Analects* has many inaccuracies. Thus, some argue that some of her renditions and notions are literally indelicate and that her attitude towards knowledge is questionable (Zhang 2007: 58). If we take one instance, we see that due to her inadequate level of understanding of classical Chinese, Yu Dan regularly mistranslates the phrase *xiaoren* (petty person) as "little person" or "child" (Nylan and Thomas 2010: 220). Daniel Bell (2008: 167) has pointed out that Yu Dan articulates in her account of the *Analects* that everybody has an equal opportunity to become an exemplary person, which might distort Confucius's original conviction in which he "takes it for granted that a minority of exemplary people can and should rule over common people. . . . [Confucius] also suggests that common people have intellectual limitations." Yu Dan does not mention such passages, perhaps because these assessments would not play well with her intended readership, but through such omissions she may be deviating substantially from

Confucius's original views. In another instance, Yu Dan interprets Confucius as teaching that "we should help the people nearest to us, and we should do so immediately, without any delay," which seems inconsistent with Confucius's own remarks which held that "what we do depends on the roles we occupy vis-a-vis the people we're dealing with. I owe more obligations to my father than to total strangers" (Bell 2008: 169).

Among those academics who are suspicious about Yu Dan's works, there are ten from Tsinghua University (the top university in China) who published a collection of essays slating Yu entitled *Jiedu Yu Dan: gaosu ni yige meibei zaota de kongzi he zhuang zi* (*Detoxing Yu Dan: To Inform You of an Unspoiled Confucius and Zhuangzi*). In addition to this, they demanded that Yu deliver an open apology to the general public for her reckless comprehension of the *Analects*. Besides *Detoxing Yu Dan*, books entitled *Kongzi hen shengqi: cong Yu Dan hong xianxiang shuoqi* (*Confucius Is Deeply Angry: Discussions about the "Yu Dan Red/ Poison" Phenomenon*) and *Zhuangzi hen zhaoji* (*Zhuangzi Is Deeply Worried*) also decried Yu's work and actually called for a rejection of it. To compare the Yu Dan Red with Sudan Red, a highly poisonous traditional Chinese herbal medicine, the authors of the book show their frustration and even censure to Yu Dan's "slanted" interpretation of the *Analects*. The recognized writers Li Yue and Li Fang also joined the movement to denounce Yu Dan by co-authoring a book entitled *Pipan Yu Dan: zhengshuo Lunyu zhihui* (*Criticizing Yu Dan: Orthodox Interpretation of the "Analects"*). In this book, they systematically scrutinize and deconstruct Yu's reading through chapters such as "Yu Dan does not deserve to be 'a watcher of culture.'" By their united efforts, these writers seek to deprecate and de-authorise Yu and her ideas. In the conclusion of their arguments, the authors likewise metaphorically compare Yu to Sudan Red. Apparently, Yu Dan's works have made many people feel uneasy and offended, and personal attacks on Yu have emerged including labelling her as "the shallowest author" who pushes Chinese culture to the brink of collapse (Yu Dan zhizheng: wenhua fuhao haishi liyi boyi 2007). More dramatically, one Chinese netizen, in order to show his discontent, wore a T-shirt with the words "Confucius is deeply worried," when he disrupted a Yu Dan book promotion (Sohu News 2009).

Apart from her mistranslation and "skewed" analysis of the *Analects*, Yu Dan's works summon inquisition due to their "alliance" with mainstream ideology and their likelihood to harm public intellectuals and their function as social critics. The utility (not the content) of Yu's Confucianism is akin to the role of early Han dynasty Confucian discourse which was embraced by the Wu emperor to bolster the regime's rule and control the population. In other words, Yu's Confucianism, which was aired at prime time via the official media platform, voiced the state's appropriation of the Confucian principles including nurturing a loyal, conformist and considerate citizenry with a "settled" and noble heart. According to Daniel Bell (2008: 174), Yu Dan's account is "complacent, conservative, and supportive of the status quo." The harshest of Yu's critics on the mainland "compare her unfavourably to the 'scholar-officials from feudal society,' who were simply determined to uphold 'the vestiges of the old society'" (Nylan and Thomas 2010: 221). As Guo (2004: 74) states:

> Confucianism has little to offer to Marxism, but it certainly has elements [to offer to others], including the concern for the affairs of the state and well-being of the people, the notion of great unity, loyalty to the ruler and love of country, and filial piety.

Besides its "partnership" with the government ideology, the movement to criticise Yu Dan reflects another concern that relates to the forfeit of public intellectuals' role as social decriers. Seizing the Confucian canon, Yu urges people to face misery without complaint and live introspectively. However, if everyone submits to Yu's tuition, no one, including the liberal social criticisers, would slate social injustice, work on behalf of injured parties, or question the government. Therefore, China's human rights and democratic progress would be postponed to an unknown future.

Though Yu Dan's construal of the *Analects* invites broad condemnation from the academic circle, her fulfilment as a celebrity professor who relishes regard from a massive group of public fans shows that the production strategies employed by *Lecture Room* are successful. Through "feminising" and "de-sacralising" the classics, the show reconciles traditional and ideological paradigms which then soften and personalise the tone of the propaganda. *The Yu Dan Show* is a prototype cultural product that parades the official propagation's clever appropriation of the Confucian discourse and creates a renewed tie between the two paradigms. Enlisting a previously unknown, but lively and attractive (to many of Yu's fans), female scholar to lecture the public on Chinese national classics constitutes one of the crucial marketing ruses of the show. Yu Dan said in an interview:

> Being on TV and having people see that a young woman could be so into Confucius was a very important tool for me. I want to popularise Confucius; not to have him as something elitist which only older male scholars are interested in.
>
> (Interview with Yu Dan 2009)

Confucius's "old man" and "conservative" image is deeply embedded in the Chinese people's minds. Therefore, Yu's casual and subtle reintroduction of Confucius and Confucianism from a contemporary young woman's perspective has revivified Confucian thought. In so doing, Yu advantageously transmitted her "inferior" female label into an operative publicising expedient that has contributed immensely to her feat.

For a formerly ordinary female professor to intrude unexpectedly into the male-dominated scholarly discourse of Chinese national studies is disconcerting and threatening for some of Yu Dan's (especially) male colleagues. For example, Professor Yi Zhongtian tried to tease Yu when he asked her, "Are you beautiful women, also interested in Confucius?" "Beautiful woman" (*meinü*) is a popular phrase that was used widely by young Chinese netizens to describe females, regardless of their appearance, stature and age. Yi borrowed this catchphrase to mimic Yu's female identity, thus adding a gender perspective to the Yu Dan phenomenon. When Yu responded to Yi's question, he retorted, "What a smart little girl and what a brilliant answer." Through his remark, Yi exposed his fear of emasculation. From Yi's comments, to the labels given to Yu – such as "academic Super Girl," "scholar beauty," "cultural nanny" and "spiritual nurse" (Wu 2009) – Yu's gender status highlights one of the selling points of her works and adds to the reasons why she is predominantly disliked by male scholars.

Celebrity professor and the commodification of culture

Another celebrity professor, Ji Lianhai (cited in Yu Dan zhizheng: wenhua fuhao haishi liyi boyi 2007), stated in an interview that *"Lecture Room* caters to the taste and satisfies the needs of the common people, and through this programme the masses have been familiarized with some traditional cultural classics." From Ji's words, it is not hard to detect that, as a cultural product, Chinese traditional classics have been tailored commercially to the demands of the audience. In the process of commodification that is intrinsic to the market economic system, literature and culture have to concede to business and become consumable. The conventional scholarly and folk classics, including the *Analects*, have enormous potential for sale as cultural merchandises. Many scholars are angry with Yu Dan for her exclusive possession of the national classics resources. According to them, Yu uses the authorised and leading media platform (CCTV) to exploit traditional Chinese culture, which has led to her monopoly of this market. Yu's case clarifies that in the modern-day Chinese cultural marketplace, the old-fashioned cultural masterworks intertwine well with both the top-down instrumentalization of the Confucian discourse (making them a kind of cultural mascot for contemporary Chinese nationalism) and the bottom-up revival of popular Confucianism (such as the foundation of private schools in which Confucian ideas and behavioural manners are taught and practiced). The Yu Dan phenomenon fits well into both the official and popular Confucian homilies, which provides the argument that Confucian thought may not exist independently of an economic-political-social matrix in contemporary China.

Another Chinese scholar, Wu (2009: 8), also points out:

> In pursuit of profit, classics circulate broadly and rapidly on the market as a special cultural product. And in this so-called classics craze, the status and situation of the classics underwent dramatic alteration; they are no longer unattainable sacred masterpieces but commodities which can be purchased with money. The commodification of culture is an indispensable part of a market economy, which stimulate the market and improve the economy.

Another archetypal feature of this fashionable trend of the commodification of traditional culture is that it manufactures academic celebrities, adding another layer to the idiosyncratic classics cultural marvel. "Celebrity or star professor" is a new title that has surfaced within China's cultural industry in recent years, highlighting the latest spectacle spawned by the intermarriage of cultural products, academics and the media. By espousing ancient classics for domestic consumption, mainland Chinese intellectuals not only reasserted their image of the "exemplary Confucian scholar" but also gained a novel position of discursive power as transmitters of the great cultural heritage (Song 2003: 98). By following Yu Dan and the Yu Dan phenomenon, many Chinese scholars have grasped a previously inconceivable celebrity status and have gradually moved from an unfavourable position in the periphery to the focal point of public attention. If the reality-show program *Super Girl*,[8] presented by Hunan satellite TV station, is the venue that breeds artistic celebrities, then *Lecture Room* correspondingly yields academic idols.

The mainstream broadcasting stage, CCTV, gives rise to the recognition of celebrity professors, albeit with social implications regarding the status of scholars and their relationship with the public. Along with procuring veneration, celebrity professors' lectures become bestsellers, and the consequent book sales, news conferences, interviews, paid appearances and guest lectures all enhance their economic and social position. A report entitled "Why Confucius Matters Now: When Yu Dan Updated the Ancient Sage's Teachings, She Didn't Expect to Sell 10 Million Copies – or to Anger Chinese Academics," which was published in *The Times* on 25 April 2009, provides a glance into Yu Dan's celebrity lifestyle:

> The Beijing professor is a picture of petite perfection on a London hotel sofa, wearing what we might call Westernised Chinese Smart: a blindingly white designer tunic, precisely tousled hair, short black skirt and patent-leather ankle-boots. Only a snag down the knee of her tights leavens her impenetrable neatness.

As an expert in media studies, Yu Dan is acquainted with the weight of the public impression she makes. "When Yu Dan faces the masses, she contemplates more on how to please them than on how her ideas will affect them" (Wu 2009). The celebrity professor sensation has changed the status of contemporary Chinese intelligentsia by making them not only the manufacturers of knowledge and culture but also the salespersons and brokers of these intellectual capitals. Chinese scholars have now moved away from the verges to the hub of the cultural stage of China. Yu Dan's successful transformation from a professor to a celebrity has altered the traditional designation and connotation of knowledge production and circulation.

As another Chinese scholar, Zhang (2009), argues:

> The powerful appeal of modern media has completely "fansified" the audiences without many exceptions; and the relationship between fans and idols has changed the structure and nature of the distribution of culture. The "idolization" of professors and the "fansification" of audiences, deviates from, and betrays the scientific spirit of knowledge. What the fans need is neither culture nor knowledge, and not even entertainment, but habit-like mental dependence on their idols.

While the audiences are "fansified," the scholars are being "starised" and "white-collarised." Dongcheng Wang (2009) and Junqi Wang (2007) define the tendency of the "white-collarisation" of contemporary Chinese intellectuals; specifically, Dongcheng Wang (2009) writes:

> Along with the development of the Chinese economy and the expanding power of capital, the people and the intellectuals alike are drawn closer to capital and become more pragmatic and secular so that they can have a share of the feast of wealth. And for the intellectuals this means to some degree that they surrender their role and obligation as social critics. Yu Dan can be considered as one of the archetypes of these scholars who sacrifice their pursuit of freedom, democracy and human rights in their effort to pursue profit.

The comments of these two critics may be somewhat unfair to Yu Dan, but their arguments about the deterioration of Chinese intellectuals are worth meditating on by every sensible and conscientious Chinese intellectual. From Lu Xun to Li Ao, and from Wei Jingsheng to Liu Xiaobo,[9] intellectuals have gallantly shouldered the responsibility of honestly presenting only facts to the public. However, the commodification of cultural products, the starization of academics, and the appeal of wealth might be the paramount obstructions that contemporary Chinese intellectuals have to overcome in order to properly fulfil their duties.

Conclusion

Over the past decade, Yu Dan's lectures and her book about Confucius and the *Analects* have indisputably been one of the leading and most thought-provoking cultural sensations in the socio-media sphere of China. They are symbolic products of the national studies craze and bear the marks both of top-down ideological instrumentalization of the Confucian canon and of bottom-up popular Confucianism. The Yu Dan phenomenon unveils some nascent developments in the trajectory of Confucianism as a discursive power in the political and cultural domains of modern-day China. Through "feminising" and "de-sacralising" the classics, Yu Dan's show on *Lecture Room* experiments with merging traditional and ideological paradigms provided by the revival of the Confucian discourse, which not only mollifies and personalises the pitch of government propaganda but also accommodates the public's taste and expectations towards cultural commodities in a consumer-driven marketplace. The production and marketing devices adopted by *Lecture Room* are fashionable and effective, which enables Confucius's "old man" and "conservative" image to be transformed through Yu Dan's vivacious and intriguing interpretation of the *Analects*.

Despite their popularity, Yu Dan's broadcasts and texts beckon interrogation for their implicit cooperation with mainstream ideology in upholding the constraining and "inhuman" Confucian principles, particularly in cultivating an ideal Confucian persona featuring a loyal, conformist and thoughtful citizenry with a "settled" and generous heart who are incompetent of critical thinking, lack independent personality, submit to social discipline and stick to moral principles. The utility of Yu's Confucianism is in line with the established core of the Confucian school which assists the rulers to control their population. Yu Dan's celebrity/star professor identity also expands the role of contemporary Chinese intelligentsias by moulding them into traders of intellectual resources, which not only relocates the Chinese scholars from the margin to the centre of the cultural fair but changes the customary notion and overtone of knowledge making and distribution. This "white-collarisation" and "starization" of academics risks having Chinese intellectuals jettisoning their public function as social critics and entering into a position of the "ultimate level of enslavement," which serves more as an obstacle than as catalyst in a positive political reconfiguration of contemporary China. Thus, the restoration of Confucian doctrine that is most representative of the national studies craze to such high esteem is historical revisionism and regression.

Glossary

A Q zhengzhuan 阿Q正传
Baijia jiangtan 百家讲坛
Chen Duxiu 陈独秀
Du Weiming 杜维明
duanzi 段子
Fang Keli 方克立
Fubaba qiongbaba 《富爸爸 穷爸爸》
Gu Mu 谷牧
guocui 国粹
guoxue 国学
Guoxue yanjiu 国学研究
hexie 和谐
Heshang 河殇
Hu Shi 胡适
Ji Lianhai 纪连海
Jiang Qing 蒋庆
jugong 鞠躬
Li Zehou 李泽厚
Liang Qichao 梁启超
Li Fang 李放
Li Yue 李悦
Liu Xiaobo 刘晓波
Lu Xun 鲁迅
Lujiang wenhua jiaoyu zhongxin 庐江文化教育中心
meinü 美女
Mou Zongsan 牟宗三
nuhua jijing 奴化极境
pingshu 评书
Qufu 曲阜

ruxue 儒学
Su Dongpo 苏东坡
Sun Yuanming 孙远明
Tao Yuanming 陶渊明
wenhua xinli jiegou 文化心理结构
xiao er du jing 小儿读经
Xinling jitang 《心灵鸡汤》
xishuo 戏说
Yi Zhongtian 易中天
Yidan xuetang 一耽学堂
yidezhiguo 以德治国
Yu Dan lunyu xinde 《于丹论语心得》
Yu Ying-shih 余英时
Zhongguo wenhua shuyuan 中国文化书院
Zhonghua Kongzi yanjiusuo 中华孔子研究所
zijue de nuxing renge 自觉的奴性人格

Notes

1 *Lecture Room* is a popular program run by CCTV, China's official media platform, which invites scholars to give public lectures on interesting historical, literary and cultural topics. *Lecture Room* is a program that explores the humanities – combining entertainment and academic features – and it enjoys great popularity among its Chinese audience and has created many celebrity scholars, such as Yu Dan, Yi Zhongtian and Ji Lianhai. For more on *Lecture Room*, see Zhu 2012; Bell 2008.
2 *River Elegy* is a six-instalment documentary program made by CCTV that was broadcast in 1988. The program enjoyed great popularity among Chinese people. The documentary series clearly repudiates Eastern civilisation and demonstrates an apparent longing for Western civilization as a cure for Chinese problems.
3 The *Analects*, *Mencius* (*Mengzi*), *5000 Years of Ups and Downs* (*Shangxia wuqiannian*), *Twenty-Four Histories* (*Ershisishi*), and *Historical Records* (*Shiji*) have all become bestselling books, and the popularity of these classic works reflects the revival of traditional Chinese philosophy and culture among the population.
4 According to John Makeham (2008: 319), between 2000 and 2003, a private company, Beijing Sihai Children's Recitation of the Classics Recitation Guidance Education Center (*Beijing sihai ertong dujing daodu jiaoyu zhongxin*), had a total of 3.5 million students in several tens of cities who participated in recitation of the classics programs.
5 The playful narrative method has been widely used in creating contemporary Chinese novels, television dramas and films. In 1991, companies in mainland China and Taiwan co-produced the television drama *Playful Narrative of the Qianlong Emperor* (*Xishuoqianlong*). This became very popular and successful, which established an example that was followed by similarly themed literary and cultural products.
6 These bestselling books are widely read by contemporary Chinese readers who seek "quick tips" to enable a successful career and life in contemporary China's extremely competitive and harsh economy and society.
7 As Michael Nylan and Thomas Wilson have observed in *Civilization's Greatest Sage through the Ages*, "The 2006 PRC annual state reports speaks of 87,000 violent incidents involving one hundred people or more. Yu Dan nonetheless insists that the 'harmony'

advocated in the *Analects* can already be found in today's blessed PRC . . . citing PRC polls that claim the Chinese are happier than Euro-Americans – polls that contradict other polls conducted elsewhere" (2010: 221–222).
8 *Super Girl* was a famous idol selection program aired by Hunan satellite television. It is very similar to *American Idol* in content. The show was cancelled because it challenged state ideology.
9 Li Ao is a well-known contemporary Taiwanese liberal intellectual who was jailed for his critical and anti-government speeches and writing. Wei Jingsheng is a famous mainland liberal and radical figure who supports and promotes changes in the political system of mainland China. As a political dissident, he spent eighteen years in prison and currently lives in exile. Liu Xiaobo was the 2010 Nobel Peace Prize winner and one of the most famous political dissidents of contemporary China. He was imprisoned for his participation in the 4 June 1989 democratic demonstration. After he was released in 1991, he lost his right to make public speeches in the PRC. In addition, he was monitored and subjected to residential surveillance (1995–1996) and was forced to receive reeducation through labour (1996–1999). Liu is currently serving an eleven-year sentence, handed down in 2009 in mainland China for the crime of inciting subversion of state political power.

References

Bell, Daniel. (2008) *China's New Confucianism: Politics and Everyday Life in a Changing Society*. Princeton, NJ: Princeton University Press.

Billioud, Sebastien. (2007) "Confucianism, 'Cultural Tradition,' and the Official Discourse at the Start of the New Century" (Christopher Storey [trans]). *China Perspectives* 3: 50–65.

Billioud, Sebastien and Thoraval, Joel. (2007) "Jiaohua: The Confucian Revival in China as an Educational Project" (Nina Levin Jalladeau [trans]). *China Perspectives* 4: 4–20.

Billioud, Sebastien and Thoraval, Joel. (2009) "*Lijiao*: The Return of Ceremonies Honouring Confucius in Mainland China." *China Perspectives* 4: 82–100.

Chen, Jiaming (2011) "The National Studies Craze: The Phenomena, the Controversies and Some Reflections" (Stacy Mosher [trans]). *China Perspectives* 1: 22–30.

Detournier, Guillaume and Ji, Zhe. (2009) "Social Experimentation and 'Popular Confucianism': The Case of the Lujiang Cultural Education Centre" (Michael Black [trans]). *China Perspectives* 4: 67–81.

Ding, Weizhi. (1995) "Wanqing guocui zhuyi lunshu." (Comments on the National Essence Campaign of the Late Qing Dynasty) *Jindaishi yanjiu* 2: 1–16.

Dirlik, Arif. (2011) "Guoxue/ National Learning in the Age of Global Modernity." *China Perspectives* 1: 4–13.

Guo, Yingjie. (2004) *Cultural Nationalism in Contemporary China: The Search for National Identity Under Reform*. New York: Routledge.

"Interview with Yu Dan." (2009) *Time Out Hong Kong*, 26 Aug, accessed on 28 Jun 2014, available at: http://www.Timeout.com.hk/books/features/26750/interview-with-yu-dan.html

Kong, Shuyu and Hawes, Colin S. (2015) "The New Family Mediator: TV Mediation Programs in China's 'Harmonious Society,'" in Ruoyun Bai and Geng Song (eds) *Chinese Television in the Twenty-First Century*. Hoboken: Taylor and Francis: 33–51.

Leibold, James. (2010) "The Beijing Olympics and China's Conflicted National Form." *The China Journal* 63: 1–24.

Li, Jian. (ed.) (2007) *Zhuangzi hen zhaoji* (Zhuangzi is Deeply Worried). Beijing: Scientific Documents Press.

Li, Mei. (2007) "Dui jingdian lai yichang wenrou de egao – tan Yu Dan xianxiang." (Spoof the Classics – Reflect on the Yu Dan Phenomenon) *Dangdai xiaoshuo* 7: 54–55.

Li, Ying. (2010) "Yu Dan: meili ciyu de shengchanzhe – Yu Dan yuyan xianxiang fenxi." (Yu Dan: The Producer of Wonderful Words – Analysis of the Yu Dan Language Phenomenon) *Xiandai yuwen* 6: 158–160.

Li, Yue and Li, Fang. (2007) *Pipan Yu Dan: zhengshuo Lunyu zhihui* (Criticizing Yu Dan: Orthodox Interpretation of the *Analects*). Beijing: Democracy and Construction Press.

Makeham, John. (2008) *Lost Soul: "Confucianism" in Contemporary Chinese Academic Discourse.* Massachusetts: Harvard University Press.

Makeham, John. (2011) "The Revival of Guoxue: Historical Antecedents and Contemporary Aspirations." *Chinese Perspectives* 1: 14–20.

Meissner, Werner. (2006) "China's Search for Cultural and National Identity from the Nineteenth Century to the Present." *China Perspectives* 68: 41–54.

Naish, John. (2009) "Why Confucius Matters Now: When Yu Dan Updated the Ancient Sage's Teachings, She Didn't Expect to Sell 10 Million Copies – or to Anger Chinese Academics." *The Times.* 25 Apr, accessed on 21 May 2014, available at: http://www.women.timesonline.co.uk/tol/life_and_style/women/relationships/article616066

Nylan, Michael and Wilson, Thomas. (2010) *Civilization's Greatest Sage Through the Ages.* New York: Doubleday.

Song, Xianlin. (2003) "Reconstructing the Confucian Ideal in 1980s China: The Culture Craze and New Confucianism," in John Makeham (ed.) *New Confucianism: A Critical Examination.* New York: Palgrave: 80–104.

Wang, Dongcheng. (2009) "Yudan xianxiang: zhishifenzi de bailinghua."(The "Yu Dan Phenomenon": The "White-Colorization" of the Intellectuals) *Wang Dongcheng's Blog*, 22 Feb, accessed on 28 Jul 2014, available at: http://www.wlcguide.blogbus.com/logs/35557528.html

Wang, Junqi. (2007) "Chaoyue jingying yu dazhong de jinzhang: cong Yu Dan xianxiang kan chuantong wenhua de shenmeihua chuanbo." (Surpassing the Tension Between Elites and the Masses: Reflections on the Aesthetic Spread of Traditional Culture from the Yu Dan Phenomenon) *Dangdai wentan* 5: 50–53.

Wu, Zequan. (2008) "Dazhong chuanmei shidai jingdian de puji yu kaifa – guanyu Yu Dan xianxiang de fansi." (The Popularization and Development of the Classics in the Mass Communication Era – Retrospection on the Yu Dan Phenomenon) *Jining xueyuan xuebao* 29(8): 8–12.

Wu, Zequan. (2009) "Sanwen Yu Dan xianxiang." (Three Questions on the Yu Dan Phenomenon) *Website of the Post-Doctoral Research Station of the Chinese Academy of Social Sciences*, 28 Aug, accessed on 21 May 2014, available at: http://www.rsj.cass.cn/bshbgs/jl/200802/200802/rdts/wzq.htm

Yan, Cuiting and Yang, Cunchang. (2009) "Dazhong wenhua beijing xia de 'xueshu mingxing' xianxiang." (The 'Star Academic' Phenomenon in a Mass Cultural Background) *Jianyu kexue wenzhai* 3: 65–68.

Yan, Shenghua. (2007) *Kongzi hen shengqi* (Confucius is Deeply Angry). Beijing: Scientific Documents Press.

Yu, Dan. (2006) *Yu Dan Lunyu Xinde* (Yu Dan's Interpretation of the *Analects*). Beijing: Zhonghua Shuju.

Yu, Dan. (2009) *Confucius from the Heart: Ancient Wisdom for Thoday's World*, Esther Tyldesley (trans). New York: ATRIA Books.

'Yu Dan zhizheng: wenhua fuhao haishi liyi boyi." (Debate Over Yu Dan: Cultural Symbol or Profit Struggle). (2007) *Xinhua Net*, 29 Apr, accessed 28 Jul 2014, available at: http://www.cq.xinhuanet.com/news/2007-04/29/content_9928074.htm

Zhang, Min. (2009) "'Yule zhisi' de wenhua kuanglan – 2007nian wenhua xianxiang pipan." (The Cultural Tide of Entertaining to Death: Critique of the 2007 Cultural Phenomenon). *Utopia*, 28 Aug, accessed on 21 May 2014, available at: http://www.wyzxsx.com/Article/Class12/200803/34178.html

Zhang, Taopu. (2007) "Huaer weishenme zheyanghong? – Yu Dan xianxiang fenxi." (Why Are the Flowers So Red? – Analysis of the Yu Dan Phenomenon) *Nanfang dianshi xuekan* 2: 58–60.

Zhu, Ying. (2012) *Two Billion Eyes: The Story of China Central Television*. New York: The New Press.

6 A cultural reading of three contemporary Chinese revolutionary spy-themed TV drama serials

Undercover, *Plotting* and *All Quiet in Peking*

Introduction

As a recognized TV drama subgenre, the revolutionary spy-themed TV serial is unique within the contemporary Chinese media sphere. Similar to the majority of the Red classics and revolutionary-themed films and TV shows produced in the consumer-led marketplace, the subgenre follows an overall depoliticizing and humanizing trend. Moreover, the revolutionary spy-themed TV drama enlists suspense and mystery to surreptitiously serve its official ends through intrigue, thus hijacking the viewers into a position of dominant reading. This nuanced merging of official ideological discourse ("mainstream melody" or *zhuxuanlu*)[1] with highly skilled professionals and the thrills and fantasy associated with the dangerous job of spying embedded in the spy-themed TV narratives set in the revolutionary eras, reveals a new pattern of state propaganda. Furthermore, revolutionary spy-themed TV shows engage with topical social problems in contemporary China and graft them into the official ideology. Meanwhile, the revolutionary suspense TV serial coincidently generates an aesthetic public sphere where ordinary citizens are able to discuss and criticise civil and political issues, thus illustrating the subversive potential of the entertainment media in articulating doubts and criticism of the government. This chapter examines three popular revolutionary suspense TV drama serials – *Undercover* (*Qianfu* 2008), *Plotting* (*Ansuan* 2006) and *All Quiet in Peking* (*Beiping wuzhanshi* 2014) – which span the period from the War of Resistance against Japan, to the following Chinese Civil War, and into the early socialist period. This chapter will reveal the production mechanism of the revolutionary suspense drama, the contributing factors to its success, the nexus between this TV drama subgenre serials and official ideology, and its subversive potential to mirror the corrupt reality of contemporary Chinese society.

Since the Opening Up period, and coinciding with the overall decentralization and marketization of China's media industry, Chinese TV drama production has experienced significant growth. In particular, from the beginning of 1990s, the Chinese TV drama market in both volume and genre has been likened to witnessing "a hundred flowers blossom" (Zhu 2008: 9–10). In recent years, suspense TV drama, especially revolutionary spy-themed TV drama, has developed into a popular subgenre on Chinese television.[2] Generally speaking, suspense TV drama ranges from the criminal investigation type such as *Major Case Group Six* (*Zhongan liuzu* 2000), to pre-liberation (mainly civil-war-period) spy war dramas including *Undercover*, *Bloody Dense Fog* (*Xuese miwu* 2008) and *All Quiet in Peking*, to post-liberation counter-espionage dramas such as *A Pair of Embroided Shoes* (*Yishuang xiuhuaxie* 2003),[3] and *Silent Vow* (*Shiyanwusheng* 2003)[4]. The revolutionary espionage and counter-espionage TV serials specifically focus on depicting the struggles of the Chinese Communist Party (CCP) secret agents against Nationalist Party spies stretching from the War of Resistance against Japan to the subsequent Chinese Civil War and the initial socialist epochs. In its nascent decade when the revolutionary spy-themed TV drama subgenre emerged, the first espionage drama to achieve any substantial success was *Silent Vow* in 2003. This success was followed in 2006 by *Plotting*, which was very popular and created the enthusiasm for watching revolutionary suspense dramas. In 2009, *Undercover* initiated a new round of spy-themed TV show hits, which is reflected in the most recent release of *All Quiet in Peking*.

Due to the official suppression of criminal investigation TV shows, revolutionary suspense TV drama has filled the audience's need for this kind of entertainment. Revolutionary spy-themed dramas are not only popular but also considered to be a safer conduit for the media investors. In April 2004, the State Administration of Radio-Film-Television (SARFT, *guojia guangbo dianying dianshi zongju*) banned the broadcasting of crime dramas before 11 p.m. because of their overwhelming violence and sexual content, and, even after 11 p.m., only mild violence was allowed according to the new rules (Zhu 2008: 8). This suspension of crime dramas by SARFT created more space for revolutionary spy-themed TV serials to flourish (Hao 2008: 297), as these shows are considered less violent, yet they manage to retain the same elements of suspense that are attractive to the contemporary Chinese audience.

The contemporary revival of the spy-themed media texts and the social phenomena and cultural impact they have engendered both within and outside mainland China have been the subject of a number of studies. Haosheng Yang (2012) has, for example, studied three spy-themed commercial films (*A Time to Remember* [*Hongse lianren* 1998]; *Lust, Caution* [*Se, jie* 2007];[5] *The Message* [*Fengsheng* 2009]) to verify the romanticizing and sensualizing of revolutionary martyrs and national heroes in the post-socialist cultural milieu. In their efforts to renovate the canonized role models of the Communist cause and national salvation, these films delve into the buried memories of the revolutionary martyrs and patriotic figures through embellishing their erotic and quixotic experiences and by "stressing the essential role of Eros" in their lives (Yang 2012: 183), and this novel approach caters to the viewing expectations of TV and film audiences in China today. In another example, Shuyu Kong (2012: 6) examines the "affective alliance" between the popular revolutionary spy-themed TV drama *Undercover* and its fan community. Through an intriguing and creative engagement with the characters and plots of *Undercover*, its fan group activities provide an insightful illustration of the interactions and interrelationships of internet media, popular culture consumption, virtual community, and public space, which serve as a platform for the netizens to share their views regarding social realities and malaises of present-day China. Yang's and Kong's studies centre on the more innovative facets of the rewriting of the revolutionary past and the unexpected social effects it generated. Their research confirms that these cinematic and TV scripts have been uniquely shaped to reconfigure revolutionary history. They are unconventional in terms of their courageous and rare rehabilitation of the voluptuous elements and body narratives and their couched, almost hidden, reproach of the social unease of contemporary Chinese society.

While Yang's and Kong's work is concerned with highlighting the erotic and entertainment facets of the spy-themed movies, this chapter is more focused on the coded propaganda revealed in the revolutionary suspense TV serial. This novel mode of propaganda appears to indicate an innovative bond between the CCP official rhetoric and the commercial media entity – another pattern and reflection of a "mainstream commercial" discourse, to borrow Yang's (2012: 203) argument, which exploits suspense, mystery, thrills, fantasy and the aura of highly skilled professionals to capture the viewers with its "dominant" reading. Attention will also be given to how the storylines and plots of espionage in TV shows relate to key social topics, workplace relations and intrigues, corrupt officialdom, identity matters, and the desire for higher social status and its corresponding materialism. However, although revolutionary suspense TV serials construct a niche for conformist entertainment products, there also exists a seditious potential for mainstream-cum-commercial cultural products as they also function as an aesthetic public sphere where civic and political issues are discussed and judged by the general audience.

Plotting, Undercover, All Quiet in Peking

When *Plotting* was released in 2006, it became an immediate hit in China. *Plotting* tells three individual but correlated stories of CCP secret agents working during the War of Resistance against Japan, the Chinese Civil War, and the early decades of socialist China. The first story is about a young blind boy whose hearing is extraordinarily sharp, and his acute hearing ability enables the communist intelligence agents to decode wireless messages from the Nationalist Party. The second story tells of a female foreign-trained Chinese mathematician who successfully deciphers a high-level code which is being used by the Nationalist Party. The third story deals with a communist spy who worked within the ranks of the Nationalist Party before the liberation, and who eventually dies in order to carry out his objective and to pass on vital intelligence information.

In *Plotting*, An Zaitian, one of the main characters of the first two stories, is a gifted, courageous, composed, and well-trained CCP secret agent. Played by Liu Yunlong – an actor turned director, who is also the director of the show – An Zaitian is a man with a charming demeanour and appearance, and a brilliant agent who is versatile and able to complete various challenging covert operations. As a master of espionage, An Zaitian notices the blind boy and the mathematician and assists them to complete their tasks – tasks which play an important part in the

CCP's history. Qian Zhijiang, An Zaitian's father, is the lead male character of the third story. Qian works as a mole within the Nationalist Party, and his efforts are critical in the eventual triumph of the CCP revolution.

After its release in 2009, *Undercover*, another classic TV spy serial, became an audience favourite. Many lines and phrases from the show, such as "undercover" itself, have become popular with the Chinese people.[6] The plots of *Undercover* cover the period from the War of Resistance against Japan and into the civil war period. Patriotic college student Yu Zecheng joins the Military Statistics Bureau (MSB, *juntong*), one of the two principal intelligence organizations of the Nationalist Party, and, after he successfully completes an assassination mission, he gains appreciation and trust from Dai Li, the person in charge of the MSB. Just when Yu's career is steadily advancing and his future at MSB seems assured, he discovers that his fiancé, Zuo Lan, works for the CCP and that his supervisor Lu Zongfang is also an undercover operative of the CCP. After his supervisor sacrifices himself for the communist cause, and after struggling with his own painful dilemmas, Yu Zecheng defects to the CCP, taking the place of his former supervisor.

While Yu is working undercover in the MSB, the Party sends a female soldier, Zhang Cuiping, to play his wife in order to help the cover story of Yu's identity. Cuiping was born and raised in a peasant family and never received any formal education, while Yu Zecheng came from a well-off, well-educated background. Their different upbringings often lead to some mild and absurd humour. However, their common belief and loyalty to the communist cause brings them together, despite their dissimilar lifestyles and personal habits. Using their professional skills and previous experiences, they head off numerous disasters and complete all the tasks allocated to them by the CCP. In their everyday struggles with the enemy, they find comfort and companionship in adversity, and these two young, outwardly contrasting people build a strong friendship and eventually fall in love. After the founding of the PRC, Yu Zecheng is sent to Taiwan by the CCP to continue his undercover work, and another CCP undercover, Wanqiu, is sent to play his new wife, while Cuiping remains on the mainland to work and raise their child. The story ends here, and their reunion is left as the assumed conclusion.

All Quiet in Peking continues the trend of the revolutionary spy-themed TV drama. The show gathers together a group of fine actors; and although it focusses less on professional spying techniques and methods, and although the plots are less suspenseful and thrilling than *Plotting* and *Undercover*, *All Quiet in Peking* is still a compelling and intriguing spy-themed TV drama serial. Having shifted its focus from the contest of professional skills between the CCP spies and those of the Nationalist Party, the show's plots concentrate more on the psychological confrontation between the two parties. The storyline of *All Quiet in Peking* revolves around the currency reform plan promoted by the Nationalist Party just before it lost control of the Chinese mainland and retreated to Taiwan. Having predicted its unavoidable failure to win the Civil War, and in order to secure large amounts of gold and silver and repatriate it to the island, the Nationalist Party enacted the currency reform policy to raise money from the people. CCP and Nationalist

Party moles become locked in a battle to either implement or stop the plan. Two of the senior management personnel of the Peking branch of the Central Bank of the Nationalist government, Cui Zhongshi and Xie Peidong, who are really CCP undercover operatives, know the inside story of corruption within the financial system of the Nationalist administration. Fang Mengao, a young Nationalist military pilot who has defected to the CCP, and Liang Jinglun, a revolutionary and progressive professor of the Peking University who is actually a Nationalist Party mole, are selected by Chiang Ching-kuo (the elder son of Chiang Kai-shek) for the mission, code-named "peacocks fly to the Southeast," which is to secretly smuggle gold and silver to Taiwan. At the same time that the final decisive battle is about to break out between the Nationalist and the Communist forces, the CCP decides to peacefully liberate Peking in order to avoid civilian casualties, which allows the Nationalist government to safely transfer the money to Taiwan. Based on the Party's instruction, Fang Mengao completes the flight mission and continues to work undercover in Taiwan after the CCP assumes overall control of the mainland.

Revolutionary suspense TV serials in the post-socialist, post-revolutionary era

Within an environment of marketization and commercialization during the post-socialist and post-revolutionary era, a transformation ensued in the Chinese media sphere. These changes affected TV drama, which remained as a key component of Chinese media space; however, the media reforms did not reduce the media's function as a mouthpiece of the Party (Hong, Lu and Zou 2009: 47). In contemporary China, private and independent investors still need approval from SARFT to produce a TV drama serial. SARFT is thus able to manipulate the manufacture of TV shows according to their "suitability" of "serving the people" and "the government." The CCP promotes TV plays that epitomise the so-called "socialist mainstream melody" (*shehui zhuyi zhuxuanlu*) (Hong 2001: 32), and the government has consistently upheld the policy that TV drama is "an ideological enterprise," and therefore the Party must provide "guidance, management and supervision" (Hong 2001: 36).

The revolutionary spy-themed TV drama serial has emerged from this backdrop of CCP guidance of TV drama production with no clear evidence to suggest that the making of this subgenre is fostered or backed by the official ideological apparatus, since the investors are mainly private and since the shows are usually released via local TV stations. Nevertheless, what we can argue is that the acceptance of the revolutionary espionage and counter-espionage drama is largely due to a compromise or "cooperation" between the commercial market and the state (Hao 2008: 302). While it is clear that there is still some conflict within the TV drama industry, as commercialization confronts the "centrality of official ideology" with hedonist or individualist values, which oppose the moral tenets sponsored by the state (Hong 2001:33), the revolutionary suspense TV drama, to a large degree, finds ways to alleviate the tension between the commercial pursuits and the state by re-igniting feelings of collectivism and honourable principles.

This may be viewed as the commercial market "cashing in" on the "mainstream" discourse by repackaging the Red classics (*hongsejingdian*) and by utilizing its official canonical status while remaking it in a fashion that caters to the demands of the marketplace (Qian 2008; Liu 2010).

The revolutionary suspense TV serial is a good example of an up-and-coming mainstream-cum-commercial entertainment medium. By the end of 2009, the popularity of counter-espionage and spy-war TV shows had increased by 9.3 per cent among all TV drama genres in mainland China (Li 2009: 128). This unique type of TV show combines the suspense features of a detective drama with the idea of defence of country as propaganda. In 2001, the then Party secretary-general, Jiang Zemin, proposed the idea of a "rule of ethics" and called for the launch of "a new ethical and moral system based on patriotism, collectivism, Marxism, and traditionalism" (Guo 2006: 52), and the revolutionary spy-themed TV play is in line with Jiang's initiatives in that they foreground nationalism, heroism and a call for individual sacrifice for the country (Hao 2008: 290–312). In contemporary times, the propaganda machine of the Xi Jinping administration continues and is even stronger, and this particular TV serial subgenre stimulates a nostalgic mood for the socialist revolutionary past among the mass TV viewers (Wang 2009: 53; Gao 2009: 89–90). In the modern-day Chinese cultural market, nostalgic sentiment is motivated by the cultural producers and brokers as "a consumer-oriented cultural fashion . . . [which is] able to cultivate uncontainable imagination" (Zhang 2008: 147). Thus, the cultural appeal of the revolutionary spy-themed TV serial coincidently conjures contemporary Chinese audience's positive imagination about the CCP and its revolutionary past.

Moreover, the revolutionary suspense TV model is acceptable to the ideals of Confucian discourse that nurtures disciplined people who conform to rules for the sake of the larger society (Zhu 2008: 27). The work of spying and the role as an undercover agent commands outright submission, discipline and sacrifice of the underlings to their superiors, and of individuals to the collective and the country. In *Undercover*, *Plotting* and *All Quiet in Peking*, the CCP agents display unyielding self-control and total allegiance, and they are willing to forgo their own safety and interests for the CCP and their nation. In order to realize their ideals, they cannot enjoy a normal family life, and they cannot live with people they fall in love with – their mission must take first priority. They never doubt their superior's orders, and they always act conscientiously when allocating tasks to their underlings. Here, the guidelines for the spies provide a rationale for loyal and disciplined citizens which mirror contemporary CCP propaganda and ideology.

In mainstream Western suspense shows, there is usually a strong lead character, ably assisted by a group of highly competent associates who exemplify the ideals of heroism and humanism. Just as its Western counterpart exudes its own self-endorsed high cultural ideals, so too does Chinese revolutionary suspense TV drama allow the high ideals of the CCP dogma of patriotism and collectivism to be aired as high cultural norms. Rather than just relying on straight didacticism and hollow heroic images typical of Chinese mainstream TV and filmic works, the revolutionary spy-themed TV serials centre on weaving captivating, suspenseful and thrilling plots into the official discourse, which creates audience interest and enthusiasm (J. Zhang 2009: 36–37; L. Zhang 2009: 56–57). Heroes, in novels and movies, have always overcome countless dangers, and the crime sleuths cleverly outwit their most evil adversaries to provide the audiences with suspense, mystery and excitement. Drama, suspense and daring offer entrenched recipes to entertain the readers and audiences over and over again (Silvia 2002). While watching suspense dramas, viewers are guided to constantly interact with the unfolding plots and deliberate the probable progresses of the storyline, which brings their deductive and inductive powers into play. The audience receives pleasure from this sense of participation and involvement, while together with the characters they brave the overwhelming odds of success and survival. In *Undercover* and *Plotting*, the characters of Yu Zecheng and Qian Zhijiang are seen as indestructible icons of the world of spies and sleuths, masters of all the special spying skills required to undertake their mission, and experts in signals, code cracking and monitoring, decryption, surveillance and counter-surveillance, and assassination. Their range of expert skills usually has no intersection with the daily life of ordinary Chinese people, and they therefore act as conveyors of "unknown knowledge" and have an illuminating association with the viewers who form a relationship with the protagonists bordering on worship. The spectators envisage Yu and Qian overcoming every single threat and that they will complete all their undertakings effectively, although they are never certain as the odds of victory are always daunting. It is this feint doubt, mixed with prospects of triumph, which seizes and rivets the audience.

In *Undercover*, the suspense level of the serial is further increased by the role of Cuiping. The characters of Cuiping and Yu Zecheng could not be more different, at least superficially. They vary enormously in education, family and social credentials, and the way they act and speak are poles apart. The outward disjunction between the two (apparent but not real as they are bonded by a sense of purpose) often creates difficulties for them and increases the risk of exposing their identities. For example, when other military officers' wives dress Cuiping in a very chic cheongsam which reveals her legs, Cuiping is embarrassed, and, as she is ignorant of current dress fashions, she cries out, "Are you making fun of your mother?" Her inexperience at this social level – and with bourgeoisie fashion, along with her unrefined spoken manner – repeatedly lands herself and Yu Zecheng in trouble.

In another scene, Cuiping plays mah-jong with the officer's wives, who discuss lovemaking. Cuiping states that she most likes to make love on the slope of the mountains, and the vulgarity of her boorish remarks causes some social discomfit with the other women, and they burst into laughter. Every time Cuiping's social skills and mannerisms lead to her almost revealing her identity, the audience experiences the thrill of the moment together, and, whenever she manages to head off a misadventure, the viewers are contented by a state of amusing exhilaration about an expected event.

Likewise, in *Plotting*, one plot tells the story about the detention of a group of codebreakers affiliated to the Telecommunications Department of the garrison headquarters of the Nationalist Party. They are interrogated for three days in a vain attempt to uncover the true identity of a suspected CCP mole. Several suspects, including the CCP operative Qian Zhijiang, are unrelentingly questioned over this entire period. It is a scene of persistent psychological suspense, and the audience is filled with endless uncertainty, leading to a rousing and final crescendo of pain and pleasure. Similarly, throughout *All Quiet in Peking*, psychological confrontations, much like those in *Plotting*, are ever-present.

While viewing the shows, the audience not only experiences an orgasmic delight brought about by the suspense, thrill and gratification but also identifies with the protagonists as they subjectively read the plot "dominantly." Durleavy (2009: 60 [italics in original]) employs Hall's ([1973] 1980) concept of a "dominant" reading to explain viewers' responses and affinities with the white male police detective heroes in Western police drama:

> In the police drama, the "dominant" reading that is ingrained, and according to which compliant viewers are subjectively situated, is one of identification with the (usually) white, male, police detective hero. In accepting this "dominant" reading, rather than "negotiating" or "resisting" it as they might, viewers are invited to embrace the detective hero as *their* guardian of law and order, and forgive his "maverick" tendencies along with his individualised flaws. It is primarily through their intense identification with the detective hero that viewers are also positioned to *accept* the legitimacy of the "right-thinking" society he works to uphold.

If we transpose Durleavy's analysis of the "dominant" reading to explain the Chinese revolutionary suspense TV drama, we can see that viewers are passively manipulated by the "dominant" reading and that they compulsorily identify with the omnipotent and charismatic CCP spies. Consequently, the viewers are "positioned to accept" the beliefs and teaching of the official ideology the CCP spies advocate. When considering the impact of the "Red Classics" visual texts on Chinese viewers, Qian's (2008: 165) study reveals the following:

> Viewers were forced to adopt the dominant-hegemonic position of the creators; over time, they internalized the feelings and ideologies encoded in these works. In other words, the individuals were hailed into a subject position by the state.

Following this logic, we see that the watchers of revolutionary suspense TV serials are also summoned into a skewed view in which they are imposed to consent to the dominant official discourse which has been repackaged by the commercial TV shows. As the revolutionary spy-themed TV serial has become an established and popular TV drama subgenre in the contemporary Chinese cultural market sphere, the "dominant" reading, which is to identify with the iconic CCP spies, also becomes more entrenched and impressed and carves out more space for government propaganda.

Topical social problems as selling points of the revolutionary suspense TV serial

By engaging with topical social problems such as official corruption, informal workplace rules, bourgeois romance, identity crisis and middle-class/high-class lifestyle, the revolutionary suspense TV serial shows its performative aspect of mirroring social reality. This is not only a marketable selling point but also a new space for mainstream commercial entertainment products. The portrayal of venal officials in *Plotting*, *Undercover* and *All Quiet in Peking* is a double-edged sword in that it not only criticised the then Nationalist Party but also casts aspersions on present-day officials of the CCP government. In recent decades, corruption has been rampant in Chinese business and bureaucratic circles. Although the CCP administration has enacted several new laws and policies to combat corruption and although some high-level government bureaucrats were jailed or given the death penalty, the anti-corruption campaign has yet to prove effectual in effectively reducing official fraud (Chen cited in Guo 2006: 51; Zhu 2008: 37). In the literary domain, with the tacit endorsement of the state, and despite mild discontent expressed by official literary critics hinting that the genre is pushing boundaries (Morison 2009: 18–9), the bureaucracy depravity genre has swamped all literary formats and frequently made the bestseller lists (Yu 2004). Noticeably, the plot devices of officialdom literature that "set readers' pulses racing are underhanded power plays, hidden alliances and devious sexual favors" (Lim 2013: 27). Texts about official corruption deliver a panoramic picture of the unspoken rules of the Chinese official circle and are read by beneficiaries or victims of these routines as textbooks that offer useful and practical information and tips.

In a similar fashion, in contemporary TV drama narratives, the inclusive adverse trend within the Chinese officialdom is revealed. Yet, instead of setting the story in present time, the bureaucracy TV serials often travel back through time to recite and divulge the tainted actuality of Chinese officialdom. For example, historical costume plays that render and dissect the corrupt practices of the Qing government are much admired by the general audience. Another trait of recent bureaucracy TV shows is that they displace the political and social context of contemporary China with the bygone collective memories of a chaotic China ravaged by both the Japanese invaders and the debased Nationalist administration. In so doing, many sensitive themes, unspoken rules and derelictions within the official circle of contemporary China, which originally are very likely to invite censorship, become possible and safe for the investors. In *Undercover*, Yu Zecheng's beliefs in the Nationalist Party and the causes it is fighting for reach a breaking point when he sees the director of the MSB Tianjin Station use his power to confiscate and then extort antiques from a local businessman. Yu is further disenchanted when he discovers that the head of the MSB, Dai Li, is transferring his lover's personal belongings instead of military supplies during the heydays of the War of Resistance against Japan. He is also disillusioned when he sees the special envoy of Dai Li flirt with Japanese prostitutes.

In *All Quiet in Peking*, when Fang Mengao sees that fraudulent senior administrators of the Nationalist Party embezzle public money and food, he is confused and disappointed, and he ultimately defects to the CCP. In the same show, even the most steadfast follower of the Nationalist Party, Liang Jinlun, comes to understand that the perverse bureaucracy and its ensuing social injustice are the prime movers of the destruction of the Nationalist Party. The corruption that is revealed within the Nationalist Party in the revolutionary suspense dramas that persuaded its members, such as Yu Zecheng and Fang Mengao, to change their allegiance to the Communist cause and the CCP strikes a contemporaneous chord with today's Chinese audience who read between the lines of the TV texts and reflect on the corrupt social reality of modern-day China.

Similarly, the incorporation of modern workplace culture norms, with all their shrewd and cunning schemes and ruses, in the plots of revolutionary spy-themed TV serials is instructional to many contemporary Chinese people, who are struggling to understand workplace practices in many government and private enterprises (Wang 2009: 53–54; J. Zhang 2009: 36–37; Gao 2009: 89–90; Lu 2009: 114–116). The freshly devised CCP idols are gurus of office politics and bureaucratic power plays. They use flattery, duplicity, mischief-making, circumvention, backstabbing and any number of other "usual" strategies they need to achieve their missions. In *Plotting* and *Undercover*, both Qian Zhijiang and Yu Zecheng are shown as experts of these less-valiant methods which are used to trap and kill the enemy. For example, in *Plotting*, Qian Zhijiang frames Yan Jingsheng, a loyal Nationalist Party general, which leads eventually to Yan's suicide. Analogously, in *Undercover*, Yu Zecheng uses his guiles to ferment dissension among his colleagues and rivals at their workplace. Making use of the conflicts of interests among them, Yu successfully sets them at loggerheads. Waiting patiently, he lets his adversaries fight it out to exhaustion, and then Yu decisively catches them all. As high-ranking undercover agents operating in key positions in rival organizations, the role obliges the characters to be more hypocritical, sneaky and sadistic than their opponents in order to get the end result.

There also exists an identity issue relevant to the undercover characters in the revolutionary suspense TV serials. Undercover means under the cover of an assumed identity; so they have two identities. As Yu Zecheng remarks, "Every nerve I have is highly sensitive every minute I play another person." The undercover agents' constant need to change between roles and identities makes them susceptible to a crisis of identity. In other words, there is an asymmetry between their public identity and real beliefs and between their hidden identity and actual behaviours. This identity crisis echoes the dilemma and perplexity facing many ordinary Chinese who regularly find themselves struggling with their identities and asking questions about who they are and who they should be: whom do they really "identify" with? For instance, some government officials and cadres propagate the ideals of a noble morality to their underlings in the workplace while at the same time they are taking bribes and keeping mistresses; some Chinese act subserviently to their superiors in the workplace and treat their family members in a tyrannical manner at home in order to let off steam; some men act as dedicated husbands at home and perform as wild lovers in their mistresses' places.

In *Plotting*, *Undercover* and *All Quiet in Peking*, all of the Qian Zhijiang, Yu Zecheng, Cui Zhongshi and Xie Peidong characters are senior government executives of the Nationalist administration, and they live in the lavish style of people with such high status; however, for them, alongside and underneath this well-to-do lifestyle is the unceasing threat that their real identities may be exposed. Nonetheless, their resolute belief in the revolutionary cause enables them to cope in their clandestine roles, for there is rarely any overt sign of identity predicament exhibited in the shows. Why is it that they do not cultivate any ideas of betrayal? How is it that they relentlessly carry out all forms of villainy yet are so ethical when it comes to their own commitments in the CCP? Remarkably, in *Undercover*, the single identity crisis for Yu Zecheng seems to be at its most critical when he must choose whether he is a real or bogus husband of Cuiping. As an undercover agent, Yu plays Cuiping's husband, yet, when he falls for Cuiping and wants to be her real husband, he hesitates and questions himself. Would this role and identity makeover encumber their work together? Does this requirement go against the CCP rules on undercover work? At this point, Yu is unsure whether he is a disciplined Party member or a self-interested person who chases individual goals. Although Yu finally manages to marry Cuiping, their life together is suspended by Yu's departure to Taiwan where he continues his undercover work. In Taiwan, Yu is asked to form a new undercover family with another female CCP comrade, Wanqiu.

The lavish lifestyles, much coveted by many Chinese people, is another aspect of the revolutionary suspense TV plays. All of the three shows under examination in this chapter present to the viewers characters and scenery which are imbued with a certain elevated standard of living and a focus on the good things in life. *Plotting* and *Undercover* are set in Shanghai and Tianjin respectively during the national and civil war periods, and the shows have the characters' homes located in the foreigners district (Western or Japanese), as there were many concessions in both cities.[7] Similarly, *All Quiet in Peking* has the administrative bureaucrats of the Nationalist Party accommodated in traditional Beijing-style courtyard houses with high-quality furniture. Imported cars, pianos, Western cuisine and dance parties reflect a lavish style of living of the shows' characters, implying excessive living criteria and aesthetics. In so doing, the shows cater to the viewing anticipations and aspirations of the city dwellers of contemporary China, in particular the white-collar middle-class social echelon living in the metropolitan regions.

Together with a lavish lifestyle, the hint of bourgeois romance also adds to the allure of the revolutionary suspense show. In *Plotting*, the Western-trained female mathematician, Huang Yiyi, acts as a signifier of the middle-class eroticism in the early socialist era which promotes a stoic proletarian saintliness. Unrestrained by Maoist moral bindings, Huang Yiyi hunts her prey using the allure of sex, thoroughly flouting Party education and morality. When asked to comment on one of her male colleagues, she says:

> He is very careful but lacks courage and creativity. . . . I have cooperated with him on many aspects. At work, we operated in the same research group. In other facets, that is private. You can guess, anyway.

Huang Yiyi means of course that she had had sex with her colleague. Huang's openness and careless attitude towards sex and her sensuous demeanour and good looks counter any ascetic plebeian ethics and placate the expectancies of a contemporary Chinese audience who seeks more sensual delight. In the current Chinese cultural arena, feminine beauty and the female body, desires and sexuality have become a commodity which is much in demand, which is likewise evident in revolution-themed commercial visual texts which persevere in representing women as spectacles and sex objects (Qian 2010: 299) – for instance, in *A Time to Remember*, where the half-nude female body is used both as a promotion strategy and as a ploy (Yang 2012: 197), and in *The Message*, which is an erotic thriller that cautiously makes use of graphic sex and violence, in conjunction with its more predictable revolutionary subject, for commercial incitement (Yang 2012: 203). Also in *Plotting*, an extramarital love affair is commissioned to accentuate the middle-class passion, which is apparent in Tang Yina's (a female codebreaker) longing for Qian Zhijiang, her good-looking, married boss, who is coincidently also a skilled and charismatic spy. In one sequence of the show, Qian and Tang dance a tango which draws everybody's attention at a Western-style evening party. Qian's understanding of the tango illustrates the nature of the undercover work and his devotion to this profession and to the CCP:

> Tango is the wild passion emitted from desperation
> Man and woman with graceful bearing
> Keep distance between their upper bodies
> However there is peerless passion under their feet
> They move fast forward
> However they are hesitant
> . . .
> It is dance on the blade
> It is the cruelest but most romantic

Qian's dance and words produce a graceful, refined and dreamy image where the revolutionary passion and the bourgeoisie lifestyle merge together. Middle-class eroticism is also found in *Undercover*, one example being the budding extramarital liaison between Yu Zecheng and Wan Qiu, an heiress (and temptress) from a wealthy and illustrious family, who has much more in common with Yu than Yu does with Cuiqing. Wan Qiu even tells Cuiping that she must imagine and pretend that she is having sex with Yu when she and her husband make love.

In *All Quiet in Peking*, a love triangle is formed between two rich girls and Liang Jinglun, a Nationalist Party mole working undercover as a revolutionary and progressive professor. First attracted by his intellect and knowledge, the two girls are further enthralled by the image of a Communist utopia created for them by Liang. Fang Mengao and his younger brother Feng Mengwei, who are more striking and enjoy a higher social status than Liang, are deeply in love with these two girls respectively; however, the girls fall in love with Liang. Interestingly, within the three shows, all these love stories are doomed to have a sublime, politically correct ending. Huang Yiyi jettisons her voluptuous and sexual impulses and devotes herself entirely to work and succeeds in decoding an extremely intricate cipher with the highest level of sophistication ever used by Taiwan. Tang Yina's longing for Qian Zhijiang is aborted by Qian's death, which was necessary so that important intelligence could be passed on.[8] Wan Qiu's love for Yu Zecheng also ends in her submission to the CCP, and she is sent to Yanan. Eventually, Wan Qiu realizes her dream to (really) marry Yu and to undertake the undercover work with him in Taiwan after the liberation.

Aesthetic public sphere and unattainable nostalgia spawned by the revolutionary suspense TV serial

Based on the analyses of previous sections, the revolutionary suspense TV drama could on one hand be read as an official-cum-commercial device that trials how the media utilize the canonic leitmotif and subject of Red Classics; on the other hand this TV subgenre ingeniously implants topical social concerns of Chinese society in order to promote the show to the consumer audiences. Meanwhile, the recognition of this one-off TV prototype also produces an "aesthetic public sphere" where the general audience can confer about civic and political issues. This is of particular significance in China where the political rights of citizens are exploited by the governing administration. In this way the revolutionary suspense TV serial uses the past to satirize the present, illuminating the seditious flexibility of the show.

> Through sharing their aesthetic and viewing experiences, the fans of *Undercover* find a way to publicly discuss the politically sensitive topics of social injustice, corruption, public morality, and ultimately the meaning or meaninglessness of revolution. . . . *Undercover* fans do not simply accept the orthodox meaning of the text; instead, they appropriate and hijack its content to inject alternative meanings into its mainstream frame. In this crystallizing process of turning fan talk into a public forum, TV drama has become one of the most productive sites of discourse in contemporary China.
> (Kong 2012: 24)

Entertainment programs and cultural products were originally disparaged by Habermas (1991) and the Habermasian scholars, as they lacked political utility and weight; instead these intellectuals advocated for a true functional "political public sphere." According to these scholars, amusement programs and artistic commodities merely direct the audience's attention to consumption and enjoyment rather than fixing on serious civic issues; they fail to enhance civic education, and they decrease the viewers' time for involvement in civic activities (Postman 1986; Putnam 2000). However, in response to the Habermasian opinions, Wu (2011) echoes Jacobs (2007, 2011) by urging a revision of the conventional reading of public sphere. By merging and blurring the line between fact and fiction, and between news and entertainment, there emerges the foundation for the notion of an "aesthetic public sphere" (Wu 2011: 49). According to Jacobs (2007; cited in Wu 2011: 49–51), entertainment programing combines people's aesthetic experiences with their discussions about common concerns and serious social issues, which explains people's strong moral investment in cultural texts, and in this way people fulfil their most significant civic practices. In the case of *Undercover*, through the "affective alliance" (Kong 2012) formed between the fans and the TV show narratives, the fans fulfil their rights as politically functional citizens via the platform of the "aesthetic public sphere."

Apart from serving as a functioning "aesthetic public sphere," the contemporary Chinese revolutionary suspense TV shows share a common feature in that they arouse a nostalgic sentiment for the revolutionary eras among the viewers. However, when this revolutionary nostalgia jumps over the temporal space and reflects on contemporary Chinese social reality, it coincidently turns itself into a sharp satire of it. Boym (2001; cited in Lu 2007: 132) categorizes two nostalgia patterns: restorative and reflective nostalgia discourses, where "[r]estorative nostalgia stresses *nostos* and attempts a transhistorical reconstruction of the lost home . . . [whereas] [r]eflective nostalgia thrives in *algia*, the longing itself, and delays the homecoming – wishfully, ironically, desperately." Here, the revolutionary spy-themed TV serial could be interpreted in regard to both of these types of nostalgia. First, mainstream propaganda entrenched in the shows resonates with a restorative nostalgia which calls for the return of revolutionary traditions and beliefs. From the official perspective, the past could be and should be restored to carry on the patriotic, collective and devotional spirit espoused by the CCP ideology. Second, the serials also produce a reflective nostalgia that yearns for an idealized revolutionary memory rather than actually returning to the past.

There is, I suggest, a third nostalgia discourse that may be called unattainable nostalgia, which denotes a past worthy of longing for, yet it would contradict how the present reality is understood. In *Undercover*, *Plotting* and *All Quiet in Peking*, the audience is moved by the sacrifice made by the old-generation CCP revolutionaries who overthrow the corrupt Nationalist government and bring about a happy life for the ordinary people. However, when the audience grasps that the previous devious social existence under the control of the Nationalist Party essentially serves as a mirror image for the present unethical Chinese society controlled by the CCP, they seem to reach an understanding that the nostalgia is inaccessible. In other words, if the nostalgic past is reinstated, then new revolutionaries should stand up and bring down the current CCP government, which is just as corrupt as the Nationalist Party of old. In this case nostalgia is only partly imagined, a fleeting glimpse of some good old times, treasured but unattainable and unreachable.

An examination of both the "mainstream commercial discourse" and the subversive potential of the revolutionary suspense TV serial indicates that there is an emerging crisis of identity regarding the show itself. If the serial has within it an official propaganda purpose, it may also be read as a mirror image for the inequalities and the socio-political evils in contemporary China. The show risks alternative readings which may go against its original intentions. However, if the popularity achieved by the serial comes primarily from its enlistment of the past in order to satirize the present, the renewal of revolutionary ideas and memories conveyed by the show causes a nostalgic sentimentality for the socialist heydays. The dilemma in regard to revolutionary suspense TV shows is that they act as a broker between official propaganda discourse and market forces and consumer pursuits, which then leads to this crisis of identity. The financially successful revolutionary suspense TV show surreptitiously conveys a mainstream ideology which verifies the ideology-cum-profit ecology of the contemporary Chinese cultural landscape, where the audience passively receives official education while consuming the delight brought about by the commercial viewing process.

Conclusion

As an established TV drama subgenre, the revolutionary suspense serial is unique within the contemporary Chinese media sphere. Although different from "mainstream" dramas directly produced and openly promoted by the official propaganda machine, the subgenre's revolutionary context nevertheless gives it a similar undisputed eminence and aligns it with official ideology. Following the overall commercializing trend of the revolutionary-themed cultural products, and through the suspense, mystery and fantasy associated with spying, and by allowing the audience to "participate" in the skills and knowledge of undercover operations, the spy-themed TV serial set in the revolutionary eras has assured its popularity. By portraying the CCP spies as unbeatable, suave and charismatic, as Chinese "James Bonds," the shows move the audience into a "dominant" reading situation where they are intrigued and identify with the spy icon dedicated to the CCP cause. Furthermore, by merging topical social problems with the characters, plots and scenes, the revolutionary suspense plays cater to the viewing demand and aesthetic of the contemporary Chinese audience.

Meanwhile, revolutionary suspense TV serials have another reading, in that they serve to mirror the corrupt socio-political environment of modern-day China and offer an "aesthetic public sphere" where the Chinese public can practice their political citizenship and speak against the government. The rebellious potential of the revolutionary spy-themed play generates an alternative conception which divulges the identity dilemma of this TV subgenre. Should it be understood more as a Red Classic text enjoying canonic rank? Or should it be regarded more as counter-rhetoric to the official ideology? Or is it purely an entertainment media device? This subgenre, I would suggest, has at least three comprehensions. Whether they are interpreted simultaneously or separately is a question still to be answered. What is not in doubt though is that the juxtaposition of commercial needs and state propaganda pursuits occurs in this genre.

Glossary

An Zaitian 安在天
Ansuan 暗算
Beiping wuzhanshi 北平无战事
Cui Zhongshi 崔中石
Cuiping 翠萍
Dai Li 戴笠
Fang Mengao 方孟敖
Fang Mengwei 方孟韦
Fengsheng 风声
guojia guangbo dianying dianshi zongju 国家广播电影电视总局
hongsejingdian 红色精典
Hongselianren 红色恋人
Huang Yiyi 黄依依
Jiang Zemin 江泽民
juntong 军统
Liu Yunlong 柳云龙
Qian Zhijiang 钱之江
Qianfu 潜伏
Se, jie 色，戒
Shiyanwusheng 誓言无声
Wanqiu 晚秋
Xie Peidong 谢培东
xinzuopai 新左派
Xuesemiwu 血色迷雾
Yan Jingsheng 阎京生
Yishuang xiuhuaxie 一双绣花鞋
Yu Zecheng 余则成
Zhonganliuzu 重案六组
zhuxuanlu 主旋律
Zuo Lan 左蓝

Notes

1 In the cultural domain of contemporary China, mainstream / main melody (*zhuliu*/*zhuxuanlu*) narrative, be it literary creation or filmic work and so on, embodies the cultural expressions of the orthodox ideology endorsed by the ruling regime – the CCP. The mainstream / main melody discourse discussed in this chapter indicates the official, orthodox Party ideology of the CCP government, which carries on the revolutionary traditions of the Mao era and promotes the rule of the CCP and the spiritual heritages of socialist revolutionary China. The mainstream cultural narrative of contemporary China has been

undertaking a commercializing trend, which is best illustrated by *Founding of the Republic* and *Beginning of the Great Revival* (these two films are also under investigation in this book) – two commercial mainstream blockbusters. For more discussion, see chapter 2 ("*Founding of a Republic* and *Beginning of the Great Revival*: propaganda-infused blockbusters in present-day China") in this book.
2 In the early stage of socialist China, there was a tradition to produce suspense films, which are normally spy-themed and serve as a propaganda tool for the CCP to educate and control the Chinese people. These films, such as *Struggles in an Ancient City* (*Yehuochunfeng dou gucheng* 1963), *Secret Post in Canton* (*Yangchenganshao* 1957), focus mainly on espionage during the wars between the Nationalist Party and the CCP. Arguably, the re-emergence of the revolutionary suspense theme in the form of TV serial carries on the convention of this specific genre.
3 *A Pair of Embroided Shoes* is adapted from a hand-written novel of the same title, which was widely circulated among the Chinese population during the Cultural Revolution. The play foregrounds the tremendous courage and wisdom of the CCP public security workers in a battle with Nationalist Party spies on the mainland who seek the opportunity to cause trouble for the newly founded socialist government.
4 *Silent Vow* leads the first round of the revolutionary suspense TV serial hits which raise the interest of the viewing public towards this unique TV subgenre. The storyline of the show revolves around how a group of CCP counter-espionage experts detect and destroy the activities of the Nationalist spies on the mainland as they intend to assassinate the scientists who work for the CCP government to construct submarines.
5 Ang Lee's *Lust, Caution* is an adaptation of the famous Republican-era writer Eileen Chang's novella of the same title. The novel shocked Lee when he first read it due to its poignant depiction of the combination of patriotic passion and eroticism. Lee's work in bringing Chang's story to the big screen displays a deep psychological and sensual interpretation of the national heroes and martyrs, which is misread by many modern-day viewers as a pure drama of desire and sexual passion.
6 Kong (2012: 20) provides a sample list of "the best dialogue" from *Undercover*: "If you cut off their money supply, they will cut off your blood supply." "Their mouths sprout noble ideas, but their hearts only care about business." "They have taken so much money, they'd better run away before they get into trouble!" "If it weren't for these 'special perks,' who the hell would become an official?" "You see these two gold bars: can you tell me which one is clean and which one is dirty?" "Any government that ignores 'human relationships' will be short lived." "All the dynasties in the past, from Qin and Han down to Ming and Qing, were the same, so how will things be any different in the future?" For more discussion about the popularity of *Undercover*, see Kong 2012.
7 The pursuit of a lavish and glamorous lifestyle – which includes dressing, dining and decorating in Western fashions – constitutes a critical aesthetic inclination of the emerging Chinese middle class. For example, the nostalgia for old Shanghai – including its chic Western-style restaurants, cafes, department stores and architecture – leads to it being widely recognized as the oriental Paris.
8 Qian swallowed his prayer beads (he always has his beads with him) on which the intelligence is carved, and, when his wife (a CCP party member as well) failed to find the beads on his body, she knows that they are in his belly. Therefore, Qian's corpse was the only means to pass on the information at a critical moment.

References

All Quiet in Peking (Beiping wuzhanshi). (2014) Directed by Kong Sheng and Li Xue, co-produced by Bejing Ruyixinxin Film Company, Beijing Helichenguang International Culture Media Co., Ltd, Chuntianronghe Film and Television Culture Co., Ltd, and CTV Cultural Enterprise Company.

Beginning of the Great Revival (Jaingdangweiye). (2011) Directed by Huang Jianxin and Han Sanping, produced by China Film Group Corporation.

Bloody Dense Fog (Xuese miwu). (2008) Directed by Liu Yunlong, produced by Beijing Film & TV Serial Production Center.

Boym, Svetlana. (2001) *The Future of Nostalgia*. New York: Basic Books, 2001.

Chen, Zewei. (2006) "Zhongguo fan fubai zhanlue de xindongxiang." (New Trend in China's Anti-Corruption Campaign) *Liaowang Magazine*, published on 3 Jan.

Durleavy, Trisha. (2009) *TV Drama: Form, Agency, Innovation*. London; New York: Palgrave Macmillan.

Founding of the Republic (Jianguodaye). (2009) Directed by Huang Jianxin and Han Sanping, produced by China Film Group Corporation.

Gao, Wangjue. (2009) "Taojin huangsha shi jianjin – dui diezhanju de shuli he sikao." (The Fold Finally Appeared After Scouring the Sand: Reflection on the Counter-Espionage TV Serials) *Shitingjie* 3: 89–90.

Guo, Baogang. (2006) "China's Peaceful Development, Regime Stability and Political Legitimacy," in Sujian Guo (ed.) *China's "Peaceful Rise" in the 21st Century: Domestic and International Conditions*. Burlington, VT: Ashgate Publishing: 39–60.

Habermas, Jurgen. (1991) *The Structural Transformation of the Public Sphere: An Inquiry Into a Category of Bourgeois Society*. Cambridge, MA: MIT Press.

Hall, Stuart. ([1973] 1980) "Encoding/decoding," in Centre for Contemporary Cultural Studies (ed.) *Culture, Media, Language: Working Papers in Cultural Studies, 1972–79*. London: Hutchinson: 128–138.

Hao, Jian. (2008) *Chinese TV Drama: Cultural and Genre Studies*. Beijing: China Film Press.

Hong, Junhao, Lu, Yanmei and Zou, William. (2009) "CCTV in the Reform Years: A New Model for China's TV?" in Ying Zhu and Chris Berry (eds) *TV China*. Bloomington: Indiana University Press: 40–55.

Hong, Yin. (2001) "Meaning, Production, Consumption: The History and Reality of TV Drama in China," in Stephanie Donard, Michael Keane and Yin Hong (eds) *Media in China: Consumption, Content and Crisis*. Richmond: Curzon: 28–40.

Jacobs, Ronald. (2007) "From Mass to Public: Rethinking the Value of the Culture Industry," in I. Reed and J. Alexander (eds) *Culture, Society, and Democracy: The Interpretive Approach*. London, England: Paradigm: 101–128.

Jacobs, Ronald. (2011) "Entertainment Media and the Aesthetic Public Sphere," in J. Alexander, R. Jacobs and P. Smith (eds) *Oxford Handbook of Cultural Sociology*. New York: Oxford University Press: 318–340.

Knobloch, Silvia. (2002) "Suspense and Mystery," in Jennings Bryant, David R. Roskos-Ewoldsen and Joanne Cantor (eds) *Communication and Emotion: Essays in Honor of Dolf Zillmann*. Mahwah, NJ: Lawrence Erlbaum: 379–396.

Kong, Shuyu. (2012) "The 'Affective Alliance': Undercover, Internet Media Fandom, and the Sociality of Cultural Consumption in Postsocialist China." *Modern Chinese Literature and Culture* 24(1): 1–47.

Li, Hongling. (2009) "Shushuo fante/diezhan dianshiju." (On the Counter-Espionage TV Serials) *Shichang guancha* 12: 128–129.

Lim, Louisa. (2013) "Masters of Subservience." *New York Times Book Review*, 3 Feb, BR. 27.

Liu, Kang. (2010) "Reinventing the Red Classics in the Age of Globalization." *Neohelicon* 37: 329–347.

Lu, Cheng. (2009) "Diezhan ticai dianshiju zhong de nuxing xingxiang jiedu." (Circulation of TV Serial – Perception on the Female Figures in the Spy Themed TV Serials) *Dongnan chuanbo* 56(4): 114–116.

Lu, H. Sheldon. (2007) *Chinese Modernity and Global Biopolitics: Studies in Literature and Visual Culture*. Honolulu: University of Hawaii Press.

Lust, Caution (Se, jie). (2007) Directed by Ang Lee, produced by River Road Entertainment, Haishang Films and Sil-Metropole Organisation.

Major Case Group Six (Zhongan Liuzu). (2000) Directed by Xu Qingdong, Co-Produced by Hai Run Movies & TV Production Co., Ltd and Beijing Forbidden City Film Co., Ltd.

The Message (Fengsheng). (2009) Directed by Gao Qunshu and Chen Guofu, co-produced by Huayi Bros. Media Group and Shanghai Film Group.

Morison, Stephen. (2009) "A New Genre in Chinese Fiction." *Poets & Writers Magazine* 37(5): 18–19.

A Pair of Embroided Shoes (Yishuang xiuhuaxie). (2003) Directed by Xu Qingdong, co-produced by Chongqing TV Station, Chongqing Media Co., Ltd and Hai Run Movies & TV Production Co., Ltd.

Plotting (Ansuan). (2006) Directed by Liu Yunlong, co-produced by Sichuan Satellite TV Industrial & Commercial Corporation.

Postman, Neil. (1986) *Amusing Ourselves to Death: Public Discourse in the Age of Show Business*. New York: Penguin Books.

Putnam, Robert. (2000) *Bowling Alone: The Collapse and Revival of American Community*. New York: Simon & Schuster.

Qian, Gong. (2008) "A Trip Down Memory Lane: Remaking and Rereading the Red Classics," in Ying Zhu, Michael Keane and Ruoyun Bai (eds) *TV Drama in China*. Hong Kong: Hong Kong University Press: 157–172.

Qian, Gong. (2010) "Red Woman and TV Drama," in Christopher Crouch (ed.) *Contemporary Chinese Visual Culture: Tradition, Modernity, and Globalization*. Amherst, NY: Cambria Press: 295–315.

Secret Post in Canton (Yangchenganshao). (1957) Directed by Lu Jue, produced by Haiyan Film Studio.

Silent Vow (Shiyanwusheng). (2003) Directed by Mao Weining, produced by China Public Security Culture Media Co., Ltd.

Struggles in An Ancient City (Yehuochunfeng dou gucheng). (1963) Directed by Yan Jizhou, produced by August First Film Studio.

A Time to Remember (Hongse lianren). (1998) Directed by Ye Daying, produced by Beijing Forbidden City Film Co., Ltd.

Undercover (Qianfu). (2008) Directed by Jiang Wei and Fu Wei, produced by Dongyang Qingyu Television Culture Co., Ltd., Beijing.

Wang, Cen. (2009) "Bei xunhuan de zhuti yu bei guixun de xingxiang – cong qianfu dao diezhan dianshiju de wenhua yanjiu." (The Tamed Subject and the Disciplined Image: A Cultural Study on Undercover – the Spy Themed TV Serials) *Dianying pingjie* 23: 53.

Wu, Jingsi. (2011) "Enlightenment or Entertainment: The Nurturance of an Aesthetic Public Sphere Through a Popular Talent Show in China." *The Communication Review* 14: 46–67.

Yang, Haosheng. (2012) "Myths of Revolution and Sensual Revisions: New Representations of Martyrs on the Chinese Screen." *Modern Chinese Literature and Culture* 24(2): 179–208.

Yu, Kai. (2004) "Against Corruption." *China Daily*, 7 Jan.

Zhang, Jinhua. (2009) "Guochan diezhanju de yici huali zhuanshen – dui dianshiju qianfu de shenmei jiedu." (A Wonderful Turn of the Chinese Domestic Spy War TV Serials – An Aesthetic Analysis of Undercover) *Shengping shijie* 9: 36–37.

Zhang, Liang. (2009) "Duochong meili de diezhanju – qianfu." (The Multiple Charming Spy Themed TV Serials) *Dianying pingjie* 22: 56–57.

Zhang, Xudong. (2008) *Postsocialism and Cultural Politics: China in the Last Decade of the 20th Century*. Durham: Duke University Press.

Zhu, Ying. (2008) *TV in Post-Reform China: Serial Dramas, Confucian Leadership and the Global TV Market*. London, New York: Routledge.

Conclusion

The CCP's propaganda strategy of adoption and appropriation of mass entertainment vehicles to mobilize and manipulate the Chinese people to follow the Party rule and its ideology has proven to be extremely effective in the pre-liberation and the early stage of socialist China. From the Yan'an period, to the heydays of Maoist China, to the decade of the Cultural Revolution, folk performance arts and popular recreational artistic and cultural genres played a vital role in unifying the Party's demand for good publicity. This positive preaching requires a dominant and common faith in the CCP's legitimacy, authority and capacity to govern the country and to bring about well-being for the Chinese people and enthusiasm of the people to participate in socialist construction. Through participation in mass entertainment activities or by reading, listening or watching repetitiously, those prevailing mass recreational literary and artistic works, or folk-art performances, the official propaganda paradigm, and its upholding have been engraved in the minds of their audiences.

After entering into the post-Mao, post-socialist new era, where revolutionary passion receded and market logic and consumer rule paralleled the official ideology and became one of the prime pushing hands in modern-day China's entertainment industry, the previous prosperous and unmatched government-led, propaganda-driven mass entertainment sensation had lost its monopolizing and overriding position. Though "mainstream," or "main-melody," rhetoric is still employed by the Party propaganda apparatus in creating popular cultural products to spread the official ideology in favour of the rule and legitimacy of the CCP, its appeal and influences amongst the audiences have been greatly lessened and abridged. The revolutionary films that assumed supreme esteem during the Mao era evolved into a "mainstream / main melody" film genre in the 1980s, which does not garner overwhelming attention as its forerunner did, and which subsequently loses a considerable amount of volunteer filmgoers.

In order to retake its lost ground in the popular cultural domain, and furthermore to regain the leadership and impact of the official ideology in the "public opinion struggle" through enlisting mass amusing modes that are prevalent within present-day China's entertainment business, the Party's propaganda machinery, in collaboration with commercial media practitioners, remodels and renovates its publicity devices and vehicles. The case studies examined in this book map out to some extent the scope, degree and outcome of the makeover and progression of the mainstream propaganda discourse in terms of its merging, cooperation and "compromise" with the commercial features and ruses on both the traditional and the newly emerged media channels, which are basically found in popular visual media creations such as movies, TV drama serials, festival galas, online web documentaries and education and science programs.

All six independent chapters of this book detect some ingenious and active publicity strategies, techniques and conduits that have been used in an endeavour to recover and renew the Party's influence and ascendency in the popular media discursive space. This unmasking of the Party's efforts of control show the continuing endeavours made by the CCP's propaganda machine during the Jiang Zemin era and the following Hu Jintao and Xi Jinping administrations. As I have shown in the discussion throughout the book, Party propaganda continuously attempts to creatively engage with official ideology that focusses on promoting the legitimacy and efficacy of the CCP rule. Its main strategy is to appropriate various influential entertainment and popular cultural events and products that best illustrate the prevailing cultural patterns and aesthetic tendencies in the daily life of the Chinese people.

Through conducting a plethora of original, adventurous and sometimes "avant-garde" experiments, the mainstream propaganda rhetoric rejuvenates itself through "comedilising" and "starising" important historical figures, "feminizing" and "desacralising" the national classics, "secularizing" and "eroticizing" communist heroes, "rehabilitating" and "romanticizing" the Cultural Revolution, "sublimating" sports events, recounting military history in an enchanting but "slanted" manner, and poignantly and vividly appropriating traditional cultural emblems and relics. In summary, the Party propaganda paradigm renovates and revamps itself mainly via following a depoliticizing and commercializing path, thus converting solemn and tedious political and moral preachings into engaging and intriguing mass entertainment programs and activities.

These "risky" and unconventional efforts by the CCP propaganda apparatus point to some inventive and ground-breaking modifications in the propaganda strategies of the Party as it promotes the official ideology in a nuanced and natural way which provides greater appeal to the general public. During this transformation, the Party's strength of rule is supported by commercial mainstream blockbusters and online web documentaries; the core value system of the CCP government regarding its notions and principles of governing the country are conveyed by festival galas, and popular education and science programs; and the past accomplishments of the CCP, together with its revolutionary history and ethos, are revived by revolution-themed nostalgia and suspense TV drama serials.

These rewarding investments of collaboration with entertainment and popular culture forefronts the ongoing efforts of the CCP propaganda as it is resolved to hold onto "positive propaganda" through an intense "struggle for public opinion." In other words, the revitalized government propaganda discourse in China's profitable entertainment industry attests to the Party's will to keep controlling and deploying the thought and outlook of the Chinese people. Successive CCP governments, in particular the current Xi Jinping administration, have insisted that the Party should assume a dominant position in the ideological domain and securely grip the "cultural leadership" in the society. Compared to previous administrations, the Xi Jinping government appears to be heralding in a more energetic and stringent system of monitoring and disciplining its ideology.

Soon after Xi Jinping assumed the reins of power in China, he tightened control of the military and public opinion domains. Xi's crackdown on corrupt forces and his reshuffling of power within China's military arena has attracted worldwide attention. Meanwhile, his tightening of regulations pertaining to the ideological field also became clear, as evidenced in the new discipline rules enacted by his administration that were recently unveiled in order to ban "comments" which stray too far from the official line or which openly articulate "inappropriate" remarks on, or challenges to, the Party's key policies and directions amongst the CCP members. Those CCP members who "improperly" discuss government policies could be removed from their jobs and expelled from the Party. These newly enacted and implemented guidelines verify the tightening of disciplinary control by the Xi Jinping administration in the ideological domain. Xi believes that if the Party loses leadership and control over the ideological domain it will inevitably lead to mistakes. According to many political and cultural critics' understanding of Xi's opinion and directives relating to propaganda, newspapers, magazines, TV stations and websites should be run and managed by "politicians" who identify closely with official ideology and conform to its regulations and who further agree with the tightening trend of the government's control over ideological matters.

In addition to overseeing stricter regulations concerning the Party's ideology, the Xi Jinping government emphasized that the CCP cadres working on the propaganda front should strive forward with initiative in their promotion of the core value system of socialism along Party lines. Apart from enhancing the moral quality of the citizens, cultivating a healthy atmosphere including righteousness and dedication in the society, one of the most significant themes of Xi's directive on propaganda is that it should be strengthened in a correct political stand which firmly upholds the authority of the central government and spreads official ideology. In his remarks, Xi instructed the Party propagandists that "positive propaganda" should be foregrounded at this crucial historical stage as the CCP is facing unparalleled questioning and suspicion from the Chinese public. Therefore, to stimulate mainstream thought in the struggle of guiding and dominating public opinion is extremely vital. In implementing the mainstream ideology, propaganda should confidently espouse the validity and proficiency of the CCP rule and its association with the well-being of the ordinary Chinese people.

Moreover, Xi Jinping orders and envisages a more widespread, effective and competitive type of propaganda that is capable of assisting his government to consolidate the rule, lawfulness and reputation of the Party. In his speeches regarding the continuance of propaganda in the new period, Xi highlighted the significant role of the internet and the social networking media vehicles such as microblogging (Weibo) and WeChat (Weixin). Based on the latest statistics, China currently has 0.6 billion netizens, among whom 0.3 billion netizens engage in various forms of microblogging which generate 0.16 billion microblog postings on a daily basis, and those netizens who use WeChat produce 12 billion messages per day. The internet and its derivative mass communication platforms have become a major conduit of opinion exchange, combination and confrontation. The connection and interaction between the cyberspace and the real world have penetrated into the diverse aspects of social life and impacted the ruling environment of the Party and its ideological ecology. Under this overall situation, information transmission has become freer and multifarious, and the power of the new media to guide public opinion is expanding and escalating. In particular, many young-generation Chinese, who seek information from only the internet, seldom consult any traditional media outlets. Having recognized the challenge postulated by the new media, Party propaganda has to renovate and advance itself in order to become proficient in utilizing new media devices and techniques in its dissemination of mainstream rhetoric and furthermore to gain the initiative in the cyber battlefield of public opinion struggle.

One chapter of this book has tapped into the combined effort made by traditional mainstream media channels and online commercial media outlets to spread official ideology to the online audiences, which has been shown as fruitful and impressive. Other chapters of the book reveal how a diverse range of traditional and new media resources including TV, film and internet have been integrated to form a multi-pattern and multi-faceted positive propaganda structure. These popular and subtle propaganda devices and tactics conveyed by the mass recreational vehicles available in contemporary China's entertainment industry reclaim a fertile ground for the circulation of the Party's ideological discourse and catapult the "invisible" political publicity that appeals to and moves the general public. In so doing, the solemn and serious concepts and themes of mainstream propaganda are intelligently and skilfully embedded in the storylines, plots and details of film, TV and documentary narratives. These exploratory and progressive endeavours made by the official publicity machinery in collaboration with business media practitioners mark a watershed and a great leap forward in the trajectory of the CCP's propaganda work. In summary, this book has completed a comprehensive study of the government-led mainstream propaganda of modern-day China that is incorporated in China's thriving and profit-focused entertainment industry. The ambitious goal of the CCP to dominate the "struggle for public opinion" that continues in contemporary China's entertainment industry has been exposed to some degree by this book. Further research is desperately needed to explore the infiltration of the Party's "positive propaganda" into the cyberspace during the Xi Jinping epoch, which reflects the novel characteristics and spotlights of the CCP's propaganda discourse.

Glossary

Weibo 微博
Weixin 微信

Index

Academy of Chinese Culture (*Zhongguo wenhua shuyuan*) 109
affective alliance 128, 140
All Quiet in Peking (TV drama) 10, 127–8, 130, 132, 134; nostalgia 140; topical social problems 135–7, 139
Analects 123n3, 123n7; Yu Dan's elaboration of 10, 106–7, 112–15, 116–18, 121
anti-Japanese TV series (*kangrishenju*) 96Au
An Zaitian 129–30
architect state model 84
Association of Chinese Journalists 86
Autumn Gala: CCTV 19–21, 22, 24, 26–9, 32–3

Baby, Angela (Yang Ying) 44, 50
Ba Jin 78n3
Barme, Geremie 63, 68, 78n4, 91
Battle of Pingxingguan 98
Battle of Taierzhuang 53, 98
"Beautiful Chinese Dreams" (song) 32–3
Beginning of the Great Revival (film) 9, 38, 41–4; conformist approach to reconstructing historical figures 47–51; heretical approach to reconstructing historical figures 51–3
Bei Dao 120n4
Beijingers in New York (TV drama) 91, 102–3n6
Beijing Municipal Publicity Department 94
Beijing TV Station (BTV): collaboration with Sohu Web 94–6, 100
Bell, Daniel 116–17
Bid for the Olympic Games (documentary) 93–4
Blackie Ko (Ke Shouliang) 93, 103n7
Bloom of Youth (TV drama) 10, 59, 63; revolutionary nostalgia 67, 71–2, 74–5, 78n6

Brady, Anne-Marie 8, 24, 34, 44
Bulletin Board Services (BBS) 23, 85

Cai E 50–1
Cannes International Film Festival 48
Cao Guilin 102n6
CCTV *see* China Central Television (CCTV)
Central Committee of the Communist Party Archives Bureau 95
Central Committee of the Communist Party History Research Office 95
Chahar 97
Chan, Jackie (Cheng Long) 29–31, 44
Chen Daoming 44
Chen Duxiu 46, 107
Cheng Long (Jackie Chan) 29–31, 44
Chen Kaige 43, 48–9, 63
Chen Kun 49–50
Chiang Ching-kuo 45, 49–50, 131
Chiang Kai-shek 44–6, 103n9, 131
Chicken Soup for the Unsinkable Soul (*Xinling jitang*) 112, 113, 123n6
China Can Say No (Song Qiang) 18
China Central Television (CCTV): Autumn Gala 19–21, 22, 24, 26–9, 32–3; *Lecture Room* 106, 112, 116, 118–21, 123n1; Mid-Autumn Festival 9, 15, 19–21; Moon Festival Gala series 9, 15, 19–21; Spring Festival Gala 19, 21–2, 33, 52, 56n8; Yu Dan using 119–21
China Film Group Corporation (CFGC) 42
China Online Media Forum 86
Chinese Civil War 51, 86, 97, 127–30, 137
Chinese Communist Party (CCP): *Beginning of the Great Revival* (film) 41–4; CCTV programs 19–21; ethnic attraction of the moon 23–5; *Founding of a Republic* (film) 41–4; ideology and collective memory 77–8n1; media

152 *Index*

manipulation 83–6, 100–101; merging ideology with arts 1–6; Moon Festival Gala on CCTV 21–3; nationalism as lifeblood of 15–19; nationalist themes of nostalgia and love 25–9; revolutionary films 39–41
Chinese Confucius Research Institute (*Zhonghua Kongzi yanjiusuo*) 109
Chinese dream: Xi Jinping 20, 23, 29, 32–4
Chou, Jay (Zhou Jiehun) 27, 35n4–5
Chow, Stephen (Zhou Xingchi) 43
Chow Yun-fat (Zhou Runfa) 44, 46, 47, 56n5
"clean officials" 7
collective memory: CCP ideology 77–8n1; Cultural Revolution 10, 59–62, 75–6; pastism 60–1; presentism 60; TV-constructed 62–4
collectivism 131–2
conformist method: reconstructing historical figures 47–51
Confucianism 46, 63; bottom-up 111, 119, 121; Confucian learning 108; criticism against 107; culture and 110; dual role for government 109; Jiang Qing promoting 111; Lujiang Cultural Education Centre 110; national essence campaign 108; New 108–9; propaganda tool 18; Yu Dan 106, 111, 114, 117–21, 122
Confucius from the Heart: Ancient Wisdom for Today's World (Yu Dan) 10, 106–7, 113, 115–19
"Country" (song) 29–31
creative industries 84
Crimson Romance (TV drama) 10, 59, 63; revolutionary nostalgia 67, 69–71, 74–5, 78n6
crosstalk (*xiangsheng*) 1, 2, 51–3, 56n9, 78n2
Cuiping 130, 133, 137–8
Cui Zhongshi 131, 137
Cultural and History BBS (bulletin board service) 23
cultural-cum-state nationalist discourse 29–33
cultural governance 5, 7
cultural leadership 3, 11, 84, 149
cultural nationalism 9, 15, 17–19, 22, 26–7, 29, 34
Cultural Revolution 2–3, 6; Chinese Communist Party (CCP) 108; collective memory 10, 59–62, 75–6;

educated youth 64, 78n6; *Farewell My Concubine* (film) 48, 63; *In the Heat of the Sun* (film) 78n5–6; Misty Poems 88, 102n4; performance arts 147–8; popular postmodern recollection of 67–75; radical and social nostalgia 64–6; Scar Literature 10, 62, 76, 78n3, 79n11; sexuality 69, 73–5, 78n5; TV-constructed collective memory 62–4; xiangsheng's role in criticising 78n2

Dai Li 130, 136
Deng Xiaoping 17, 62, 65, 108
Duan Qirui 52
Du Weiming 109
Du Yuesheng 49

economy: free market system 5, 41
educated youth: Cultural Revolution 64, 78n6
Eight Model Operas 3

Falun Gong 22
Fan Bingbing 44
Fang, Vincent (Fang Wenshan) 27–8, 35n5
Fang Keli 109
Fang Mengao 131, 136, 139
Fang Mengwei 139
Fang Wenshan (Vincent Fang) 27–8, 35n5
Fan Wei 52–3, 56n8
Farewell My Concubine (film) 48, 63
Feng Gong 52–3
Feng Guozhang 52–3
Feng Xiaogang 49, 52, 56n7
Feng Yuxiang 48
film industry: *Beginning of the Great Revival* (film) 41–4; blockbusters for propaganda 53–4; China 41; *Founding of a Republic* (film) 41–4; rehabilitating reputation of historical figures 44–6; revolutionary films 39–41
Five-anti Campaign 88, 102n2
Flying Over: Annotation to the Year of Return (documentary) 93
Forbidden City 71
Founding of a Republic (film) 9, 38, 41–4; conformist approach to reconstructing historical figures 47–50; heretical approach to reconstructing historical figures 51–3; profitable blockbuster 56n6
free market economic system 5, 41

Gang of Four 3, 62, 78*n*2
Ge You 52, 56*n*7
Global War against Fascism 95
Great Famine 60, 78*n*1, 102*n*3
Great Leap Forward 9, 54, 60, 88, 102*n*3, 150
Great Wall 18, 78*n*4, 89
Gu Cheng 102*n*4
Gu Mu 109
Guo Degang 53, 56*n*9
Guo Jihong 21
Guo Yan 102*n*6

Hai Yan 78*n*3
Han Han 30
Han Sanping 42
harmonious society 20, 25; CCP 94; Hu Jintao 6, 23–4, 35*n*2; Moon Festival Gala 23–5, 29; Moon Festival Galas 25, 29, 32, 34; Yu Dan 114–15
harmony 18, 73, 101, 109, 123*n*7
Hebei 19, 97
heretical approach: reconstructing historical figures 51–3
He Yunwei 53
history: CCP 38–40, 42, 65; conformist approach to reconstructing historical figures 47–51; heretical approach to reconstructing historical figures 51–3; Hong Kong 93; Mao 79*n*11; nostalgia in TV dramas 67–75; popular 10, 59–61, 63–7, 75; postmodern recollection of Cultural Revolution 67–75; rehabilitating reputation of historical figures 44–6; *Search for Modern China* 83, 87–94, 100; socialist China 39, 83–4, 92; Sohu Web 103*n*8; television's construction of 60–1, 75–6; Xi'an Incident 103*n*9
Hooligan Literature 68–70
Hou Baolin 2
Houston International Film Festival 20–1
Huang Jianxin 42–3
Huang Yiyi 137–9
Hu Jintao: harmonious society 6, 23–4, 35*n*2; nationalism 17, 18; PRC anniversary 88; propaganda 107, 148
Hu Shi 46, 107

imagined community 22, 24
In the Heat of the Sun (film) 63, 78*n*5–6

Jameson, Fredric 60, 64, 66
Japan: War of Resistance against 10, 60, 83, 86, 94–100, 127–30, 136

"Jiang Cheng Zi" (song) 26–7
Jiang Baili 51
Jiang Jieshi 45
Jiang Jingguo 45
Jiang Qing 3, 111
Jiang Wen 63, 78*n*5, 103*n*6
Jiang Zemin 17, 35*n*1, 84–5, 132, 148
Ji Lianhai 119, 123*n*1

Kangxi (Emperor) 6
Ke Shouliang (Blackie Ko) 93, 103*n*7
Kingsley, Edney 8
Kong Shuyu 128–9, 143*n*6

Land Reformation 88
Lao Nie 114
Lao She 2
Lau, Andy (Liu Dehua) 30, 44, 50–1
Lau, Jeffrey 56*n*5
Lecture Room (CCTV program) 106, 112, 116, 118–21, 123*n*1
Lee, Ang 21, 143*n*5
Leibold, James 106
Li, Jet (Li Lianjie) 44
Liang Jinglun 131, 136, 139
Liang Qichao 107
Li Ao 121, 124*n*9
Li Dazhao 46
Li Fang 117
Li Jing 53
Li Lianjie (Jet Li) 44
Li Ruihuan 6
literature: classical 110; folk 1–3; Hooligan 68–70; Scar 10, 62, 76, 78*n*3, 79*n*11
Little Fengxian 50
Little Red Books: Mao 65, 106
Liu Dehua (Andy Lau) 30, 44, 50–1
Liu Nianchun 4
Liu Xiaobo 111, 121, 124*n*9
Liu Xinwu 78*n*3
Liu Yuanyuan 29
Liu Yunlong 44, 51, 129
Li Yuanhong 52
Li Yue 117
Li Zehou 116
lofty-noble-perfect images (*gaodaquanxingxiang*) 51
love: theme of state nationalism 25–9
Lujiang Cultural Education Centre 110
Luo Changpei 2
Lust, Caution (film) 128, 143*n*5
Lu Xun 46, 115, 121
Lynch, Daniel C. 8

mainstream/main melody (*zhuliu/zhuxuanlu*) genre 3–11; CCP propaganda 39–41; paradigm 12n2; Party ideology 55n1, 142–3n1; propaganda 3, 7–8, 38–9
Makeham, John 123n4
Mang Ke 102n4
Mao Zedong 2, 46, 52, 78n7, 79n8, 97, 102n2; Little Red Books 65, 106; Maoism 16, 87
Marriage Law 2
Marxism 15–16, 40, 87, 118, 132
May Fourth Movement 25, 44, 46, 107, 111, 115
"May You Live Long" (song) 28
media: CCP manipulation 83–6, 100–101; People's Republic of China (PRC)'s control of 84–5; socialist China 83–4
Mid-Autumn Festival Gala: CCTV 9, 15; CCTV signature program 19–21
military channel: Sohu Web 95, 103n8
Military Statistics Bureau (MSB) 130, 135–6
mine warfare 98–9, 103n10
Ministry of Information Industry (MII) 85
Misty Poems 88, 102n4
moon 34; ethnic attraction of 23–5
"Moon Enchanting Bird" (song) 24–5
Moon Festival Gala series 9, 15, 35n3; CCTV signature program 19–21; cultural-cum-state nationalism 29–33; ethnic attraction of moon 23–5; ideology of political leadership 33–4; softened state propaganda 21–3; spreading ideology 33–4
"Moonlit Night on Spring River" (song) 25
Mou Zongsan 109
music 20, 71, 74, 88: Chinese style of 27–8, 35n4–5; nostalgia 89; popular 24, 29, 89
musical storytelling art of Suzhou 1–2
"My Requirement Is Not That High" (song) 33

National Conference for Cinematic Production 3
national essence 2, 107–8, 110, 116
nationalism 9, 15; Chinese commercial media 83–4; cultural 9, 15, 17–19, 22, 26–7, 29, 34; cultural-cum-state discourse 29–33; as lifeblood of Party-state 15–19; nostalgia and love themes 25–9; popular 17–18, 100, 110; propaganda in new post-socialist era 86–7, 102n1; state 15–18, 29, 32, 83, 94

Nationalist Party 16, 44, 46, 48, 72; CCP competing with 86, 143n2–3; Chiang Kai-shek 103n9;
codebreakers 134; rule of mainland 108, 130–1; TV serials criticising 135–7, 139–41; War of Resistance against Japan 95–7, 99–100, 128, 129
national learning 108
national studies craze 10, 106, 107–11, 121–9
New-authoritarianism 132
New Confucianism 108–9
New Culture Movement 46
New Left 6, 132
New Storytelling Movement 2
New Yangge Movement 1
North Song Dynasty 26
nostalgia: Cultural Revolution 64–6; music 89; restorative and reflexive 140–1; revolutionary suspense 139–41; theme of state nationalism 25–9; TV drama genre 10; *see also* revolutionary nostalgia
Nylan, Michael 123n7

Olympic Games 8, 22, 88, 93–4
Opening Up reforms 16, 39–40, 67, 84, 86, 88, 92, 108, 127

A Pair of Embroided Shoes (TV drama) 128, 143n3
pastism: collective memory 60–1
patriotism 10, 16, 21, 31, 94, 100, 108, 132; new post-socialist era 86–7, 102n1
peach blossom garden 20
Peking Opera 1; CCP using 2–3; film stars and directors 42
People's Liberation Army 8, 17, 39, 52
People's Republic of China (PRC) 1–2; films released in sixtieth anniversary of 41–4; founding of 59, 64, 84, 86, 90, 102n2, 130; Hong Kong's allegiance to 30, 50, 93; Liu Xiaobo 124n9; media control 84–5; polls 123n7; sixtieth anniversary of 9, 22, 38, 41–4, 64, 87–8
The Pillar Standing in Midstream (documentary) 10, 83, 94–100
A Place Where Dreams Start (TV drama) 10, 59, 63; revolutionary nostalgia 67, 70–1, 74–5, 78n6
playful narrative (*xishuo*) 112, 123n5
Plotting (TV drama) 10, 128–30, 132–4; nostalgia 140; story line 51; topical social problems 135–8

popular nationalism 17–18, 100, 110
positive propaganda 3–4, 7, 11, 12n3, 39, 148–50
presentism: collective memory 60
propaganda: cultural-cum-state nationalism 29–33; festival galas 33–4; merging ideology with arts 1–6; Moon Festival Gala as platform 21–3; nationalism 86–7; nationalism as, in new post-socialist era 86–7; patriotism 86–7; patriotism as, in new post-socialist era 86–7
public opinion, struggle for 4–5, 11, 16, 148, 150
public opinion guidance 4, 16

Qian Zhijiang 130, 133–4, 136–9
Qing Dynasty 19, 45, 50, 108
Qingping ode 27, 28
Qiqihar 102n1
Qufu 109

Rafting – The Yangzi River Flows East (documentary) 92–3
Red Classics 10, 41, 65, 127, 132, 134, 139, 141
Remi Award 20, 21
Research on Guoxue (*Guoxue yanjiu*) (journal) 109
revisionist Qing dramas 6–7
revolutionary films 1, 3, 5, 39–40, 147; CCP propaganda 39–41
revolutionary nostalgia: *Bloom of Youth* 10, 59, 63, 67, 71–2, 74–5, 78; *Crimson Romance* 10, 59, 63, 67, 69–71, 74–5, 78n6; genre 10; *A Place Where Dreams Start* 10, 59, 63, 67, 70–1, 74–5, 78n6; revolutionary ideals 39, 71, 73, 141
revolutionary suspense TV drama 10–11, 127–9; aesthetic public sphere and unattainable nostalgia 139–41; post-socialist post-revolutionary era 131–5; *Silent Vow* 128, 143n4; topical social problems as selling points 135–9
Rich Dad, Poor Dad (Fubaba, qiong baba) 112, 113, 123n6
"Riding the Wind" (song) 31–2
River Elegy (documentary) 63, 78n4, 108, 123n2
romance: propaganda 9, 15, 19, 22, 25–6, 28; social problems 135, 137; TV drama 65, 68–9, 72–5

Scar Literature 10; authoritarian rule of Mao 79n11; Cultural Revolution and 62, 76; emergence 78n3
Schneider, Florian 7
The Search for Modern China (documentary) 10, 83, 87–94, 100
sexuality: Cultural Revolution 69, 73–5, 78n5; social problems in TV serials 128, 135–40, 143n5
Shanxi 97
Silent Vow (TV drama) 128, 143n4
Sina Web: online news portal 23, 85–6
Sino-American Association of Science, Technology and Cultural Exchange 4
soccer 88, 91–2; *Soccer: A Game and a Dream* (documentary) 91–2
socialism: advancement of 56n2; CCP's ideology 149; Chinese characteristics 18, 115; contemporary China 38; state ideology of 17–18
Sohu Web: Beijing TV (BTV) collaboration with 94–6, 100; *Bid for the Olympic Games: Current Roaring in the Carnival* (documentary) 93–4; documentary programs 10, 83, 87; *Flying Over: Annotation of the Year of Return* (documentary) 93; military channel 95, 103n8; nationalism 86–7, 92, 102n1; patriotism 86–7, 102n1; *Rafting – The Yangzi River Flows East* (documentary) 92–3; *Search for Modern China* (documentary) 83, 87–9, 100; *Soccer: A Game and a Dream* (documentary) 91–2
Song Qiang 18
Soviet Union 46, 70, 72
Spielberg, Steven 21
sports: games and events 89–92; national pride 89–91; Olympic Games 8, 22, 88, 93–4; rafting 92–3; soccer 88, 91–2; table tennis 89–90
Spring Festival Gala: CCTV 19, 21–2, 33, 52, 56n8
State Administration of Radio-Film-Television (SARFT) 128, 131
State Council Information Office (SCIO) 85
State Council's News Office 86
state nationalism 15–18, 29, 32, 83, 94; nostalgia and love themes 25–9
Stockmann, Daniela 8
storytelling 1, 2, 112
struggle for public opinion 4–5, 11, 16, 148, 150

Su Dongpo (Su Shi) 112
sun 34
Sun Yet-sen 45
Sun Yuanming 116
Sun Zhongshan 45
Super Girl (reality show) 120, 124n8
Su Shi (Su Dongpo) 26, 28–9
Suzhou: musical storytelling art 1–2

table tennis 89–90
Tangshan Earthquake 88
Tang Yina 138–9
Tao Yuanming 20, 112
Telecommunications Department: Nationalist Party 134
television: *All Quiet in Peking* 127–30, 132, 134, 135–7, 139–40; anti-corruption 7; *Bloom of Youth* 10, 59, 63, 67, 71–2, 74–5, 78; collective memory of Cultural Revolution 62–4, 75–6; construction of histories 60–1; *Crimson Romance* 10, 59, 63, 67, 69–71, 74–5, 78n6; mainstream ideology in 5–9; *A Place Where Dreams Start* 10, 59, 63, 67, 70–1, 74–5, 78n6; *Plotting* 127–30, 132–8, 140; radical and social nostalgia of Cultural Revolution 64–6; *River Elegy* (documentary) 63, 78n4, 108, 123n2; sexuality in serial dramas 128, 135, 137–9, 143n5; *Undercover* 127–30, 132–40
Teng Wenji 63
"A Thousand Rivers" (song) 27–8
Three-anti Campaign 88, 102n2
Tiananmen Square: 1989 demonstrations 4, 6, 16, 40, 60, 65, 86–7; collective memory 77n1; commemoration of 88; post- era 5–6, 17, 63
A Time to Remember (film) 128, 138
Transport Security Movement 2
The True Story of Ah Q (A Q zhengzhuan) 115
tunnel warfare 98–9, 103n10
Tu Weiming 109

Undercover (TV drama) 10, 127–8, 130, 132–3; aesthetic public sphere 139–40; dialogue 143n6; topical social problems 135–8

Wang Dongheng 121
Wang Fei (Wong, Faye) 28–9
Wang Junqi 121
Wang Qiming 91, 102–3n6
Wang Shuo 68–9
Wang Xing 96
Wanqiu 130, 137, 137–9, 142
War of Resistance against Japan 10, 60, 83, 86, 94–100, 127–30, 136
Wei Jinsheng 121, 124n9
Wilson, Thomas 123n7
Win Honour: To Conquer the Enemy with Twelves Smashes of the Ball (documentary) 89–90
witty skits (*xiaopin*) 51–3, 56n8
Wong, Faye (Wang Fei) 28–9
Woo, John (Wu Yusen) 44
World Table Tennis Games 89–90
Wu, Daniel (Wu Yanzu) 46
Wu Gate of Forbidden City (*wumen*) 71
Wu Yanzu (Daniel Wu) 46
Wu Yusen (John Woo) 44

xiangsheng (crosstalk) 1, 2, 51–3, 56n9, 78n2
Xi'an Incident (Xianshibian) 97, 103n9
Xiannong Temple of Beijing 71
Xiaofengxian (Little Fengxian) 50
xiaopin (witty skits) 51–3, 56n8
Xie Jin 62
Xie Peidong 131, 137
Xi Jinping: CCP propaganda 3–5, 15–16; Chinese dream 20, 23, 32; mainstream media corporations 42; nationalism 15–18; propaganda 21, 34, 39, 107, 132, 148–50
Xinhai Revolution (1911) 44–5
Xu Lin 51

Yan'an Forum on Literature and Art 12n1, 56n2
Yan'an injunctions 3, 40
Yan Geling 76, 79n11
Yang Haosheng 128–9
Yang Jiang 78n3
Yang Jingyu 97
Yang Ying (Angela Baby) 44, 50
Yan Jingsheng 136
Yearnings (TV drama) 6
Ye Jing 63
Yellow Crane Tower 19
Ye Xin 78n3
Yidan School (Yidan xuetang) 110
Yi Zhongtian 116, 118, 123n1
Yongzheng (Emperor) 6
Yuan Shikai 45–6, 53

Yu Dan 10; celebrity 121–2, 123*n*1; explanation of *Analects* 112–15, 123*n*7; harmonious society 114–15; lectures and writings about Confucius 115–19; media and commodification of culture 119–21; national studies craze 10, 106, 107–11, 121–2; phenomenon 10, 106–7, 119–21
Yu Yingshih 109
Yu Zecheng 130, 133, 135–9

Zhang Chaoyang 87
Zhang Xiaoling 7
Zhang Xueliang 103*n*9
Zhang Yimou 49, 63, 106
Zhang Yinde 78*n*3
Zhao Benshan 22, 44, 52, 56*n*8
Zhou Enlai 50
Zhou Jielun (Jay Chou) 27, 35*n*4
Zhou Xingchi (Stephen Chow) 43
Zhu Rongji 6
Zuo Lan 130